Also by Linda Perlstein

Not Much Just Chillin'

TESTED

ONE AMERICAN SCHOOL

STRUGGLES TO

MAKE THE GRADE

LINDA PERLSTEIN

HENRY HOLT AND COMPANY • NEW YORK

Henry Holt and Company, LLC
Publishers since 1866
175 Fifth Avenue
New York, New York 10010
www.henryholt.com

Henry Holt® and 🏛® are registered trademarks
of Henry Holt and Company, LLC.

Distributed in Canada by H. B. Fenn and Company Ltd.

Library of Congress Cataloging-in-Publication Data

Perlstein, Linda, 1971–
    Tested : one American school struggles to make the grade /
Linda Perlstein.—1st ed.
        p. cm.
    Includes bibliographical references and index.
    ISBN-13: 978-0-8050-8082-7
    ISBN-10: 0-8050-8082-1
    1. Tyler Heights Elementary School (Annapolis, Md.) 2. Education,
    Elementary—Standards—Maryland—Annapolis. I. Title.
    LD7501.A493P47 2007
    379.1'580975256—dc22   2007006599

Henry Holt books are available for special promotions
and premiums. For details contact: Director, Special Markets.

First Edition 2007

Designed by Victoria Hartman

Printed in the United States of America

10 9 8 7 6 5 4 3 2 1

For John

CONTENTS

A NOTE TO THE READER

To protect the privacy of Tyler Heights Elementary School students and their relatives, their names—but no other details—have been changed.

TESTED

Ain't No Stopping Us Now

You could not tell by looking that Tina McKnight was in pain. Her hair was perfectly curled and she sat up straight in her desk chair, underneath a series of watercolors of Taxco, the Mexican town she loved to visit. That morning Tina had chosen a pantsuit of salmon pink and pinned a matching silk flower to her lapel, as if she could will good news through cheerful attire. Her back throbbed, sore from hours of bending over the toilet, possibly from food poisoning but more likely from stress. It was a week and a half before the end of the school year, and McKnight, the principal of Tyler Heights Elementary School in Annapolis, Maryland, had a lot on her mind.

She was worried about her sick mother, whom she could not care for the day before because she'd been stuck babysitting strangers who had appropriated the playground for an illicit soccer tournament. (Corona bottles and Pampers had been scattered all over the grass until Tina appeared with trash bags; god knows what was still left.) Today drops of water plopped rhythmically into strategically placed trash cans on the fifth-grade hall—trouble with the air conditioning, one more thing that needed to be fixed.

Other problems obsessing McKnight: It didn't look like she'd get the school uniform plan in place by fall, as she'd wanted to. The discipline data had stopped improving, even with all the prizes given to students as behavior incentives, so McKnight hoped another principal in the district would call to chip in for the five-thousand-dollar consultant whose book promised "discipline without stress, punishment and rewards." Then there was the secretary whose father had suffered a stroke, the assistant whose dad was headed to the hospital for his heart, and the kindergarten class that at the moment had neither teacher nor assistant nor substitute.

On top of all that, something far bigger was looming.

It was the first Monday in June 2005, a D-day of sorts for the principals of Anne Arundel County: They were about to receive their students' scores on Maryland's annual standardized test. For McKnight, and educators across the nation, test score day had accrued such monumental importance that it provoked more jitters than the first day of school, more emotions than fifth-grade graduation. Since McKnight's arrival at 6:30 a.m., she had spent much of the time intensely drumming her hands on her prized Harvard desk blotter, a gift from her son. She had dug through the mailbag and found nothing. She kept looking out the window for deliveries but saw nothing.

"Good morning!" McKnight called to one little boy who came into the office to sign in. She greets every child she sees coming in tardy—and at Tyler Heights there are many, particularly in the last days of school. "Running late?" she said. "We're glad you're here."

"Why is it so quiet?" the boy asked.

"Because everybody's learning," the principal told him.

She signed checks, one after the other, to keep up with the school's bills. When the phone rang but no secretary picked up, she grabbed the receiver. "Hello, Tina McKnight, Tyler Heights." Ms. McKnight—no longer Mrs., since her divorce had become final months before—dispatched the call and greeted another latecomer. "Good morning! Running late? We're glad you're here." Then a man in a ball cap and khakis appeared in the outer office, holding a manila envelope.

McKnight walked over to greet him, and he handed her the envelope, marked MARYLAND SCHOOL ASSESSMENT.

"Am I going to be happy after I open these?" she said.

"I have no idea. I'm just the delivery man."

The principal shut her office door, bracing herself for the moment she had anticipated with anxiety pretty much every day for three months, ever since her third, fourth, and fifth graders took the state reading and math exams. McKnight pulled a sheaf of papers from the envelope, columns and columns of numbers, and paged through them. What she saw just didn't make sense—not for a school that so many middle-class parents had rejected, not for a school that mainly served the poor, not for children who had arrived in the building with so few skills and so many problems. Such was the school's reputation that when McKnight was appointed principal five years back, colleagues had said, "Congratulations, *I think.*"

Baffled, McKnight flipped back and forth to assess the numbers. Her hand was at her chest.

"Oh, I have to be sure I'm digesting what I'm digesting, because I'm, like, really . . ." She couldn't finish her sentence. She sniffed. Her brows scrunched behind her glasses, her dark brown eyes practically closed. "I don't know if I'm really looking at the right numbers."

Overall, according to the results, 86 percent of the students passed reading. Eighty percent passed math. Black fourth graders—91 percent passed reading! Hispanic third graders—100 percent passed math! McKnight compared the county numbers and the school numbers, side by side. Hers were higher in many categories. "I don't believe this. It's, like, what . . ."

Maybe, she wondered, she had been sent some other school's results. Maybe this was a mistake.

Or maybe not. Definitely not.

McKnight screamed. The reading teacher came in, saw the numbers, and she screamed too. McKnight grabbed a compact disc from her desk and went to the PA system in the outer office. She was forbidden to officially reveal the results to teachers yet, but she couldn't resist giving them a clue. She put the disc into the boom box and pointed the intercom mike at it. The whole building heard the song—fuzzy, but clear enough. *"Ain't no stopping us now, we're on the move!"*

In the classrooms, the students danced, not because they knew the song's hidden meaning but because music, even a cheesy disco tune, meant dancing. The teachers had no problem understanding what the song signified: For them, it was a deliverance of sorts. Most came out of their rooms as McKnight raced down the hallway to high-five them, like she was finishing a marathon.

At the end of the hall, she let out a shocking, triumphant scream.

◆ ◆ ◆

A person could live in Annapolis for a lifetime unaware of its poverty.

The city of forty thousand is best known as an exemplar of preppy, nautical affluence; it is home to the buttoned-up U.S. Naval Academy, the pristine, historic State House perched on a hill, and an array of yacht clubs. Those who visit from Washington or Baltimore, forty-five minutes away, or who head down Forest Drive to pick up a bushel of steamed crabs at the Seafood Market en route to million-dollar homes on the Chesapeake Bay, probably don't know that tucked blocks away are rows of garden apartments that are modest at best, dilapidated at worst, and two glum housing projects known to few beyond their residents and the police.

Before Tina McKnight received the envelope that would tell the world that Tyler Heights Elementary School was a compelling example of educational accountability done right, it might have been possible to live in Annapolis and never know the school existed either. Located a curvy block off Forest Drive and announced by no sign on the main road, the low-slung brick building with its Mondrian wall of windows and red panels is, like most schoolhouses built in the early 1960s, neither attractive nor ugly. The houses closest to the school are new four-hundred-thousand-dollar colonials where Tyler Heights students are unlikely to live: Well-off families in the area have sought refuge in private education, at a rate triple the national average. The public middle school across from the Seafood Market has fewer than five hundred students in a building once crowded with two thousand.[1] The U.S. Census says the area is about half white, but Tyler Heights counts only about one white child per classroom.

Tina McKnight had arrived at Tyler Heights in 2000 to find the front office crammed with misbehaving children, like emergency-room patients awaiting triage. The test results were so dismal—a schoolwide index suggested that only 17 percent of students performed satisfactorily on the state exam her first year—that at county principals' meetings, McKnight had wanted to disappear. Adding to the distress, both her mother and son were ill; by the spring she would wind up in the hospital herself, from what had looked like a heart attack, though doctors couldn't figure it out. Two years later, two-thirds of her students still failed the state reading test. The line chart of children who scored "advanced" looked like a dead man's EKG.

In a 2006 poll, 70 percent of Americans said that society, rather than schools themselves, was to blame for problems like those found at Tyler Heights.[2] But over the last decade, a dramatic transformation of American education has changed the way teachers teach and students learn—a revolution based on the idea that those 70 percent of respondents are wrong. By the time McKnight had taken over at Tyler Heights, education was being driven by a new expectation: Every school has the responsibility to bring every student up to par. "No excuses" is the mantra; test scores are the measure. No longer should children like those at Tyler Heights—mostly poor, mostly minority, deprived of the fundamentals commonly considered catalysts for a good future (educated parents, family stability)—be expected to score low. No longer should the benefits of high academic expectations accrue only to those born into advantage. The country, it is thought, can no longer afford to let any student slide.

This attitude has its genesis in the mid-1980s, when America's political and business leaders decided that if employees weren't as productive as their bosses liked, if the gross national product was faltering, if the future of science and industry lay not in this country but in Asia, schoolteachers were to blame. A Nation at Risk, a federally commissioned 1983 report, warned in stark prose that America was allowing its schools to bob along on "a rising tide of mediocrity."[3] In the 1990s, policymakers decided that the tide could be turned back, and the "achievement gap" between test scores in high-poverty districts and well-off ones could be narrowed, if educators were held accountable for their schools' successes and failures. To make this happen, states were encouraged to create lists of what students should learn, specific ways to assess whether those standards were being met, and sanctions for schools that failed to prove progress.

Reforms adopted throughout the decade captured the spirit of the accountability movement, but they varied in content and impact, from negligible to sort-of-strong. Only when George W. Bush became president did the system begin to change significantly. From his first day in office, Bush pressed for a version of educational accountability that would force real reform in every state, in every school, in every classroom. A year later the No Child Left Behind Act, which had been passed overwhelmingly by both parties of Congress, was signed into law. The act set up a tangible set of criteria and consequences. All American public school students must be tested in reading and math each year from third through eighth grade and once in high school. Not only must scores increase overall each year, they must also rise for every "subgroup" of children in a school: minorities, the poor, students who receive services such as special education. By 2014, the law states, 100 percent of students must pass the tests.

For schools with populations affluent enough to be funded only by state and local money, failure to meet test-score targets might mean no more than public embarrassment—inclusion in the local newspaper's "Failing Schools" list, for example—and community hand-wringing. Schools like Tyler, on the other hand, which receive federal funding because of their large numbers of children in poverty, face many more consequences. In 2002, because of its low test scores, Tyler Heights had to allow students to transfer to other schools. In 2003, the school had to fund a specific kind of after-school tutoring because too few black children passed the reading test. In 2004, Tyler Heights did well enough so that it didn't move to the next level of reform. But barely half the students had passed the state test, and the school was still not off the hook. Steps backward could have resulted in a number of changes down the line: a longer school day or year, the firing of teachers, a new curriculum, a new leadership team that might or might not have included the principal.

◆ ◆ ◆

Tina McKnight often presents herself as the ultimate optimist, somebody who could see the silver lining in a mushroom cloud. Even if she has to fake it, McKnight would never let on that goals are unattainable.

With this sort of energy, and well aware of the stakes, McKnight wasted little time at Tyler before introducing what she called a "laser-sharp focus" on improvement. Her changes, as well as those imposed by the county's new highly paid, hard-charging superintendent, looked a lot like those taking place across America. Students at Tyler Heights now got at least two and a half hours of reading and ninety minutes of math instruction each day. Floundering children who once might have been allowed to flop undetected from grade to grade were pulled aside daily for special attention. Kindergartners learned to write not just words but paragraphs. Students were taught strategies for taking tests, including a formula for crafting written responses, and given all manner of rewards for good answers and good behavior.

Anything seen as irrelevant to the Maryland School Assessment—field trips, talent shows, Career Day—got pushed back until after the March testing dates. Under pressure to cover all the state standards before the exam but often short on time, teachers were not allowed to just close their classroom doors and choose what they taught. When Eric Smith became superintendent of Anne Arundel County schools in 2002, he mandated new reading and math programs that laid out exactly what to teach and how, hour by hour and day by day. While McKnight couldn't simply fire teachers she felt were not up to the challenge, she "encouraged them to hang their hat elsewhere," as she put it.

In the new world of education, school systems have sought salvation in business strategies that emphasize continually increasing returns. At Tyler Heights, the progress of children as young as five was monitored by regular, formal tests and laid out in spreadsheets. On orders of the county, McKnight hired consultants to help her shape her goals, missions, and objectives. (In this newly jargon-filled world, these are all different things.) Her supervisor visited constantly, checking classrooms to make sure everybody stayed on track. A dry-erase board markered in different colors with past test scores and future targets was brought out at every opportunity.

McKnight, a workaholic even before the laser-sharp focus, usually stayed at school until 10:30 p.m. on weeknights, when the custodians went home, and until dark on Saturdays. (She used to stay later, until a bullet zinged through the office window.) Breakfast was often supermarket-brand Rice Squares out of the box, lunch an apple she may or may not finish. Since she arrived at Tyler Heights her social life disappeared, as did her season tickets to the theater. Tina, who was fifty-six, never used up her vacation time; it vanished at the end of each calendar year with the Christmas trash.

It was worth it to her when she thought of how much Tyler Heights had accomplished on her watch. The place was no longer as dangerous as during her early years, when the police were a regular presence. Students by now had been taught new rules, a new school culture, a new vocabulary for learning. But in this era of provable results in education, where "increasing achievement," "improving student learning," and "demonstrating progress" are just synonyms for upping test scores, McKnight knew that little of that would matter if the numbers didn't come down in her favor.

◆ ◆ ◆

On the day in 2005 when they did, some county principals—the ones with good scores—gathered at a press conference in the Anne Arundel County school board chambers. They greeted one another, sharing their numbers and hugging, then took their seats. Superintendent Smith approached the lectern, two television cameras pointed at him. McKnight looked up from her score sheets, which she was marking with a highlighter.

Like principals, superintendents these days focus more than anything on bringing up the abilities, and scores, of poor and minority children. Smith, named the nation's best urban educator while in Charlotte, North Carolina, and lured to Maryland for more than three hundred thousand dollars a year, had staked his claim in one of the nation's largest and most visible school districts on narrowing the achievement gap. To read one of the three newspapers that covered him was to see the archetype of today's big-district chief. Dogmatic and evangelical, dynamic and bossy, Smith was as much politician as educator, prone to exclamations like "All children can learn!" and "All children can succeed!"

At the lectern he announced the "tremendous success of our educators and certainly our children." He used the word *exceptional*. He told the cameras, "It's a very significant day in Anne Arundel County."

For the first time, at least three-quarters of the county's students had passed the reading test and three-quarters had passed in math. Giant charts, with bars in the shape of extremely lanky children, showed score increases for black students, for poor students, for students in special education. As Smith mentioned each increase, the audience applauded. "We have gains that moms and dads, elected officials, business leaders, community members should and will be proud of," the superintendent said. "To all of you, thank you very much."

Later that day, bouquets of flowers arrived at Tyler Heights. The marquee out front was changed to read:

OUR MSA SCORES
ARE GREAT

In a few months, the scores would secure Tina McKnight a place as one of five finalists for county principal of the year. Smith would tell an aide, "We should nominate Tyler Heights for Blue Ribbon School," a national honor. More immediately, the school's improvement merited attention in articles in the *Washington Post*, the *Baltimore Sun*, and both the editorial and news pages of the Annapolis paper. "In some troubled schools," the *Capital* editorial said, meaning Tyler Heights, "teachers and staff have performed minor miracles—and set an example for others."

◆ ◆ ◆

"Miracle" was exactly the word Alia Johnson thought of when she heard how her third graders had scored on the Maryland School Assessment. "An example for others," though? She wasn't so sure.

As McKnight had waited for the results in her office that Monday, Johnson had been sitting on the rocking chair in her classroom, teaching a math lesson. While she looked put-together as always, her curly dark hair pulled back tight, she, too, had been sick to her stomach waiting for the results. MSA, MSA—sometimes it felt like that was all she was supposed to think about. McKnight had been in and out of her room almost weekly until the test. McKnight's supervisor had also been a regular presence. Johnson had drilled her students in the proper written response to any reading question they might encounter, taught them the process of elimination, given practice test after practice test, talked about stamina (demonstrating the lack of it by falling out of her chair). She felt like she'd done all she could to prepare her class.

But in March, when Johnson had looked over her students' shoulders as they took the MSA, she grew scared—it didn't seem like they knew much. Their answers betrayed their nerves. A lot rode on these scores, Johnson knew. Vindication for the school. A bonus to teachers of $1,500 apiece, to add to a forty-thousand-dollar paycheck in a county with the lowest salaries around. A degree of autonomy. The way things worked now, the higher the test scores, the more freedom a teacher was given to choose how she taught. Johnson already had to adjust to the superintendent's new reading and math curricula, and she knew that if Tyler Heights didn't make what the law called "adequate yearly progress" she could expect a whole new slate of programs and meddlers, a burden that might push her out of her job, if the state didn't first.

So when Johnson heard "Ain't No Stopping Us Now," she was bathed in relief. (Her students carried on with math instead of dancing; she was strict that way.)

The next day, at a staff meeting in the library, McKnight put on the music again.

"Was our reading score sixty-five? No way! Seventy-five? We left it in the dust. Eighty-five? Higher! Off your feet!" The principal sang along, working herself up to a pant.

The scores were put on the overhead projector, grade by grade, and Johnson was stunned to see that 90 percent of the third graders passed the reading test—compared to 35 percent just two years before. As much as the results pleased her, though, they frightened her, as they raised the stakes. Rumor had it lots of teachers were going to quit over the summer, and she wondered if her new teammates would be up to the challenge. The children that Johnson would have for third grade in the fall, whom she had taught as first graders, were very low in skills, and No Child Left Behind wouldn't count their improvement so much as how they compared to this year's group. Johnson, who was twenty-seven, had been at the school four years and had hoped to quit by the time they caught up to her in third grade. But those plans fell through. She knew that come August she'd be back in Room 18 at Tyler Heights.

Alia Johnson had wanted to make a difference for poor children. But she wasn't sure how much she was, 90 percent proficiency notwithstanding. The "no excuses" thing bothered her: No matter how little help students got from parents, no matter if they came to school hungry or abused, lead-poisoned or learning disabled, they had to pass that test. But did the test really tell anyone all they needed to know about the children? Throughout the year, so much was sacrificed to achieve that score. Was it worth it? This revolution had begun with students like Alia Johnson's in mind. But teachers like her wondered: Were they doing the best by their children?

"I don't know what to say, except it's been a really, really long journey to get Tyler Heights to where it is," McKnight told her teachers at the staff meeting. Alia listened as the principal went on to talk about the $1,500 bonuses, and about next year: where she stood in hiring new teachers, where to submit school-supply lists, and, of course, next year's test.

"We can see the kids who almost made it," McKnight said. "We have names and faces, and they're not going to get away."

No amount of relief could erase the fact that the clock had restarted that day. The staff of Tyler Heights felt the pressure. They had exactly one year to prove that this was not a fluke.

1

You Ready?

When jazz poured out of her clock radio at 5:50 on August 29, the first morning of the new school year, Alia looked at it and thought, *Yeah, right.* One snooze cycle later she was up, and an hour after that she was zipping around her sunny, spacious classroom, humming and talking to herself as she got everything ready. Before the weekend she had left things in order: books and binders inside the desks, folders in denim pouches hanging on the chair backs, cards with letters and sounds magneted to the front of each desk.

On the board, Miss Johnson had written a schedule and the day's objectives:

> *We will review school rules and procedures.*
> *We will discuss the code of conduct.*
> *We will listen to the story of Amos and Boris.*
> *We will discuss the theme of friendship and preview vocabulary.*
> *We will tell time to the hour and solve elapsed time problems.*

Next to that, it said,

Welcome
To
3rd grade!

Except that the exclamation point wavered a little, so it looked as much like a question as a greeting.

Alia had spent the weekend in Norfolk saying good-bye to her boyfriend, Frankie, before his deployment to Iraq. She got her crying out of the way, then drove four and a half hours home. Alia Johnson is a matter-of-fact woman. "I might not see him again for six months, or I might not see him again ever," she said. Because Frankie was in the Navy, she figured he probably wouldn't be in direct combat. But fleets had been fired upon; she kept track. "I'm not afraid to die," Frankie had told Alia, but she wished he would be, at least for her sake, and for his family's.

Jennifer Johnson, the guidance counselor and one of Alia's closest friends since they started at Tyler Heights four years before, came in to say hi. "Is it hot in here?" Alia asked, while she hunted for her spelling tests.

"Did you have a nice trip this weekend?" Jennifer asked.

"It was all right."

"Everyone's coming back from their happy trips."

"It wasn't happy. I had to say ' 'bye.' Where the hell's this folder?"

Alia was wearing black slacks and a slit-sleeved white Old Navy top she had bought for Frankie's cousin's wedding rehearsal dinner. She doesn't usually wear her nicest clothes to school, because the kids accidentally write on her, and she writes on herself. The first day, though, everyone dressed a little better than normal—Jennifer in a pantsuit, the fourth-grade teacher across the hall in a jazzy white dress with turquoise rectangles, Nikki Facchine next door in a black tank and long, striped skirt.

"*Buenos días,*" Nikki, a new third-grade teacher, said as she came into Alia's room. "Did you see I left you Skittles?"

"I'm going to get you the spelling pretest. I made a recess schedule. Do you have everything? You ready?"

"Yeah," Nikki said. "Are you?"

Ready? Maybe. Nauseated? Literally. She knew how nasty these kids were to one another in first grade, how little they knew, and over the twenty days of summer school, she had grown more concerned as she watched them count on fingers to subtract three from four. She thought, do the new third-grade teachers have any idea what they're up against? Are they prepared to teach these kids? Ninety percent on the MSA: Right now it felt like there was nowhere to go but down.

◆ ◆ ◆

Over the weekend Ms. McKnight had cleaned the copy room and set out a sign she had typed and laminated: PLEASE KEEP THIS COUNTER TOP NEAT AND ORGANIZED. She put a perfect-looking Red Delicious apple in each staff member's mailbox with a cheerful note. Several times Tina checked the weather forecast, because when it rains on the first day "some just don't come—they don't want their new sneakers to get wet." She bought a skein of black yarn to string hall passes on and prepared a presentation to parents, who are always invited to Tyler Heights on the first day of school. It's hard to get parents to school in a poor community, so as long as they were coming to drop off their kids on the first day, Tina figured she may as well try to keep them there. She flipped 250 bananas over and over again, because all Sam's Club had were green ones and she thought air circulation might help them ripen in time. She changed the marquee to say:

SCHOOL

A FAMILY

AFFAIR

McKnight had worked so hard to get this year off to a good start. But in truth, how much could she control? Half her classroom teachers were new, and several others were only in their second year. Her job interviews last as long as two hours, she always checks references, and her gut feeling was that she had made good hires. Still, she wondered if they would fit in.

She wondered too about the children. "People look at the scores and say, 'Wow.' But of the ninety percent proficient, I know there's a lot of kids just over the line." Last year Tyler Heights had fourteen kinder-gartners in each class, but this year they were starting with twenty, and the number always grows. Of those who were in pre-K last year, a few could write their names, or some letters in their names. "But I'm not sure they knew those were letters in their names," McKnight said.

The incoming third graders, who would be taking the state test for the first time, concerned her as much as they did Alia. On a different standardized test last year, fewer than half had scores that indicated they would pass the MSA this spring. McKnight had gotten as many of them as possible into summer school. When one of the two third-grade teachers moved to another job in the school, McKnight replaced her and added another, so this year's classes would be tiny, no more than fourteen students. In order for the school's scores to simply stay the same, the new third graders would have to perform above their ability, McKnight said—"or what appeared to be their ability based on past performance."

One thing she felt good about was the groove she had going. Ms. McKnight had been around since this year's fifth graders had been kindergartners. By now the children knew the ropes of the Open Court Reading curriculum, which had been brought to Tyler three years be-fore. With the Saxon Math curriculum, introduced at the same time, they knew to always look on the back of their worksheets for the homework. They knew, at least in fourth and fifth grades, the format of the MSA. They knew about walking on the silver line between floor tiles when they passed in the hall, and following with their fingers when listening to someone read. If they couldn't all follow the school's pledge, at least they could recite it: "Respect self, respect others, respect learning, respect property."

Despite her concerns, on the first morning of the school year Tina McKnight exuded enthusiasm. Shortly before the buses arrived, she gathered the teachers in the library and put a poem on the overhead:

> I took a piece of living clay
> and gently formed it day by day
> and molded with my power and art
> a child's soft and yielding heart.

"The impressions that you make today will make a lasting imprint on them, so don't take it lightly," the principal said. Teaching is, in fact, brain surgery—and heart surgery too, she added. McKnight instructed the group to stand in a circle and hold hands. She held an Energy Ball, a device designed to teach about circuits but intended in this case to show the importance of synergy. When everyone held hands in an unbroken chain, McKnight's ball lit up red and buzzed. "Have a wonderful, great, special day," she said. "Let's get started!"

◆ ◆ ◆

During the poem, during the holding-hands thing, all Mandi Milhoan wanted was to meet her pieces of living clay: her third graders. After a tiring move from Ohio for the boyfriend she had met on a football chat room, the twenty-five-year-old, who would be teaching third grade, had spent two weeks in mind-numbing teacher orientation. The buzzing ball was the least of it. There had been the welcoming address in which Eric Smith told the county's new teachers to set their students on a "trajectory for greatness," to never aspire to mediocrity, to "go get 'em"— and then he growled! There had been the training session where Mandi learned the difference between rules and procedures and routines. There had been the icebreaker game where she had to fill in the blanks: *My peers don't know I have a snake.* (A colleague with a snake? Yet another thing that would trouble Alia.)

Along the way Mandi was warned to keep track of her purse, document phone calls, and learn each child's name the first day of school. (No problem; elementary school teachers have this amazing talent for names.) She learned from Ms. McKnight that it took forty-three muscles in your face to frown yet only seventeen to smile. The principal also said that last year's MSA scores had to be posted in every room—and it was imperative they be met or exceeded.

"Where are we for reading?" McKnight asked the teachers, in a routine she would repeat throughout the year on adults and children.

"Eighty-five point seven."

"Where are we for math?"

"Seventy-nine point six."

Mandi also was told that teachers must document each item a child chooses for breakfast in the classroom, that the next day's schedule and "learning outcomes" must be written on the blackboard before going home, that faculty meetings are on Monday afternoons—and McKnight's boss is a stickler for minutes. Mandi learned that if she suspects a disability, she should keep her eye on the student for four to six weeks, then discuss it with the team. She learned that Congress mandated there be a lesson for Constitution Day, and that McKnight mandated there be no parties for Halloween. She learned that fighting automatically results in suspension; cheating doesn't. Each incidence of bullying must be reported to the state, and teachers should use the proper words with the children: "bystander," "victim," "intimidation."

The week before school started, Alia told Mandi and Nikki that Dr. Smith insists they teach Open Court and Saxon Math right away. On day one, she said, students will tell time to the half hour, decode long "I," recognize base words with inflectal endings, summarize, and make predictions with connections. The first day of school will be the last day the third graders won't write a BCR—a "brief constructed response," a paragraph-sized answer that's required on the state test. "Later you'll be doing five BCRs a day," Alia warned.

By the time the weekend had arrived, Mandi Milhoan's brain was full of what she was supposed to do with her students. She yearned to focus on what she *wanted* to do with them. Then her boyfriend tripped bringing groceries down the stairs and broke his arm in four places, so she spent twenty-one hours at the hospital.

Through all this, Mandi remained excited about the children. After McKnight's pep talk that first morning, she went outside with her clipboard and her colleagues. Three hundred kids were disembarking from buses and arriving on foot, their backpacks mammoth and their sneakers very, very white. Some children carried paper towels with which to banish dirt from their shoes; some spit-shined them with their hands.

"Hello, how are you?" Miss Milhoan said to each of her third graders as they clustered on the grass.

Miss Johnson was businesslike: "You're in my class," she told her kids.

"Hi, I'm Mrs. Facchine," Nikki said warmly to every student and parent, with a smile, handshake, and usually unrequited attempt to make eye contact. Her first introduction to classroom dynamics came immediately, when Ferric's mother saw that he was in class with a boy named Gardell. "You had that problem in first grade," she told her son, and marched across the driveway to Ms. McKnight.

Ferric—more concerned with his outfit than with Gardell—announced: "I got new clothes! Did you see Miss Rockwell on the news this summer?" Montell, standing next to him, said, "My whole last year my desk was the cleanest."

Suddenly Ms. McKnight appeared on the roof, bright against the sky in a blue top and skirt. "Good morning, boys and girls!" she shouted. "Welcome to the 2005–2006 school year at . . ."

"Tyler Heights!"

"I can't hear you!"

"Tyler Heights!!"

"Last year we did an incredible job! Our test scores were great! You were great! Tyler Heights earned incredible respect! This year we will do even better!" McKnight and Caroline, the custodian, unrolled a sign, and she told the kids to read it:

"Tyler Heights Eagles Respect!"

"I can't hear you!"

"TYLER HEIGHTS EAGLES RESPECT!"

"Are you ready to start a great year? Are you ready to follow the rules? Are you ready to come to school every day ready to learn? With no further delay, let's start the 2005–2006 school year!"

◆ ◆ ◆

Miss Johnson, her forehead sweating from the humidity, sent her class single file into school, past a first grader screaming on the sidewalk, a new arrival from Mexico afraid to leave his mother; past the lunch lady in a chili-pepper apron, who wheeled a cart of breakfast foods and said hello; halfway down the intermediate hall and into the second classroom on the right.

Miss Johnson is someone who brings a filled-out check to the car dealer and tells him exactly how much she will pay—announcing, when it comes to loan terms, that her credit score is better than 61 percent of American consumers, and don't even *think* about mud flaps or clear coat, thank you very much. She knows how important it is to set the tone from the first moment in the classroom; that hers was businesslike was very much in character. "Put your book bags on the floor," she told her fourteen students. There's a routine to mornings, she said: Take two items of breakfast, put the trash in the front wastebasket, dump leftover milk in the sink and rinse it down well. "We don't want to have a flood in the trash can and bugs in the sink."

The children were stunned a bit by the early morning, after a summer of sleeping late. While they ate breakfast they rubbed their eyes and filled in a packet of worksheets called "All About Me." "First and last name please, 'cause you're not rock stars and it's third grade," Miss Johnson said. A skinny, scrappy girl named Autumn wrote, *"Someday I want to be is a doter."* A boy named Roman drew a perfect SpongeBob. Jamila dug through her desk and turned around. "Mommy, I got two binders!" she said, with a smile that displayed both rows of teeth. Jamila, a chubby girl with neat, beaded braids and a smooth round face that made her look almost adult, nearly hadn't made it to third grade. She did so poorly in second grade that she was allowed to advance only after she completed summer school.

Jamila's mother, a former Tyler Heights student herself, was one of seven parents who watched from the edges of the room. Miss Johnson urged them to fill out the emergency phone numbers form, the emergency procedures form, and the form that shows an income low enough to qualify for free lunch, which helps the school secure federal Title I funding. "It'smoremoneyfortheschoolthatwecanputbackintothechildren," Miss Johnson said in a rush. As with many teachers, kids are no problem but talking to groups of adults flusters her. "You will get crayons at a later date," she told the children, more slowly, and passed out donut holes. "I don't hear manners," she said, and the Thank Yous began. "Please try to keep your desks in a nice row, because they're a little bit jumbled."

The parents were working on forms, the kids were working on forms; only the air conditioning made noise. The music teacher sat in the back of the room dumping school supplies from children's backpacks onto the rug and repacking them in Ziplocs. Several children brought new backpacks, decorated with Bratz or superheroes but devoid of supplies. Three children had no pack at all, and received one from the pile at the back of the room (donated by a national charity group of Jimmy Buffett fans). It frustrates teachers when parents buy expensive sneakers and hair extensions for their children but send them to school empty-handed because cool backpacks will be waiting. This wasn't the case with these three, though; Autumn, Manny, and Elena wore old, ill-fitting clothes and nothing fancy on their feet.

◆ ◆ ◆

Across the hall in Miss Milhoan's class, the new teacher had the children out of their seats, searching for a classmate whose favorite color was blue, who could touch tongue to nose, whose parents were there (four of them, one with a video camera), and who shared their eye color. This last one was easy: Miss Milhoan, who had sapphire eyes and hair streaked with various shades of blond and brown, was the only person in third grade, grownup or child, without dark brown or black hair and brown eyes.

"Just because we're getting out of our seats doesn't mean we have to act like we're in a zoo," Miss Milhoan said. This brought silence, which drew Ms. McKnight into the room.

"I was coming down the hallway, and I thought, Miss Milhoan's class has gone somewhere," the principal said calmly. "She is new to Tyler Heights so I picked the very, very best kids. Are you going to show her you're the very, very best?"

"Yes."

For telling what they learned about one another, Miss Milhoan offered Scholar Dollars, a schoolwide currency that paid for trinkets at the end of each week. Hands shot up. Each teacher uses Scholar Dollars a bit differently—to encourage good answers and participation, or temper behavior, or just for fun. So while Miss Johnson wouldn't give any out till the next day—and then only one, to the child who remembered what a "colon" was—Miss Milhoan gave five to the girl who remembered her mom's wiener dog was named Ebony, five to the boy who remembered her boyfriend was a Marine, and several to children she never got to call on.

Miss Milhoan explained that in her class, the binder where much of their work would be kept goes home every day, with a behavior chart in the front and a homework chart in the back. It must come back initialed by a parent. According to the school-wide discipline system, a student can move from green to yellow to red, "the worst kind of day you can have." According to Miss Milhoan's own system, a sticker for good behavior every day of the week would earn a trinket from her purple box. Stickers every day of the month win pizza or ice cream.

"My shoe's squeezing my feet," Alex blurted out of nowhere, invoking roomwide laughter, and Miss Milhoan began to question whether there would be many trips to the purple box.

◆ ◆ ◆

"The stuff we learn in morning math meeting is going to be on the test," Miss Johnson warned her class, hours into the school day.

"When is going to be the test?"

"March."

"What test?"

"MSA—it's hard," Miss Johnson said.

"How many pages is it going to be?"

"I love the fact that you're going to tie your shoes and stop playing with them."

By late morning, the parents were gone and Miss Johnson's kids were in the library, playing a game about the rules. "We need to have no *blank* or groaning," Ms. Borinsky, the librarian, said. "*Moaning,*" they scribbled on little dry-erase boards.

With her own classroom quiet, Miss Johnson pushed aside a pile of green bananas on the counter and said, "I think it went okay. They know me. They know I don't play."

Already four staff members had visited the room to see Malcolm, a short boy with a beautiful, smooth dark face, and now other colleagues came in to ask, "How was Malcolm?" Teachers suspected Malcolm was neglected at home, and they knew he was emotionally troubled, prone to frightening fits when he was unhappy with his progress. Miss Johnson saw immediately that Malcolm wrote slowly, and even what he wrote correctly he angrily erased. The school psychologist helped him write the day's assignment in his planner—two words, "*Respect homework*"—and that took fifteen minutes. Later in the day Malcolm began to rock side to side in his chair. "It would make me sad if you had to leave today," Miss Johnson told him. During math she called on him a lot, to read the date out loud, to show 8:00 on a plastic clock, because she knew he could. The idea was to give Malcolm the help he needed without him knowing he was being monitored so closely, to subtly build his confidence. Miss Johnson seated him up front, where she could stroke his bald head to calm him. She wanted to give him the gift of a fresh start. "I don't care how many referrals or prereferrals you got last year," she said. "It's a new year."

A new year that by lunchtime of the very first day chatty Lilia proclaimed too difficult. Cyrus agreed—"a whole lot of math"—and so did Avante, a boy who does math workbooks before school. All this MSA talk—the test sounded tricky to him. "They gonna keep on saying it to us," Avante predicted, correctly. "If they say it one more time, I not coming," he predicted, incorrectly.

Miss Johnson, Avante said, is "a little bit mean." He meant this as a compliment. It was a compliment too, coming from Ms. Borinsky, who watched Miss Johnson order her kids in line by saying in an even tone, "I should see faces and eyeballs, not ears and backs of heads. So far you're five minutes late for lunch. Do I look worried?"

Ms. Borinsky told Miss Johnson, "I can't be mean like you. I think it's great that you are."

By the end of the school day, Miss Johnson's students had been reminded to sit "criss-cross applesauce" on the carpet or, if they wore a skirt, with legs folded to the side. They had listened to a William Steig story about a mouse named Amos and a whale named Boris who became best friends forever after the whale saved the mouse's life. They had recited the days of the week and the months of the year, created number sentences that produced the answer twenty-nine, and figured out (with some help) that you got from ninety to eighty to seventy by counting backward by ten. They had written thoughts about friendship, the theme of the first reading unit, to be posted on the bulletin board: "I wod want a frend is Nice." "Do you always have to have friends and be playful?" They had learned that they could play kickball only if they didn't argue during games, and that failure to follow playground rules would mean a recess spent against the brick wall.

At 2:45, news of three classes' perfect attendance, a custodian's birthday, and, in turn, each bus's arrival came across the PA. Ms. McKnight called the staff outside, where she sent soap bubbles wafting into the air. "This is the end of our first day of oh-five-oh-six," she said. "Was it a great day or what? Go put your feet up, relax. Oprah's on."

"I know it was a great day because I didn't feel that stress," McKnight said as she walked inside. "All that planning paid off. All those kids returning, they know what to do." But Miss Milhoan, who didn't get to time-telling or "Amos and Boris," didn't know what to do. She had arrived full of spunk after a first-rate year as a long-term substitute in Ohio and two and a half decades in which she excelled at just about everything she tried. That bank of confidence had gradually been depleted all day. "They talk constantly or they hate each other," she said. "They say whatever they want whenever they want."

For Miss Johnson, the day wasn't perfect, but it wasn't dire either. She walked past the bubbles and back inside. Frankie was calling on her cell, asking what laundry detergent she used, so he could carry the scent to Iraq.

2

America's Schools Will Be
on a New Path of Reform

On an April Sunday in 1965, President Lyndon B. Johnson returned to the first school he had ever attended, the one-room Junction School in central Texas. At a picnic table on the schoolhouse lawn, the president sat next to the teacher on whose lap he had once read, while she peered through cat's-eye glasses at the law he was about to sign as if she were inspecting his arithmetic homework.

The Elementary and Secondary Education Act was, Johnson said that day, "the most sweeping educational bill ever to come before Congress." Indeed, it represented the first significant foray of the federal legislature into the business of public schools. Schools had been a local and state affair—but they were also a crucial link in Johnson's War on Poverty. Poor Americans could be lifted from despair, as he saw it, only through education vastly better than what they had been receiving. Vastly more expensive too. The law's centerpiece, called Title I, sought equity for poor schoolchildren by infusing significant funds into the schools that they attended.

"By passing this bill," Johnson said, "we bridge the gap between helplessness and hope for more than five million educationally deprived children. . . . And we rekindle the revolution—the revolution of the spirit against the tyranny of ignorance."

Over the next four decades, the money the federal government would pump into public schools, mostly through Title I, would never represent the bulk of the country's education spending: It was only between 5 and 9 percent, the rest provided by states and localities. Still, the federal share would turn out to be money most school systems couldn't do without. By 2005, nearly 60 percent of American public schools, and all districts in which poor children made up at least 2 percent of the student body, would receive Title I funds—in all, nearly thirteen billion dollars a year.[1]

At Tyler Heights, the money would mean a lot. The school had all the investment attainable by a principal with moxie—grants from the state and nonprofits, partnerships with the Navy and local businesses, even children's shoes from a neighborhood lady who donated a few pairs each month. Eric Smith had directed extra resources to schools with the most poor children. Thanks in part to Title I, Tyler Heights could employ as many teachers outside the traditional classroom role as it did inside it. In addition to the eighteen women at the head of its classrooms and a teacher each for physical education, art, library, and music, the school had seven reading and "resource" teachers, five aides for pre-K and kindergarten, two teachers for ESOL and two for special ed, two men who oversaw behavior, a speech pathologist, a community liaison, a full-time guidance counselor, and a part-time psychologist.

This funding disparity fuels no small amount of bitterness in those who work at schools with not enough poor kids for Title I money but not enough rich ones for abundant PTA budgets. Teachers who leave Tyler for such schools are taken aback when they can't get the furniture or books their children need. On hearing mention of Tyler Heights one day, a principal of an Anne Arundel County school with only 14 percent poor children grumbled, "They get all the resources." You couldn't help but think about this principal, and her working-class school with its sad chain-link fence, if you watched a group of Tyler Heights teachers race to spend thousands of Title I dollars by the end of one September day when the budget books were about to close. They paged through catalog after catalog, flagging math games and workbooks and calculators, telephones and office chairs, pencil cases and purple pens that said "I'm doing well on the test," picture dictionaries and coloring books.

Money alone, though, could not cure the most intractable ill of American education: the achievement gap. Throughout the nation, well-off students did better in school than poor ones, white students did better than blacks and Hispanics—this was clear during Lyndon Johnson's time, and a large reason why he fought for legislation. It became even clearer a few years later, with the first country-wide administration of an exam, the National Assessment of Educational Progress, whose results could be broken down by race. Since then an achievement gap has continued to show up in nearly every indicator of educational status: NAEP, state tests, college board scores, dropout rates. The gap narrowed in the 1970s and 1980s, after equal access to education became the law; the degree to which it has improved since then depends on the measure you look at.

Language is generally considered a large contributor to the achievement differential between white students and Hispanics, many of whom are immigrants or the children of immigrants. But the potential causes of the lingering gap for poor children and for black children (even well-off ones) are contentiously debated, interrelated, and complex. To what degree do community economics and culture contribute? Innate cognitive skills? Do educators expect less of, and provide less to, disadvantaged children? What is the role of the attitude of parents? Of the children themselves?

Whatever the causes of the achievement gap, whatever its quantifiable degree, there is no debate that the nation's worst schools—the ones with the shabbiest facilities, lowest morale, and most ineffective instruction—are attended mostly by poor, minority students. Even when those children attend better schools, their classmates usually outperform them.[2] Most Americans surveyed say the achievement gap is not mainly related to quality of schooling, and nearly half say it is not the responsibility of schools to close it—but how can they not try?[3]

Justice should be reason enough. But throughout the last quarter of the twentieth century there was another powerful motivator: the economy. The consensus among policymakers and commentators was that the country's public schools were declining—not just on issues of minority achievement but in overall quality—and that this contributed to slumps in the economy and U.S. competitiveness. Was the gloom well-founded? There are convincing arguments on all sides—not just about schools but about the economy.[4] Was it shared by the public? Not fully: Polls showed high confidence in schools. No doubt there was great room for improvement, particularly concerning the nation's disadvantaged children and the academic neglect they were subject to.

When it comes to the economic correlation, frankly, there are too many steps between K-12 education and outputs such as worker productivity and the gross national product for it to be convincing: fiscal policy, monetary policy, international politics, and corporate mismanagement, to name a few.[5] And no policymakers bother to credit public schools for the Internet boom or impressive medical advances or the nation's prosperity in general. Still, "investment in human capital," as some speak of education reform, is seen as a prerequisite to maintaining the country's standing in the world, especially at a time unskilled jobs have dried up. It seems like a manageable idea, remaking a hundred thousand public schools, whereas reforming an economy to afford everyone a decent job is far too radical for most to accept.

"You're the ones training the workforce of tomorrow," Penny Cantwell, a local banker and Chamber of Commerce member, told a conference of Anne Arundel County educators over the summer. Cantwell presented a PowerPoint of statistics each more dismal than the last. The country is suffering a labor shortage and a skills gap, she said. China is eclipsing America in engineering degrees. In fourteen states, more than half the adults are illiterate.

No matter that China has four times our population and a far broader definition of engineering (one that apparently includes car mechanics), no matter that she either misinterpreted the reading data or relied on a remarkably stingy definition of literacy. The teachers and administrators gasped at her revelations.

The message was coming across as: This is your fault, and your problem to solve.

◆   ◆   ◆

The 1983 publication that is thought to have sparked modern education reform, *A Nation at Risk*, was peppered with fierce rhetoric. It equated the "rising tide of mediocrity" that schools were enabling with "an act of war." It stated that "more and more young people emerge from high school ready neither for college nor for work." "History," it said, "is not kind to idlers." Academic rigor must increase immediately and dramatically, the authors insisted—and not just for the elite.

A Nation at Risk had been commissioned by President Ronald Reagan's education secretary, Terrell Bell, in what many thought to be a bold gambit at a time his boss wanted to abolish his cabinet department. The report came as American schools, high schools in particular, were being criticized for an environment in which too many students were shunted into uninspiring coursework (think home ec) and many teachers had the freedom to teach whatever they wanted, which too often was not much. A diploma, detractors thought, didn't mean anything.

Insofar as A Nation at Risk made waves—and the Department of Education did not disappear—Bell's gambit worked. Some governors began considering an infusion of rigor through state standards. (Maryland standards would first be implemented in 1990 and a state test a year later.) The loudest calls for standards-based reform and accountability came from weekly newspaper columns from a national teachers union president, Albert Shanker, and a newly interested coalition: executives from many of the nation's biggest businesses, joined in organizations like the Business Roundtable and the U.S. Chamber of Commerce. The CEOs were no longer satisfied simply providing grants here and there and adopting the occasional school. They wanted to force change.

Although the idea that all students be held to higher standards appealed to many policymakers, it would be years, and in some places decades, before much bad practice was truly washed away. George H. W. Bush attempted to speed up the process by shifting federal attention on education, which had historically focused on issues of access and funding and the occasional digression like school prayer, to the quality of what was being learned. In tandem with the nation's governors, in particular Bill Clinton of Arkansas, the White House in 1990 presented Goals 2000, a set of broad aims they hoped would be achieved within a decade. Students should have to demonstrate competency in several subjects in fourth, eighth, and twelfth grades, the goals emphasized, and Americans must become first in the world at math and science.[6]

But Goals 2000, which Clinton got through Congress in 1994, never had much force. (Six years: a short time to change the world of school, especially through what turned out, due to a fear of overintrusion by the feds, to just be a pool of money.) Nor did his Improving America's Schools Act, the 1994 reauthorization of the Elementary and Secondary Education Act. The law, however, did keep the ball rolling in the direction of higher standards. ESEA had to be renewed every five to seven years, and this time around Clinton had focused not on money or services but on accountability. The act said federal funding must be used to teach higher-level skills, and that children benefiting from Title I had to take standards-based tests three times during their schooling. States were supposed to provide assistance to schools that didn't make annual improvement in scores and impose sanctions if scores remained stagnant. States could set the bar for improvement as low as they pleased, though, and seek Education Department waivers for various requirements. And they had so much time to comply with the law that few had by the time the next George Bush took office.

Still, some progress had been made toward reform. A set of voluntary national standards, some funded by the Education Department, were released over the first half of the 1990s. While some were dismissed as too controversial or too lame, states used others, particularly in math, as part of their own accountability systems. Over the decade, a good number of states pursued true reform—real tests, based on real standards, with real consequences. One was Texas, which was about to send its governor to the White House. George W. Bush arrived in Washington in January 2000 with a twenty-eight-page manifesto on reforming the nation's schools.[7] It was a plan he had begun to sell before he was sworn in, in meetings with governors, business executives, and members of Congress, and he didn't waste a moment once in the Oval Office. His first day of work, Bush announced his education proposal at the White House; the second day, he sent the plan to Congress.

For anyone eager to see quantifiable results, Bush had something to show. As governor he had presided over what would be called the

"Texas Miracle": skyrocketing test scores and a plummeting dropout rate, most notably in Houston. Improvements in the city's dropout rate would eventually be disregarded as exaggerated and the test scores questioned, but not before Houston's superintendent, Rod Paige, became the U.S. education secretary and the bulk of Bush's blueprint became law for the nation's fifty million public school students.[8]

The president's main priority was annual testing, with scores broken down by subgroup and progress expected in each group, each year. Schools that improved would be rewarded; those that didn't would be assisted, then sanctioned. Students in low-scoring schools, Bush said, would be tutored by private firms or given vouchers to attend higher-performing public or private schools.

Except for the private school vouchers, which would eventually be dropped, centrist Democrats supported the basics of the plan. After all, they and President Clinton had already proposed some similar measures. Bush's ideas included enough flexibility to appease governors— not that it mattered, because they didn't get a vote. Conservative Republicans in Congress, the ones who had wanted to exterminate the Education Department altogether, did get a vote, though, and it was a tough sell.

But Bush sold hard.[9]

Crafting legislation is a notoriously slow process, but No Child Left Behind came together fast. Congressional aides from both parties wasted no time, repairing to Capitol Hill townhouses and Starbucks when the September 11 attacks kept them out of their offices. There were only a few orchestrated hearings on Capitol Hill, and far less involvement of Education Department professionals and education associations than would normally be the case on matters affecting them. A lobbyist for the school boards association said that his organization was given twenty-four hours to look at draft legislation, when typically it got weeks or more. "The law came out of nowhere," he said. Meetings with education groups were more briefings than discussions, one aide who helped write the law said. "It was the only way to get things done, because it was so controversial."

No Child Left Behind passed Congress in December 2001, with the support of 90 percent of senators and representatives, and was signed into law the following month.[10] "As of this hour," Bush said on January 8, 2002, "America's schools will be on a new path of reform, and a new path of results." The law required states to set specific targets for graduation, school safety, and attendance. Teachers had to prove they were competent in the subjects they taught—through college majors, tests, or other criteria set by each state—a provision Hill Democrats pressed for. School districts could apply for grants that would fund reading instruction, if the Education Department decided the curricula were proven effective through empirical research. The vast majority of the law does not apply to private schools, though charter schools, which are administered and funded through public school systems, must comply.

The aspect of No Child Left Behind that changed the climate of school more than any other was the requirement that states phase in annual testing for students in grades three through eight, and once in high school, for reading and math. (Before the law, most states did not test every grade.) The exams must be specific to each state's academic standards. States decide what constitutes an acceptable score, or "proficiency," and set ever-increasing targets, approved by the Education Department, for what percentage of students must pass. Improvement in that pass rate, or what the law calls "adequate yearly progress," is measured by comparing the scores of children in a given grade with those who preceded them—this year's third graders, for example, are held up to last year's—instead of by looking at how each child progresses.

Schools that do particularly well are rewarded with money. At those that miss the pass-rate target two years in a row, overall or for any subgroup of students, children may transfer to a higher-scoring school selected by the district. After three years, the school must draw from its Title I funds to pay after-school tutors. After four years, a school faces "corrective action," which could involve decreasing management authority at the school, changing the curriculum, lengthening the school day or year, or other measures. One more year of inadequate scores, and the sanctions intensify: The school can be taken over by the state or a private firm, the staff and principal can be totally replaced. The only way to break the cycle is to make the test-score goal two years running.

In 2014, every child must pass the state tests. Several pieces of No

Child Left Behind have been criticized as idealistic, but none more than this. At Lake Wobegon Elementary, perhaps, every student can be above average, but in America as a whole, can grade-level work be expected of every single child? According to people involved in the law's crafting, any other target was politically infeasible. "No politician can come out and say, we want seventy-five percent of the kids in our country to read," one said.

◆ ◆ ◆

Tina McKnight was a year and a half into her tenure at Tyler Heights when No Child Left Behind became law. She had already begun to make changes at the school—she did not need a law to tell her the chaos needed to be tamed and the students had to be challenged.

The environment at Tyler Heights was the kind the law was intended to change, and the kind that didn't sit well with someone who likes things just so. Tina's hair is always perfectly composed; her outfits too. She favors solid-color ensembles from Hecht's, keeps a pile of shoes behind the driver's seat of her car so she can make last-minute changes, and will store a skirt in her closet for years, tags on, before she finds just the right top to wear it with. She pays the same kind of attention to every detail at school. Tina complained weekly that she needed an assistant principal, like some other schools Tyler Heights' size, but it was hard to imagine her ceding any tasks. Teachers had become used to her generous tweaking of the projects they handed in to her. When letters for the marquee arrived in the wrong size, she offered to follow up; she bought snowman wrapping paper and made fifty placemats, cut to size and laminated, for the staff breakfast.

Tina's energy is boundless. When she has a story, she'll tell it over and over again, with an animated voice and bright open face. That she sleeps only three hours a night doesn't show, except for a brief stretch after school each day when her energy is only at about 97 percent. As a classroom teacher Tina didn't ever sit down and never understood why other people needed to. If she won the lottery, she says, she would still work—though maybe not as many hours, and maybe at her own school in Mexico or Oprah's in South Africa.

The onetime college valedictorian was married for many years to an intense Air Force officer. She wonders where their son, now in medical school, got his competitive spirit; those who know her do not. When she carried this energy to her new job in 2000, it was almost as if nobody could believe she was aiming so high.

"There wasn't anybody pushing Tyler Heights to be anything more than what it was," Tina said. The first time she presided over a fifth-grade graduation, trying to connect with the parents in the audience, she mentioned that she had just been at a graduation too: her son's, from Harvard. After that she was summoned to the school board, she said, and instructed not to mention Harvard. "Be realistic about where you are," she said she was told.

While her latte skin and big almond eyes can arouse mystery about her heritage—"What *are* you?" a third grader once asked—Tina is African American through and through. People assume that means she is closely acquainted with the ghetto and with poverty. But before she dug deep in the Annapolis schools, she said, "I didn't really know about the issues."

She had taught for two and a half decades—in Ohio, Mississippi, Arkansas, and then Maryland—and served as assistant principal for two years before she got a promotion to Tyler Heights. She knew little of the school beyond the warnings of her colleagues and its reputation as a place where principals didn't stick around. The one she was replacing lasted just a year; word was the job nearly killed her. The one before stayed two years. The one before that was well-loved and entrenched but was removed to a desk job after being arrested for allegedly soliciting an undercover cop for sex.

When Tina arrived at Tyler Heights, three in five of its students lived under the poverty level or not far above it—a number that would increase within five years to 70 percent. Children of immigrants, many of them immigrants themselves, are the fastest-growing population at Tyler Heights and in America as a whole, where they comprise nearly one-fifth of elementary schoolers.[11] The school remained mostly black since it opened in 1962, but over the past five years the Hispanic population had risen from 8 percent to one-third. Many of those students had difficulty with English—either because they had never spoken it at home, or never spoken it at all. The classroom teachers, meanwhile, were all white except for Alia Johnson, who was half black. There was a Hispanic ESOL teacher and aide; blacks were well-represented among resource teachers and other staff.

In Anne Arundel County, race has long been a great, grim divide. Throughout the school system, whites outscore blacks on the SAT by nearly three hundred points; in Annapolis proper, whites are ten times as likely as blacks to have graduated from college, and five times less likely to live in poverty. Barely half the black boys who start at Annapolis High School, which Tyler Heights students attend eventually, graduate four years later.[12]

The Anne Arundel County Public Schools had long been accused of holding minorities to different academic and disciplinary standards. Turmoil in particular at Annapolis High, a place where the culture blatantly divided along race and class lines, drove a coalition to file a complaint in 2004 with the U.S. Department of Education's Office of Civil Rights, an action that is often the prelude to a lawsuit. At a press conference announcing the complaint on the anniversary of the *Brown v. Board of Education* ruling, a representative of the local NAACP chapter used the "S" word: segregation.

After months of mediation and just as the 2005–06 school year was beginning, Eric Smith and the school board signed an agreement with the NAACP, allowing that the county "has categorically denied and limited educational opportunities for African American students" through low expectations and lack of encouragement. The evidence was both anecdotal and numerical: blacks underrepresented in honors classes and overrepresented in special education, underrepresented at graduation and overrepresented in suspensions.

Smith acceded to a pact that included a number of promises about algebra completion, participation in extracurricular activities, Advanced Placement coursework, SAT scores, and discipline. Eighty-five percent of black students, he vowed, would pass the state test. At the signing, the president of the local NAACP chapter said he felt like he was signing a Declaration of Independence, awarding freedom to children. News of the agreement brought a "yeah, right" expression to

Tina McKnight's face. She was glad to see attention brought to the culture of low expectations: The Harvard incident came to mind. She herself loved to aim high. When she would present the agreement to her
staff months later, she would betray no ambivalence—as is typical for
her. (Her teachers wished that she would, about a few things at least;
they were not convinced by the constant cheerleading.)

The NAACP agreement—Tina had seen this kind of thing before.
Many years before, she had helped create a massive equity study for the
county, which sat untouched on a shelf ever since. And why should
Anne Arundel County be able to accomplish something out of reach,
so far, for every school district in America? In signing the agreement,
Smith and the board had promised to eliminate the achievement gap by
June 2007, two school years away.

◆ ◆ ◆

When I set out in 2005 to write a book about how the standards and
testing movement had changed the lives of children and teachers, I
knew I needed to write about an impoverished elementary school in an
affluent district. In five years as an education reporter for the *Washington
Post,* and thousands of hours observing classrooms, I had seen school
change a lot in the name of standards and testing, and I felt that people
outside the walls—from parents to politicians—had little idea what went
on inside them. I had seen too where the most dramatic reforms were
taking place. Large, wealthy school systems had the money to commit and the brainpower to innovate and the stability that allowed
them to focus not just on day-to-day management, as is the case in
many urban districts, but on the details of classroom instruction. Elementary schools were generally seen as a good place to inaugurate reform, since the more time passes in a child's life, the harder it is to
remedy deficiencies. In the accountability systems that predated No
Child Left Behind, Title I schools were under scrutiny; with the new
law, they faced the gravest consequences. Certainly, they had the
longest way to climb.

There were not enough white children at Tyler Heights to have an
achievement *gap.* But there were, clearly, achievement problems, the

kind that landed the school on a 2001 *Washington Post* list of "Maryland's Troubled Schools." One of Tina's first moves was to try to nudge out teachers she felt were completely ineffective but had decades of glowing reviews behind them. If she had rated them "unsatisfactory" right away, Tina figured, her superiors would have thought *she* was the problem. She would have to ease down from "satisfactory" one year to "needs improvement" the next to "unsatisfactory" after that, before she could get rid of anyone—praying for resignations and wincing all the while that every year of bad teaching meant that twenty children stagnated.

For reading, teachers in the county had been basically allowed to choose what they taught from a binder of options; Tina sought a grant for a new reading curriculum that would be started in kindergarten through second grade and then expanded throughout the school. She set a goal of 100 percent participation in parent-teacher conferences, no matter if the school had to finance a fleet of taxis. As for the wild environment, she adopted a schoolwide, structured plan of specific rewards and consequences for behavior.

But academically, the biggest changes didn't happen until Eric Smith arrived in the summer of 2002. He came from North Carolina, one of the states that had implemented standards-based reform on its own, with an ambitious agenda similar to the one he had brought to the Charlotte-Mecklenburg schools. He promised to dramatically increase the pass rate on state tests and participation in high-level coursework. He was the first to tell the county: Background doesn't matter. Children will perform no matter what.

"Man," he told school board members, "I'm champing at the bit."

The board, in the fourth wealthiest county in the fourth wealthiest state, had the resources to set Smith loose. He tore up high schoolers' schedules to get them into more Advanced Placement classes. He insisted on new countywide curricula in math and reading. And he was in and out of Tyler Heights, what seemed like all the time.

I visited Eric Smith in April 2005 with a request to immerse myself in a school that, while not dysfunctional, had been in "school improvement"—meaning it had missed targets under No Child Left

Behind at least two years in a row, and meaning the stakes were high. He immediately thought of Tyler Heights. Smith loved Tyler Heights. Really, he loved its principal.

Immediately I was impressed with Tina's lack of guile, her pride in the school paired with total honesty about its shortcomings. (With me at least.) Tina loved attention for the good things happening in her school—"I'm very big about getting in the paper," she told me—and was open, she said, to a "warts and all" portrayal. "Somebody should write a book," she and her colleagues would say when something amazing or appalling happened. Now, somebody was. I had an all-access pass to the school, starting in May 2005. I sat in on classes, on meetings, on events, on conferences. I spent lunches in the cafeteria or the teacher's lounge or conversing with individual children in whatever free space we could find. For hours after school I would talk with Tina and teachers. While the names of Tyler Heights students and families are pseudonyms, the staff I write about all chose to keep their real names. Even after I detailed what would be in the book, they felt they had nothing to be ashamed of.

It had taken a while, but the school was making strides; in 2004 it was finally among the three-quarters in the country to make adequate yearly progress, or AYP. The share of fifth graders passing the MSA in reading and math doubled from 2003, and third-grade reading was going up as well. Tina was told by her boss at the time, "The bottom line is, you can't fall back into that big pit." The stellar 2005 scores, which were released two months after I met with Smith, sent the school not to the pit but to stardom.

Tyler Heights was now, officially, a school that broke the mold—the kind of place supporters of standards-based testing point out as exemplars, as if you could order Tina McKnights out of a catalog. Every newspaper around called to find out her secrets. To one reporter she credited hard work and a focus on MSA vocabulary, to another the importance of motivation: "You have to prove to students they can do it. . . . We have to impart to them that they can learn and they can achieve." One state official, visiting the school, told me Tina was a "classic hero." An impressed school board member showed up with five hundred dollars cash in an envelope, a personal gift. The man who had warned Tina about falling into the pit said, "They are completely breaking out of that mold now, and they are going to be in good standing with the state and with us."

At a countywide conference weeks later, Dr. Smith singled out Tyler Heights for increasing the percentage of black students passing reading from 21 percent to 90 percent in two years. "If you can find a school that can make it work for children, there's no reason it can't be done everywhere," he said, as the Tyler Heights teachers cheered in the back of the big auditorium. "That statistic chokes me up a little bit. They are real gains. They are real lives."

Before he mentioned Tyler Heights, Smith said that day, "As you analyze what it's really all about, it's not about the scores." This was something county leaders were saying into microphones with regularity—"It's not about the scores"—and it made hundreds of teachers in the audience snicker. For they were living in a world where everything was judged by its effect on the scores. Researchers throughout the country were attempting to link any number of factors to quantified improvements in "student learning": The length of a superintendent's tenure. The time class starts in the morning. The composition of school boards. Character education and recess and music class and afterschool programs. The condition of school buildings—square footage per student, air temperature, natural light, street noise. Seating arrangements. Whether it's worth it to give students breakfast at school, and whether those breakfasts should include omega-3 fatty acids.

At Tyler Heights, the scores were posted throughout the school and recited at meetings, a constant reminder of the ultimate goal. This laser-sharp focus was particularly acute here, but you can find it to a degree at nearly any school with a ways to climb and the desire to do so. It is likely to become more widespread, as the nation's schools work their way toward 100 percent proficiency.

In a country full of classrooms marked by an unimaginable variety of experiences and rules and quality, test scores have been the most appealing single factor—perhaps the only possible factor—with which to measure output consistently. Test scores, a pair of influential researchers averred, "tell us precisely what we need to know if we have any hope of reforming education and closing the racial gap in academic achievement."[13] Across America, educators were changing the way they operated; it's a good bet that without the pressure surrounding tests, many schools would have continued to neglect their lowest students.

For better and for worse, then, of course it was about the scores. What I sought to explore: What were the scores about?

3

Am I Going to Be a Bad Teacher?

The day after school started, a group of teachers joined Tina McKnight in her office to make sure no third grader was left behind.

This kind of work goes on at American schools more than ever, though not always as thoroughly as at Tyler Heights. Tyler Heights is small enough so that every adult in the building knows, or at least knows of, each of the three hundred students. The school system encourages attention to individual student data, and the Title I budget provides for the personnel and packaged programs to provide small-group attention. "Data-driven decision-making" is the term often used to describe this sort of preparatory effort, which intensified in Anne Arundel County after the advent of the Maryland School Assessment and the arrival of Dr. Smith.

This Tuesday, the data being reviewed were scores from the previous year's Stanford 10, a test the county requires of its second graders. The average score for the new third graders was below 50 percent. "The work for third grade is tremendously low this year," Tina told the five Literacy Team members crowding the faux mahogany table. (She had ordered the table and removed a set of file cabinets when she learned at a seminar that her office should reflect the way she saw her job: less clerical, more collaborative.) "We've got students who don't bring much to the table."

It hadn't helped, Tina said, that one teacher last year was new to second grade, another "checked out early," and the third—"teacher of the year someplace"—had taught over her students' heads. Alia Johnson had warned two years ago, when she taught these kids as first graders, that they were low achievers and that they could use some of the extra help being given to older students facing the MSA immediately. Now a massive deployment of reading interventions had to be mustered to get these kids ready.

The plan included the use of Corrective Reading, a quick-paced series of scripted phonics lessons, and Soar to Success for reading comprehension. For the lowest readers there was SpellRead, a program recently mandated by the county that required a specially trained technician and a full hour for each of 150 days. Child by child, the group assessed the Stanford scores, as well as the students' personalities.

Some decisions were easy. Eddy, who was only in the twentieth percentile nationally in vocabulary and tended to shut down on his teachers, was slated for Corrective, as was Montell, whose greatest challenge was showing up—though he wasn't too hot with phonics either. Quiet Dantay, the only boy to arrive in Miss Johnson's class without a discipline record, was identified for Soar. So was Dena, a mildly autistic child whose "comprehension is zip," as one teacher put it, but who had an outside chance of passing MSA.

Because SpellRead takes up so much time that otherwise might be spent on MSA skills in class, Tina figured she could pretty much write off a proficient score for the kids who took part. So it was with some reluctance that she recommended SpellRead for two excruciatingly low readers, Munir, who received services in English as a second language (ESOL), and Demetrius, who was in special ed. (Tyler Heights needed both of those subgroups to have proficient scores on MSA. The test score levels are "basic," or failing, "proficient," and "advanced." Even one basic in each group could imperil the school's rating.)

Then there were children whose stories could not be told in percentiles alone. David, a student new to Tyler, had arrived with dismal scores but very little information from his old school except that he needed help in "reading" and "writing." Felicia had no file at all from her last school. For a Mexican girl named Inés who had already flunked one grade, the problem could have been reading comprehension or the English language itself—it was not clear. Michelle, teachers said, would do fine if she didn't behave like a monster. Savannah was smart, so why did she flatline while her classmates improved? Jerold had a surprisingly high Stanford score given that he was, as Yolie Marshall put it, "slow as molasses on a winter day."

"You might star him for test-taking skills," Tina said. Although Jerold had lived in America and spoken English all his life, he had been an ESOL student because his parents spoke Spanish. Children in ESOL or special education—and those who have been graduated from ESOL for up to two years—are entitled to certain kinds of help on tests, called "accommodations," to level the playing field for their deficiencies. Since, unlike the Stanford, the MSA is timed, Tina suggested seeking extra time for Jerold to take the test.

And of Miss Johnson's defiant Malcolm, Tina asked, "What's the intervention he's going to be most available for? How does he respond in a small group?"

"As long as he's not writing," said Yolie, Tyler's most veteran teacher at twenty-eight years of service.

"SpellRead is lots of writing," Tina said.

"Malcolm's problem is keeping up, erasing his writing," Yolie said, and the teachers agreed to leave the Malcolm decision aside for the time being.

"We've got an awful lot of kids we're identifying for intervention," Tina said. She didn't like canned programs like these. During her own teaching days, children weren't pulled out of class for help; she had to do it all. Even a couple of years ago, only the eight worst readers in first and second grade were pulled out for intervention. But then, teachers broke classes into small groups for reading at each student's level, so they were more likely to know how everyone was doing. Now the school had to use a curriculum that taught all children the same lessons using the same reading passages in the same amount of time. What's more, now there was the money, the mandate, and the data to channel attention to the "bubble kids," those teetering on the edge of test-score proficiency.

This meant that half the third grade was to be pulled out of reading each day. The interventions had to be scheduled without cutting into MSA objectives and Open Court and without denying the resource teachers lunch. Yolie pointed out that these kids would have to miss time spent on the county writing curriculum, but that wasn't covered on the MSA. Her comment got no response.

◆ ◆ ◆

While Nikki Facchine is prone to chatty sarcasm and storytelling among her closest colleagues, add a couple of people, call it a meeting, and she'll clam up tight. During teacher orientation in August, though, fresh off an Aruba honeymoon, twenty-three-year-old Nikki had overcome her shyness to participate fully in a session on discipline. Last year in Baltimore, her second as a real teacher, she was given the lowest kids, the ones with the most behavior problems, the ones who ran with scissors, literally, and threw themselves on the floor—so here she paid close attention. "You have to take power away from him," she had said confidently about a theoretical back-talker. "Start taking away minutes from recess. Don't deal with it in front of the class." When the trainer mentioned a book called *Conscious Classroom Management,* Nikki jotted down the title. When she put a transparency on the overhead that read *"Procedures are the railroad tracks. Content is the train,"* Nikki wrote that down too. She had thought she was ready.

By the second week of school, she learned that she was not. Seeing one child get carried, flailing, through the hall during a tantrum, she said to me, "I thought they were better than my old school, but now I don't know."

Eight-year-olds throwing straws, sucking their teeth, rolling their eyes, operating at a general setting of Smart Aleck: "It was not like this in Ohio," Mandi Milhoan said. When she had first been told Tyler's rule about "learning position"—a student must sit with feet on the floor, back against the chair, hands on the desk, head up and forward—she thought, forget it. Everyone's comfortable in their own way. A week into school, she started insisting on it.

Nikki and Mandi couldn't believe how their students would start fights just because someone looked at them wrong. Worse, they didn't seem to want to learn. Two weeks into the school year, only two of Miss Johnson's students had done all their homework. Saying "this will be on the next test" didn't have nearly the potency it had the year before, when her students were so afraid of failing you could see it in their faces. These kids didn't seem at all nervous about doing well.

The teachers, though, were beyond nervous. Now that success was measured mainly in quantifiable ways, and progress was determined by comparing this year's kids to last year's, the bad luck of drawing a bunch of children unable to write a sentence could have a major impact. So Mrs. Facchine felt no small measure of distress when she asked what adding an 's' does to a noun and every face in her class went blank. Miss Milhoan was mortified when she handed out Post-it notes for questions about friendship and got back *"How do friend go yon"* and *"The kestos is the kmbslo,"* and then again when Stella didn't know what a paragraph was ("though boy, she knew I had a Coach purse"). Miss Johnson felt nearly ill when Dantay answered "Word" to "What is the character trait that describes you?" and when Roman answered "Four" to "How much is between seventeen and eighteen?"

Last year, Miss Johnson's students aced their math facts, and increased the third-grade pass rate on MSA twenty-four points from the year before. This year it was a challenge to zip through the morning math meeting script in the prescribed fifteen to twenty minutes.

"Nineteen, seventeen, fifteen, thirteen. Roman, what are we counting by?"

"Minus one? Minus ten?"

"How many jumps do I have to go?"

"Backwards?"

"Nineteen, seventeen, fifteen, thirteen. What's the next one? Autumn?"

"Twelve? Thirteen? Fifteen?"

Repeating last year's MSA 90 percent reading proficiency seemed impossible to Miss Johnson on the eleventh day of school when her students couldn't tell consonants from vowels. She told them to take out their laminated lists of letters. Savannah held the long, skinny card by its end and watched it wave back and forth past her face.

"Which letters are consonants?" Miss Johnson asked.

"B?" Avante said.

"Which ones in general?"

Nothing.

"The black letters are consonants," Miss Johnson said slowly. "The ones that aren't red. Every letter but A, E, I, O, and U. You learned the difference between vowels and consonants in first grade. Close your notebooks and take out your black-and-white journals. Open to the first clean page and write vowels and then consonants." For four minutes, letter by letter, she said, gently, "Raise a quiet hand. Is 'A' a consonant or a vowel? Raise a quiet hand. Is 'B' a consonant or a vowel?"

Repeating last year's 90 percent reading proficiency seemed impossible to Mrs. Facchine too, if her students didn't start showing more interest. They had had some good conversations about the stories they read—one of the best times to be in class was when the children looked through the pages of a new story and imagined what it would be about—but more often, the spark was dim. "It's hard to tell if they don't know it, they're just tired, or they don't care," Mrs. Facchine said.

Generating motivation would be a problem all year for these teachers. They blamed the rigidity (and boringness) of the curriculum and the pace they had to maintain, though sometimes it might have helped if they had simply explained *why*, connecting skills or content with the real world. "Why are we learning this?" was a common question the students had. Really, it is one of the best questions a child can ask, if considered and answered seriously, but to Miss Johnson it was at best a delaying tactic. In her mind, "Why are we learning this?" was an appropriate question for sixth graders at the earliest. In third grade you learn things because your teacher teaches them. Because you want to please her. Because that's the lesson that comes next in the math pacing guide. Because Objective (c) of Indicator 1 of Topic C of Standard 6.0 of the Maryland Voluntary State Curriculum in mathematics requires that you be able to solve addition and subtraction word problems. Because subtraction is one of the fundamental skills of everyday human existence.

◆ ◆ ◆

At her apartment in a D.C. suburb, Miss Milhoan was still nursing her boyfriend and his broken arm; at school she felt like an idiot nearly every minute of every day. The previous year in Ohio she had felt so competent. Now it wasn't even the end of September and she didn't know what to do about the boy who had arrived in May with no English and didn't understand most of what she said. She didn't know what to do about the supersmart girl, because the school had formal interventions for low students but none for gifted ones. She didn't know what to do about the boy who would fart all day and announce, "I smell like salad."

There were bright spots, times when Miss Milhoan felt she had the power to improve things at least a little. First, she realized what nobody else had, even though there was no test score to confirm it: A new girl couldn't sound out words and needed to be in Corrective Reading. Then, after she wrote a note home telling parents that kids weren't turning in homework and that she would deduct points for papers without names, for a few days the work came back, properly signed. "Maybe I'm not a total loss," Miss Milhoan said.

But she couldn't keep up with the prescribed lesson pace, a problem most of the teachers had, and the day's organization often fell apart. Morning announcements and breakfast spilled into the fifteen minutes assigned to character education. Character education spilled into the twenty minutes of math meeting. Math meeting spilled into Open Court. As for the list of all the terms and skills from the Maryland curriculum that were likely to be on MSA, which she was told to do in "flextime," whatever "flextime" was, Miss Milhoan never seemed to have any.

After one week, the three third-grade classes were already behind in science and social studies. At county training new teachers had learned about the science program, complete with new textbooks and experiment kits stacked in plastic bins. Science would be taught forty-five minutes on half the days, alternating with social studies, the trainer said. But that wasn't the message teachers got at Tyler Heights. "Science and social studies is a part of the day, I will have to tell you, that often gets compacted," McKnight had said before school started. Miss Johnson had told Miss Milhoan and Mrs. Facchine, "I know they bought all this stuff for us. If you don't get experiments done, don't stress. Read the textbook and go over the terms in bold. The benchmark test, they don't ask questions about experiments; they ask questions about terms."

In planning meetings Miss Johnson would enumerate everything to be done that week and it would make sense to Miss Milhoan, until she got back to her classroom. "I almost feel like I don't know what I'm doing," she said about the reading lessons. "I need to physically see someone doing this stuff. Am I going to be a bad teacher?"

◆ ◆ ◆

Miss Johnson was pretty sure she wasn't a bad teacher, but as September progressed, she became further convinced she had a class of bad kids. She was sitting at the overhead in front of the class, filling in a social studies worksheet of concentric circles. The innermost circle, she explained, was for your town.

"Maryland!"

"Maryland is not your town. Maryland is our state. Most of you live in Annapolis. Even if you live in Harbour House or Eastport Terrace, you still live in Annapolis. I live in Glen Burnie, so I'm going to write 'Town—Glen Burnie' in the middle circle."

Then she moved to *"Anne Arundel County—county"* in the next circle.

"What's a county?" someone asked, and Miss Johnson paused to think. Anne Arundel County and its governance was a core piece of the third-grade social studies curriculum but difficult to explain to eight-year-olds who didn't yet understand town or state. "A county is where we just are," she said. "What state do we all live in?"

"Annapolis," Jamila said.

"Maryland," Roman said.

"We all live in Maryland who goes to school at Tyler Heights," Miss Johnson said. "When I go home to visit my mom in Pennsylvania, that's not Maryland anymore. That's Pennsylvania. What state do we live in?"

"Maryland."

"You should write Maryland on your paper," Miss Johnson said, and demonstrated on the overhead. "Felicia, you have been poking holes in your tights with your pencil all day. Cyrus, take that off. We live in the United States of America," she continued, but, by this point, the kids were dreadfully bored by filling in circles. They were snickering at Felicia and her tights and Cyrus and his pencil case and were talking to one another about anything but geography.

"Put your papers away in your social studies folder, and put your heads down," Miss Johnson said. "I'm done teaching for today. I'm not talking anymore. You don't want to get smarter, that's your problem. If you don't pass third grade, if you don't pass your report card, if you don't pass the MSA, you can explain to your parents why not. If you want your third-grade year to be awful and miserable, keep doing what you're doing."

At this point Summer turned to talk to Savannah. Miss Johnson ordered her out of the desk, pushed it across the room, and pulled Jamila's over to replace it. "Jamila, you're switching seats with Summer. Because *you're* not going to talk to Savannah."

"I'm not."

"I know."

Then it was time to pack up for the day. The kids straggled out for dismissal, while Alia held back tears. Nikki came in and asked, "How did the rest of your day go?"

"I'm not coming back."

4

A Bank Teller Could
Pick Up the Lesson

Think about your favorite teachers from your youth: the ones who changed your life. The ones who taught you lessons you carry with you decades later. Chances are, these were the teachers with a gift for improvisation, artists of the classroom who brought a spark of life to the most mundane subjects. Chances are, they didn't teach from a script.

At an August meeting, a woman from the county's reading office introduced elementary school principals to "explicit instruction," weekly lessons completely orchestrated for the teacher, from what questions she should ask to what answers she should look for. Open Court gave similar guidance, but not as meticulously. A line drawing of a bank teller popped up on the PowerPoint, and the presenter enthused, "A bank teller could pick up the lesson immediately. We're really proud of what we've come up with. It's really exciting."

"Explicit instruction—what a gift," said McKnight's supervisor, Lorna Leone. All around McKnight her colleagues applauded; one said, "This is fabulous!" After having scrambled all summer to fill Tyler Heights with the teachers she thought were the best educated, the best qualified, and the most creative, McKnight was not so sure. "Why don't I just go and hire a bunch of bank tellers?" she said under her breath.

The explicit lessons, and similar moves toward uniformity among teaching corps around the country, were an attempt to match each day's lessons with state standards and infuse a measure of consistency among a cadre of teachers who varied widely in ability, experience, and style. It makes great sense for teachers to know exactly *what* they need to teach; the question is whether they need to be told exactly how. The explicit lessons weren't meant to offend, but they did, insecurity in teachers' abilities oozing from the exactness of the instructions:

> SAY: *It is important to learn about character traits because it helps you understand characters and how they behave in stories. . . . Remember when Julian asked Gloria to come over to his house? She told Julian she would have to ask her mom. What is Gloria like? (teacher think aloud) Well I'd say she seems to be pretty responsible. How do I know? Because she did what her mom told her to do before leaving the yard and that is responsible.*

At Tyler's new-teacher orientation, McKnight had put a cartoon on the overhead showing a teacher facing her students from the front of a cresting roller coaster car. "Today we're going to learn about gravity," the teacher said. Mrs. Facchine liked that her principal wanted colorful, real-world teaching—and now she was being handed a script? "Why did I spend four years in school?" Nikki said. "Why am I getting my masters? It feels like anyone could walk off the street and have my job."

Particularly in a school with low scores, the twenty-first-century educator teaches the standards laid out by the state, in a manner prescribed by the school system, very often according to curricula that leave little room for maneuvering. The social studies teacher I had in sixth grade, whose class seemed to consist solely of showing slides from his vacations and making us copy country facts out of the encyclopedia, would never have cut it in today's world. Then again, the teacher who taught me fluent French by way of crepe-making, art appreciation, and the composition of goofy songs might not have either.

Shortly after Eric Smith arrived in Anne Arundel County, he said something I have heard from superintendents around the country: "We're trying to weave this place together to be not a system of schools, but a school system."[1] Just like jazz musicians master technique before they improvise, he told me later, teachers need a standard, structured platform laying out the basics before they apply their artistry. Of course, having no direction is a curse—particularly for rookies. But the message came down to teachers that a visitor should be able to go into any third-grade classroom in the county and see the same thing. Whether it was their interpretation or a clear directive, they felt they had no room for improvisation.[2] They were expected to follow pacing guides that laid out which lessons to teach each day in language arts, math, science, and social studies. (Even the guidance counselor followed a pacing guide.) Open Court Reading and Saxon Math came with consultants who made sure the programs were faithfully implemented. At Tyler Heights, teachers were told what share of their walls to devote to a math bulletin board (for a series of scripted daily exercises), a reading bulletin board, examples of student work, and a big list of vocabulary words needed to understand the Maryland School Assessment. The MSA words, teachers were warned, would fill the walls like kudzu.

At orientation, several new hires told me they liked how Open Court Reading laid out exactly what they should do each day. "We don't have to think," one second-grade teacher said, as if that were a good thing. Certainly for a teacher who doesn't want to think, who can't figure out what to do without being told—not that this particular teacher couldn't have—this kind of guidance makes sense. In some ways it can make the job more appealing for unmotivated teachers who might otherwise be scared away by rigorous standards and testing. (Which is good or bad, depending on your point of view.) At the same time, minimizing autonomy can alienate the teachers a school wants most to keep: the best, experienced ones.

These are the ones in low supply at schools with the highest poverty and the least freedom. It is no secret that in American public schools, poor, minority children have the greenest teachers.[3] (More than half of Tyler Heights' teachers were in their first or second year.) School systems have attempted to comply with the rules in No Child Left Behind that ensure that all teachers have a basic level of knowledge about the subjects they teach. The law, however, also tells states to make sure that in districts receiving Title I money, poor and minority students have teachers as experienced as those in other schools—a provision that has largely been ignored. The allocation of experienced teachers—in Anne Arundel County and around the nation—is still terribly inequitable.[4]

Experience inequity is not the only problem. There is also a common perception that schools of education does not provide a particularly rigorous program. Given those factors, you start to see why administrators have set up such highly structured systems, especially in elementary schools, that attempt to leave teachers little room to fail.[5] Innovative teachers can sneak their way around the scripts, at least if no visitors are in their classrooms. If you've proven yourself, you might get that leeway. But all in all, teachers—the good ones, the ones you would want teaching your children—complain that the more they are told exactly what to do and how, the less they feel vested in the successes of their students, and the likelier they are to leave.

◆ ◆ ◆

There is, Tina told her staff, a Tyler Heights way of doing things, one she hoped to formalize soon in a binder of Best Practices. Teachers were expected to plan lessons together. Those that did received high praise; those that didn't vexed her endlessly. The format for answering a BCR, the way student data was charted, the way lesson plans were written, the way children were supposed to quiz one another in class: Everything was formalized from above. For fairness and accuracy, Tina said, all children in a given grade should get the same quizzes and tests, and teachers should fill out report cards together, to ensure that each child's marks were determined by the same criteria.

One of the biggest current education fads is "professional learning communities," in which educators in a school work together to improve instruction through structured, continuous self-assessment. Administrators throughout the school system were required to read two books on "PLCs," and apparently their counterparts across the country were too, because at conferences I frequently heard presenters say things such as, "Schools with professional learning communities are four times more likely to be improving than ones where teachers work on their own" and "Schools where teachers bash students and parents in the teachers lounge have stagnant achievement; those where they talk about teaching and learning instead show improvement." (Nobody mentioned what happens to achievement in schools where teachers' lunchtime conversation revolves mainly around wedding plans and reality television.)

It is not necessarily part of teacher culture to watch one another in action for instructional inspiration.[6] The resource teachers met with McKnight weekly to talk about how they could help throughout the building and usually followed through, but often the teamwork sounded like this: "Let's introduce the MSA cards Wednesday for compare and contrast, and Thursday for character traits. Friday the objective is to take the comprehension assessment, the lesson assessment, the vocabulary assessment, and review the MSA cards. Tuesday do the spelling pretest. For Wednesday it's long 'a,' plural and possessive nouns, and workbook pages ten and eleven."

Most planning centered around keeping up with the pacing guides, which proved in real life hard to follow, especially for the least experienced teachers. What does a second-grade teacher do on the day the guide says to teach adverbs, but the children don't yet know adjectives? When they're supposed to learn haikus but don't yet know syllables? County pacing accounted for two brief constructed responses with each Open Court story, but McKnight wanted teachers to fit in more. If kids scored poorly on a quiz or a test, she wanted the material introduced over again. But the pacing guides, the teachers worried, didn't leave room for reteaching.

"Can we review in workshop time?" one fourth-grade teacher asked a resource teacher.

"I can't promise it won't be questioned," she was told.

Nikki Facchine figured that after lunch, recess, and daily specials (PE, music, art, library, computers), there were barely four hours of class time. In Baltimore last year she was able to spend enough time on each topic so that her students would finally get it. This year when she wanted to review common versus proper nouns, she tried to do it in thirty seconds. In education school in Delaware she learned all these great ideas on how to teach, how to apply concepts to real-life situations; now she didn't get to do any of that. When, she thought, was the last time her professors had been in a classroom?

She didn't blame her students for their languor. "It's so scripted," she said. "I want to make it fun but there's no time."

"Every time we have a new word, can we do Word Scrabble?"
Gardell asked.

"Maybe."

"Awww."

"I'm not the boss," Facchine told them. "I don't make those decisions."

◆ ◆ ◆

One boss, McKnight's new supervisor, made her first thorough visit to
Tyler Heights in October. Back when teachers each did their own thing,
Lorna Leone felt, you couldn't compare the progress between classes
or schools. So now she emphasizes uniformity—at quite a detailed
level. After Leone's four-hour visit, McKnight sat down with Alia Johnson, the lead teacher for third through fifth grades, and Sheila McDermott, the kindergarten teacher who led the primary grades. Leone was
concerned that each classroom in each grade didn't have the same
number of vocabulary words displayed on their Word Walls. Why
aren't they all the same size? Why do some teachers post the words on
the wall and some on a flip chart? Why does one fifth-grade teacher
have parts of speech on the wall but the other doesn't? How do teachers collaborate on which words are hung up?

"My kids are higher, so we had more words up," McDermott said.

Leone was also concerned, McKnight said, that one class in a grade
was listening to a story on tape while another class was taking turns
reading it aloud. One class read at their desks, another on the carpet.
One teacher used a green witch's finger as a pointer to lead children
through the story, which Leone thought would be distracting. When
she had gotten to third grade, she was pleased to see each of the three
classes working on the same BCR at the same time.

On Leone's next inspection, she told McKnight as they started
through the building that she was going to "zero in on the posted
outcomes"—the daily objectives teachers wrote on the board for each
subject. Writing objectives has become a big deal in schools. Teachers
actually take classes in this—the more jargon the better, it seems: "We
will demonstrate the ability to perceive, perform and respond to music" in music, "Develop expressive and receptive vocabulary to begin to classify things
found in the home environment" in a kindergarten play kitchen.

Passing through the gym, where kindergartners wafted a colorful parachute in the air and scampered under it in turns, Leone said of the teacher, "I can't see his goal." In pre-kindergarten, where Leone saw not only "sight words" like *is* and *and* but also the MSA scores displayed on the wall, she said, "I love the way these are all posted." In fifth grade she was dismayed to find some of Mrs. Williams's students sitting at their desks reading books while others finished a test. She encouraged McKnight to come up with a school-wide protocol for spending time after completing a test, one that didn't include free reading.

Mrs. Williams, a former Navy officer, was probably the Tyler Heights teacher least on board with the push for uniformity, the one who rarely used the overhead projector, the most maligned for not being a team player. ("Soon they're going to make us go to the bathroom together," she grumbled when told to collaborate on report cards.) Objectives, though, Mrs. Williams did well, and Leone was pleased to see her board say, "*The student will use the comprehension strategies of monitoring and clarifying, making connections, and visualizing during the first read.*" She liked that a first-grade teacher had written, "*We will identify verbs and write a sequence of events using transition words. We will blend orally to form words. We will identify spellings for known sounds.*" She even boxed key words! When Leone peeked into Miss Johnson's room, however, she saw, "*We will review for the unit assessment.*"

"We need to work on our goals," Leone told McKnight.

It's not enough to use the educationese on the board. "Students need to own the vocabulary," Leone said, and McKnight agreed. But students don't own the vocabulary. They don't even read it. They look to see what time reading will end and they'll get to go to lunch, but I've never talked to any kid in any grade in any school who actually paid attention to the bulky, abstruse outcomes. "They don't make much sense," one fifth grader told me, and they never have to me either. What is the point, exactly, of telling first graders, "Today we're going to model efficient addition and subtraction strategies," instead of "We're going to add and subtract"?

Back in McKnight's office Leone said, "Well, Tina, everything you showed me today shows you're right on task where you need to be. I don't want them to get lost in the writing of outcomes, but I want them to know what they're going to be teaching." For instance, third grade. "What a shame the whole day is review." In any case, she said, the objective should be something like *"Review reading strategies used in narrative reading,"* instead of *"We will review for the unit assessment."*

Then Leone changed the subject, asking McKnight if she had come to work on the day off Friday—knowing that, of course, she had.

"How many nights have you worked this month?" Leone asked.

McKnight opened her eyes wide and breathed deep.

"Look at me," Leone said.

"How many nights are there?"

"I want you to really start thinking about this." It's this thing they do, Leone telling McKnight to work less, and McKnight knowing that will never happen.

5

Was It a Big Scratch or a Little Scratch?

There is no better way to understand the growing responsibilities of American schools—not just to educate children, but in many ways to raise them—than by spending a day with a guidance counselor. When parents of Tyler Heights students are murdered or overdose in the middle of the night, the children usually attend school the next day, and it is up to the counselor, Jennifer Johnson, to comfort them. When kids show up for a few weeks, leave for a few weeks, come back and disappear again, it is up to Johnson to track them down. When a six-year-old burst into tears several times a day, Johnson puzzled it out until she determined the girl was seeing visions from a horror movie she had watched with her mom. Parents phone her for help with their own problems. (There is little the counselor won't do for a child. Mediating drama between exes, though—that's where she draws the line.)

Tyler Heights has a good number of children whose parents have managed to protect them from the grit of the neighborhood, navigating the home-work-church triad of much of the African American and Hispanic middle class. Nonetheless, at the lunch table most of the eight-year-olds keenly narrate the crimes they have witnessed. They talk about men "smoking the stuff" against the housing project Dumpsters. They ask if you too have seen the edgy cartoon *The Boondocks* or the drug-filled Ray Charles biopic or *Get Rich or Die Tryin'*, starring the rapper 50 Cent. "They *do it*," a third grader named Tisha told me, after watching the movie with her aunt.

When a social worker at Career Day asked a class of first graders who knew what Social Services was, hands shot up and children began sharing: "They come to make sure your house is clean." "They came when my dad got out of jail and my mom was pregnant and he threw a plate at her and then she didn't have the baby." (By third grade they'll learn: What happens at home is nobody's business.) When young children not only carried walkie-talkies in the neighborhood but were cagey about them, suspicions grew that they were being used as drug runners. One mother gave her second grader and kindergartner instructions on how to steal diapers from Rite Aid, then sent them in alone.

Johnson, who laughs even in awkward yearbook photos, navigates her days with an unrelenting optimism that her coworkers find both admirable and odd. But underneath her cheery sunshine, the counselor wants to cry several times a day. While she had already spent four years at Tyler Heights and six years teaching before that, no amount of time will harden you to the nonchalant way children speak about whom their mother is sleeping with, or how their twelve siblings each have a different dad, or going to clubs, as if this were part of their daily affairs. Johnson was sad but not surprised the morning she asked a preschooler why he was late and he said, "My mom put a knife on my dad because he was supposed to be working at Popeyes but he was with his girlfriend."

What came from the mouths of Tyler Heights kindergartners in particular fed a never-ending pool of anecdotes both pathetic and amusing: The boy who, when complimented on his new sneakers, said, "Thanks! My mom stole them! But don't steal toys from Value City or you'll get caught!" The girl who announced during sharing, "I saw my dad through the glass and talked to him on the phone!" The girl who saw a plastic wrapper at the edge of the playground and ran over to warn, "Teacher! There's a rubber over there! Dem things are dangerous!" At least, her teacher sighed, she realized the hazard.

When Casey Dunleavy, a young second-grade teacher, was asked during a lesson if parents were heroes, she said, rhetorically, "Do they give you food to eat? Do they give you a bed to sleep on?"

"No, I have to sleep on the floor with my stupid brother."

"Well, do they give you a nice warm floor instead of outside?"

When a boy in Miss Johnson's class asked what "stray" meant, as in "stray cat," Felicia piped up: "Like a homeless person." When Miss Johnson explained that a tropical storm "is not going to hurt your house like you saw on the news in Texas and Louisiana and Mississippi," Felicia announced, "I live in a shelter."

The immigrant children compare how many people are crammed into their tiny homes (seven, nine, thirteen, relatives and strangers), how much of the housekeeping they are responsible for (most of it), what it was like to cross the border. The kids are matter-of-fact about traversing the river by moonlight and laugh in the telling, but there is nothing funny about stories like Tere's. The Salvadoran girl told a teacher that she was sent on the journey with a group of people she didn't know, all ditched by their coyote in Mexico. A stranger in the group helped her patch her way to America, where she was having trouble making it through fourth grade—again.

◆ ◆ ◆

Johnson got her day started one December morning by running up-to-date attendance data. Data, paperwork, numbers, forms: Now more than ever, the load felt unmanageable. Under No Child Left Behind, average daily attendance below 94 percent would mean a failure to make adequate progress, no matter what the test scores were. This was no sure thing. It didn't matter if the Latino kids stayed home because a blue van was rumored to be trolling for illegals—absences counted against them. It didn't matter if a child was suspended—absences counted against them. "It doesn't matter if they're sick," Johnson said. "It does in my heart, but not in the data."

Her primary attendance concerns for the day were Jada, a fifth grader who hadn't been at school the past sixteen days, and Nevaeh, a first grader who had threatened a classmate. Johnson, who always keeps up on the news from home, heard that Jada's mom had disappeared, and she couldn't track the girl down. Nevaeh, she figured, had acted out because of family upheaval, but the mother blamed the school, Johnson said, and threatened to keep her out indefinitely.

Johnson had set up a bulletin board where classes earned a mark every day they had perfect attendance; each month the winning class got a snack. If you were one of the many children with more than three absences in a quarter, she talked to your mother. She got you an alarm clock. She even fetched you in her '97 Ford Probe, which everyone called Black Beauty. And she documented it all in the attendance records, stored in one of many binders that caused her bookshelves to sag ominously.

Before the bell rang, Johnson shut the binder and took her place in the lobby. Tyler Heights is a warm place and the staff, in a litigious world, is brave enough to be generous with hugs. Children are welcomed and sent home every day through an assembly line of enthusiasm, from Mr. Al opening the car door to Ms. Prater opening the school door to Ms. Johnson complimenting your outfit. "How is every*body*?" she said in her unique cadence. "How's every*thing*?"

As always, she was greeted with hugs and accusations.

"Joe hit someone," she was told.

"He told me to be quiet," Joe protested.

"Did you put your hands on another person's body?"

"Yes."

"We'll talk later," Johnson said, and continued to greet children left and right. "Oh, stop with those boots. Those are too cute. Do they come in Ms. Johnson's size? Let me fix your buttons. How come you look so stylish? How's every*thing*? Do you have a note today? Where did you put it?" This was a fifth grader who had just transferred from a charter school and spent a half-hour crying for mommy in the guidance office. Johnson came up with the idea of having a new note from her mom every day. "Where do you want to keep it? Do you want to tear it out and keep it with you, so if you need it you don't have to go to your locker? Here, fold it, put it in your pocket." As the last kids straggled in, the Pledge of Allegiance came over the PA, and Johnson stopped to join in, her hand over her heart and her face pressed against the door looking for latecomers. Tardies, too, were tallied in the binder.

Every morning Ms. Johnson met with a second grader named

Kadeem to make sure he was calm enough to start the day in class; today she headed to his room and found him absent. She greeted two tardy children and told one that she would have to do a neglected homework assignment during music class. Johnson was discussing with Mr. Dillard, the dean of students responsible for discipline, whether a new baby in the house was making a normally well-behaved second grader act out when she was called to meet with a kindergartner. The girl had just told her teacher that her brother, who had been suspended from school, was beaten at home.

Jamie settled in at Ms. Johnson's table and checked out the walls, which were covered by pictures students had drawn, Washington Redskins paraphernalia, and motivational posters about the blessings of children. Her eyes lit on a bag of candy canes.

"I might be able to hook you up a little later," Ms. Johnson said.

Jamie reached for a pad on the table, her alphabet barrettes clacking, and said, "I want to write something. I want to write a sentence."

I like to go to school.

"Jamie, why do you like going to school?"

"Because we do activities. We make snowmen. We draw hearts. Two snowmen. I want to write another sentence."

We like to go to hom.

"Tell me what happened yesterday at home."

"We played a puzzle."

Johnson leaned in. "Is Ms. Johnson your teacher?"

"No."

"Does she teach PE?"

"No."

"Her job here, her most important job, is to make sure boys and girls are good and safe."

Jamie noticed Johnson's diamond ring. "What's that for?"

"That tells people I'm going to get married."

"What's this one say?" Jamie touched the other hand.

"That one is just decoration. Jamie, I like to make sure students are safe at home. Yesterday, what happened at the house with Jemarcus?"

"I played with Jemarcus?"

"Did people get hurt? Did you see Jemarcus yesterday?"

"He got beaten."

"Does he have any marks on him?"

"A scratch on his face?"

Ms. Johnson brought Jamie's finger to her face. "Was it a big scratch or a little scratch? Show me how big." Jamie dragged her finger about an inch. "What did he say to Jemarcus?"

"Why you be bad at school."

"How did he scratch him?"

"A belt."

"Did Jemarcus cry?"

Jamie didn't answer. She wrote again: *dog log*. "I'm write you some sight words." *The we*.

"Pick your last favorite word you want to write down for me," Ms. Johnson said. *Small*, Jamie wrote, and was sent on her way.

Barely a minute passed before Ms. Johnson had another visitor: a second grader named Carla, whose cries and words tumbled out at a frantic speed. "Trina and Antoneshia, they said my mommy fights with my daddy. I said they do not—they sleep together in the same bed with my sister. They said my mommy is nasty and pooped on the floor."

Johnson's credo was to believe 50 percent of what she heard; she also knew to trace things to the origin. "How did this start? Do you live by Trina or Antoneshia?"

"Mommy took me to Antoneshia's house yesterday. She was my friend but now she's not."

"I know that is upsetting. You love your mom more than anyone else. What is something your mom does for you?"

"She makes cake and cookies."

"She washes your hair, she puts you to bed, she makes you dinner, she takes care of you. This is my question: Are you okay right now? I would like to meet with all of the girls at lunchtime. Is that okay? Do you feel they will keep bothering you if I don't speak to you all now? They are not going to be able to come to school and talk to you that way. We know these things aren't true. You did the right thing by telling an adult. Are you okay? You know your mom loves you so much. I re-member when you first came to Tyler Heights." Carla was wearing a sparkly gold bracelet. "Who gave that to you?"

"My mom."

"Does she know you are wearing it? That is bling-bling fancy."

After Carla left, Johnson said, "This is why attendance doesn't get done."

As the morning passed, Ms. Johnson watched a second grader race against Mr. Dillard—a reward the boy, one of several at the school with a special behavior incentive plan, won for being good several days in a row. She got a phone message from Trina's doctor, saying he wanted to report neglect because the girl was morbidly obese. He asked for Johnson's help in getting Trina to eat healthy and talking to the mother.

So now, Johnson sighed, the school was responsible for the girl's diet too. Many children in poverty are given bottles of sugar water or Oodles of Noodles broth as infants, Froot Loops as toddlers, and by the time they show up at school they're often overweight, undernourished, plagued with rotting teeth. Tyler Heights students laughed when I asked if they had to drink milk at home; occasionally they arrived at school at 7:45 a.m. clutching sodas from McDonald's. All American public schools provide federally subsidized lunch to poor children; at Tyler Heights, free breakfast is served too. In the bins delivered to each classroom, among the mostly untouched Wheaties and Cheerios, are packets of Pop-Tarts and Dinosaur Grahams, sugar-laden strawberry milk, iced Super Buns with enough vitamins pumped through the sixteen grams of fat to qualify as nutritious.

Johnson decided the doctor could wait. In her office she ate her weekly preemptive lunch with a troubled third grader and three friends of his choice, leaving jealous classmates behind as they carried their trays out of the cafeteria. "Will you eat with me?" was one of the most commonly uttered sentences at Tyler Heights; the kids were desperate for one-on-one audiences with Johnson or Dillard or any adult who would join them in the calm conversation they said they rarely got at home. It pained them that this privilege was awarded disproportionately to the naughty kids.

"How's everything?" Ms. Johnson asked the boys.

"Fine," they chimed.

"I can't wait to do the MSA test so I can move on to fourth grade," David said. The third graders erroneously believed that a good MSA score was required for promotion—a notion their teachers chose not to touch.

Between the first and second lunch periods, Mr. Dillard told Ms. Johnson that Felicia was going to be suspended again, for kicking. Yesterday's in-school suspension had been ineffective, they agreed. Ms. McKnight instituted in-school suspensions last year to reduce the number of regular suspensions and keep children in school learning instead of, say, going to the mall. "I hate in-school suspension," Ms. Johnson said. "If parents aren't inconvenienced, you won't get their attention. What is it? It's babysitting."

Antoneshia, Trina, and Carla came into the guidance office with their trays and sat at the table. Mother insults, Johnson told the girls, "are the worst thing you can do without touching someone. Before you say something, you have to think, would I want someone to say this to me? And would I say this in front of my parents?"

When Antoneshia changed the subject to her baby nieces, Johnson didn't protest. She saw the opportunity for detective work: Antoneshia was a half-sister to Jada, the AWOL fifth grader.

"Where do you go to see the babies?" Johnson asked.

Antoneshia told her which neighborhood, "the third building down the hill." "Is there a number, like 7401? Is your mom there? Who takes you there? Is there a phone number? Do you know it, Antoneshia?"

She did.

For Johnson, a working phone number could be as rare and valuable as a Honus Wagner baseball card. After the girls left, the counselor shook her head and grinned at her good fortune. She dialed, and Jada's aunt answered. "Hello, this is Jennifer Johnson, the guidance counselor at Tyler Heights? I'm looking for Jada because she hasn't come back from break. Pink eye? Did she see a doctor? She should be able to come back the day after she sees the doctor. She'll be back down tomorrow?"

Johnson hung up. More often than not parents sent their kids to school sick. "Pink eye. That's so much BS." The aunt had seemed annoyed that Johnson had called. "Well," Johnson told me, "if you don't want me to keep calling you, don't lie, because I will ride you to the end. These kids have to be in school." A report came over Johnson's walkie-talkie of a second grader angry he had to miss PE because of reading intervention, so she sent Mr. Al, a behavior specialist who worked with Mr. Dillard. A form letter went in the mail to Jada's aunt, following up on the phone conversation, and was documented in the attendance file.

"I can't believe she gave me a good number," Johnson said. The phone rang. It was Jemarcus's dad, who was scheduled to come for a meeting before his son could be taken off suspension. When the father asked if he had to bring Jemarcus, Johnson's smile vanished; she made a mental note to look for a mark on the boy's face.

"I need to report child abuse" is how Jennifer Johnson starts way too many phone conversations. She called Child Protective Services and asked them to visit Jemarcus's dad without letting on that Jamie had snitched. She then called the grandmother of a second grader who hadn't been showing up at after-school tutoring. She was about to call her mechanic—the Check Engine light, again—but Mr. Al came in with news that Malcolm was in the Respect Room. It was formally called the Respect Decision Making Room, in a world where no euphemism is too silly, but Mr. Al called it "South Central." Malcolm hadn't finished his writing assignment before the class moved on, and he had erupted.

By now Johnson was late for a guidance lesson in Ms. McDermott's kindergarten. When she entered the classroom, the kids swooshed in for hugs, and she directed them back to the carpet. "Today we're going to talk about a problem that sometimes happens at school. What is it called when you take something that belongs to someone else? Alisha?"

"Snatching."

"Some people call it snatching. Marquis?"

"You steal."

It was once considered a given that a child's character was shaped at home and brought to school like a pencil box or clean notebook. But just like today's children come without sharpened pencils, they often come without control of their emotions and impulses—a void that impedes academic potential more than any school supply. Many students also lack empathy, McKnight told her teachers. "If you cannot connect with other people, you're never going to make decisions based on other people's self-interest," she said.

Character education programs have become a given in many American schools. At Tyler Heights, students were explicitly taught, day in and day out, the culture of school: greeting people properly, writing your name and date on your work, answering in complete sentences, sitting in learning position. The first week students learned the school's Code of Conduct and every day they recited the Respect pledge, after the one to the flag. The children had been given blue rubber bracelets that said RESPECT, to remind them to behave, but they seemed to just remind them that they had something on their wrist to play with, so the idea was abandoned. Every Friday students were given a lesson on values—responsibility, courtesy, and so on—sponsored by Chick-fil-A, the sandwich chain. The four other days, for the first half of the year, teachers gave a fifteen-minute scripted lesson from Second Step, which aims to prevent violence through social skills. Second Step teaches kindergartners about their feelings and the meaning of concepts like "maybe later"; third graders learn how to make conversation and how to keep from stealing. (It is yet another program that hints at higher test scores on its website.)

Kim Benefield, the psychologist assigned to Tyler Heights two days a week, had regular meetings with the children most lacking in social skills, where they might play a board game called "The Helping, Sharing, and Caring Game." Questions include, "Why is it important to throw garbage in the garbage can?" and "Why is it dangerous to trip another person?" Straightforward stuff, but very often, Benefield said, it didn't translate into changed behavior. The problem wasn't that these children didn't realize it was bad to litter or trip. It was that too often they didn't seem to care.

Twice a month each class received a guidance lesson from Ms. Johnson. On her rounds today, the counselor read the kindergartners a book about a leopard who was plagued by guilt after stealing a toy truck. She showed second graders a video about managing frustration and with a first-grade class she pulled items one by one from her Anger Bag. When you are fuming mad, Ms. Johnson told the children, you might find some relief by screaming into a pillow, listening to relaxing music, or squishing Play-Doh. Ms. Johnson was doing her best. These strategies are classic. But it's expecting heroics to ask a child who feels he doesn't matter—who leaks hope even at age seven—to derive enough solace from a tightly gripped tennis ball to change his world.

◆ ◆ ◆

When education reformers say "No excuses," they mean that outside factors should not prevent educators from effecting great results with their students. Certainly all children must be expected to do their best and must be inspired beyond what they think they can accomplish. But for impoverished children in particular, living lives written off by so much of society, very often expectations, as well as the means to survive, differ greatly between home and school. To deny that what happens outside of school affects what happens inside it is to deny reality.

The disconnect between the cultures of school and home is one of the greatest issues facing the educators at Tyler Heights and places like it. Tina McKnight, when meeting with parents, cites a common quote among educators that children spend only 10 percent of their waking hours from birth to eighteen in school—she lets them know how important their role is. Except for one father who accused his son of "acting white" when a relative helped him improve in school, the parents at Tyler Heights, as far as I could tell, wanted their children to do well. When McKnight told parents crowding the library on the first day of school about "our best year of student performance, I believe, in the history of the school," the pride was evident. The math score got a big round of applause and the reading score a standing ovation from parents sick of hearing how their children's school was failing.

But the things most middle-class parents do as a rule to make sure their kids learn—things that go far toward proficiency on schoolwork and a test like MSA—often went neglected at Tyler Heights. In high school it's fair to place the blame solely on the student who doesn't hand in homework, but in third grade? Why, Alia Johnson thought, wasn't anyone making sure these eight-year-olds did their work? One of the parents, who had told Alia all about how important education was to her, never signed her daughter's biweekly contact folder. Alia hated keeping recess from the girl for her mother's neglect, but that was the rule.

When teachers in high-poverty schools are asked their biggest challenge, they most commonly say it's communicating with and involving parents.[1] The sociologist Annette Lareau, who has done some of the best work on class differences and education, explains that while upper-middle-class parents feel like they are an active part of their children's education—and possess the skills and confidence to perform that role—lower-income parents see education as the school's job, simply put.[2] Parents may be suspicious of public institutions at a time Americans' trust in them is decaying as a whole, or they may have a complicated history with authority. Their lack of education, literacy, or English skills may make helping with homework or meeting with teachers difficult or embarrassing. They may be unable to get to the schoolhouse because they lack a car or can't get time off from work. One Tyler teacher told me, "Parents are too busy smoking crack to help with homework." This wasn't the norm. But, sadly, in a few cases she was right.

In a more affluent neighborhood parents tend to maintain classroom phone trees, pay attention to the news and the Internet even while at work, and keep their emergency cards updated. At Tyler Heights, on the other hand, when school let out early one day because bad weather threatened, twenty kids sat in their parkas and watched *The Emperor's New Groove,* while in the office, seven staffers harriedly and often futilely tried to contact parents. Parents of higher-achieving students tended to show up at Tyler Heights often, to volunteer, to watch their children receive awards, to learn about the MSA, to chaperone field trips. Some others appeared mainly when they felt their children had been wronged.

Meeting with parents on the first day of school, McKnight read aloud the part of the handbook that said, "Parent involvement is critical to the success of students in the Anne Arundel County Public Schools." McKnight envisioned classes for parents in English and computers and fantasized about getting an entire social services wing from *Extreme Makeover: Home Edition.*[3] More than anything, she tried to get parents and guardians in the building. The school had a community liaison who translated at events, and activity fees were kept low, when there were fees at all. For one family night the staff rigged a drawing for tickets, hoping that a break from the admission price—two dollars for adults, one for children—would entice those who hadn't yet shown up.

Typically the greatest number of parents attended the events that centered around food. The school pulled off several joyous, crowded, notable occasions: a Valentine's Day dance, reading-in-pajamas night, a field trip to Washington museums, a magic show in the multipurpose room accompanied by piles of food from Boston Market, a giant picnic on the playground where more than half the school's families showed up to listen to Mr. Al boom music and watch even kindergartners rock "My Humps" with startling proficiency. This was a massive accomplishment for a school that a few years previous had an us-versus-them vibe going, parents and teachers usually communicating antagonistically or not at all. Enough times of Jennifer Johnson riding the bus to and from the housing projects with the kids, teachers calling parents regardless of the chances they might be cussed out, staff members doing and doing and doing for kids in ways before unseen—it became clear that they cared for the children. Trust and relationships grew.

Still, there was a ways to go. Typical attendance at PTA meetings was only about six, including the guidance counselor and principal. Teachers outnumbered parents at a relay race held at a park one beautiful Saturday, and only eighteen families participated in a well-planned Science Night with experiments and displays. Not one parent came to the kindergarten's Language Arts Night, and the annual car show and fish fry was canceled due to lack of volunteers, two days before a feature story in the *Washington Post* highlighted room-mother mania in more affluent areas nearby.

On Back to School night in September, McKnight said as people straggled into the multipurpose room, "I think we outnumber our guests. Oh well." Parents from sixty-two families would eventually show up, out of more than two hundred. Gatherings like this seemed awkward for many of the parents. In middle-class schools, parents tend to interact with teachers, but here they talked mainly with one another, if at all.

During Ms. McKnight's presentation, parents were a bit reluctant to engage in the call-and-response she initiated.

"Reading, say it with me!"

"Eighty-five point seven!"

"Math?"

"Seventy-nine point six!"

"What are McKnight's ten rules for learning?"

"Read, read, read, read, read, read, read, read, read, read."

"What day do I send the newsletter home?"

"Friday!"

"Wednesday."

"Tuesday," someone finally offered.

After a PowerPoint presentation showing photos of the first day of school and the Tyler Heights rules, after McKnight listed the reading interventions and talked about the new science books, after she said that kids who do their homework every day each quarter win a golden dollar, Jennifer Johnson asked parents to pay five bucks to join the PTA.

"Don't just say okay," she pleaded. "I want to see you at one of the meetings."

◆ ◆ ◆

The day after Ms. Johnson tracked down Jada, the impressed kids in Mrs. Williams's class called the guidance counselor "CSI." The skinny, tough-looking girl, with adorable jeans and scraggly braids, sat in the front row of class.

"She's so far behind," Mrs. Williams said.

In the hall, Ms. Johnson spotted Jemarcus. "I want to see you," she said, and scooched up his blue hat to check out his face. "Where did you get this scratch?"

"Jamie," Jemarcus said.

Johnson lifted the tiny boy up for a long hug and said, "I know it's hard to grow up with a big sister sometimes."

6

Chapter Books Are Not Bad, People

Two weeks before school started in 2002, the teachers at Tyler Heights had to learn a new way to sing the alphabet song, in which LMNOP was no longer a potentially confusing blur. They were told to rearrange classroom desks into a U shape, to strip the walls—and to totally change the way they taught children to read.

A month after Eric Smith arrived, the new superintendent told the principals of fourteen high-poverty elementary schools, including Tyler Heights, that they would be using a new reading curriculum, called Open Court, published by media giant McGraw-Hill. The textbook-based program expects teachers to lead students—the whole class at once—through a highly structured, explicitly paced course of study that includes reading comprehension, language arts, and phonics.

In kindergarten through second grade, Tyler Heights had been using a program the staff and children loved, called Literacy Collaborative. In third through fifth grades, as in most schools throughout the county, teachers had essentially been choosing what they wanted to teach from a binder of options, and Tina had already hired a coordinator to expand Literacy Collaborative to those grades too. Teachers would reminisce for years about children in Literacy Collaborative proudly toting little bags that contained all the books they could read.

Each week several centers in the classroom provided activities that integrated reading and writing with science and social studies. The children did so much creative writing: stories and dialogues and pen pal letters, even their own books. They would critique one another's work in discussion circles. With the students in small groups according to their ability, all within the same room instead of being sent out for interventions, teachers kept track of how well every child was reading. They didn't expect each group to be reading the same amount of the same story in the same time frame—so all children could reach some level of success.

Newspaper stories documented the ardor at Tyler Heights and other county schools. Teachers told reporters that the program was improving achievement, improving behavior, and inspiring the children. "I saw students go from struggling readers who just didn't know what to do with print to 'Can I read you a story? Can I read you a story?'" Tina said in one article. The percentage of students reading at grade level jumped from 51 to 71.[1]

There were two problems, though.

First, while some measures of reading ability looked better, the kids, once in third grade, still couldn't pass the state test. Second, a battle was raging about the best way to teach American children reading, and Literacy Collaborative belonged to the losing side. The program did not yet include phonics and phonemic awareness, the basic letter and sound concepts that many experts see as crucial building blocks to figuring out words. The debate between phonics-based programs and those that emphasize understanding and appreciation of text had shifted many times over a half century. By now phonics was winning, at least among those in power. Through the 1990s, phonics was not just popularized but, in many states, legislated.

The Bush administration's $1-billion-a-year Reading First grants are contingent upon use of curricula that have been scientifically proven to work—"evidence-based," as it is called—and that include instruction in phonics and phonemics.[2] Literacy Collaborative didn't make the cut. A recent study found only "limited" evidence that Literacy Collaborative positively affected student achievement. (This didn't mean that the program was necessarily bad, the study warned, just that the research asserting its worth wasn't scientifically rigorous enough.)[3] Reid Lyon, a former chief of child development at the National Institutes of Health and President Bush's primary adviser on reading, told Anne Arundel educators at a conference in the summer of 2005 that programs without the science to back them up were clutter and relying on them was no less than child neglect. "We've let down so many kids," he said, after an introduction that included bow-tied elementary schoolers singing "Let's get reading, America" in three-part harmony. "If we don't do this right, we're in trouble."

A website from Open Court's publisher, McGraw-Hill, displays several reports showing how "the most complete, effective reading program available!" has raised test scores for poor kids, for immigrant kids, in districts big and small.[4] There are plenty of press releases too, taking credit for improvements—although *these* proclamations don't seem evidence-based. For example, one headline, SRA'S OPEN COURT CREDITED FOR HELPING BALTIMORE ELEMENTARY STUDENTS IMPROVE, linked to a nine-paragraph *Baltimore Sun* article about rising test scores for first and second graders. Only the last sentence mentioned Open Court: "Though the system has used the same scripted reading program, Open Court, for several years in the early grades, schools did not always implement it as faithfully as they did this year, Chinnia said."

The Bush administration's fervor for phonics took an embarrassing turn in September 2006, when an Education Department inspector general's report confirmed what many had suspected: Even though agency officials weren't supposed to promote specific curricula, they fell over themselves to do so. Internal e-mails published in the report show the Reading First director eagerly admitting to stacking the deck in favor of specific phonics programs, and Bush adviser Lyon advising about how to do so.[5]

In 2001, when Lyon was advising President Bush, he spoke to business and civic leaders at a Charlotte conference on reading, where Dr. Smith, then the superintendent, introduced him as "one of America's great heroes."[6] Asked which curricula work best, Lyon said he wasn't allowed to recommend any. He went on to say that according to research, for low-skill readers "the Open Court series has been the best we've seen to date." Later that year, Smith became the first large-district superintendent to introduce Open Court to all of his elementary schools, at a cost of seven million dollars. The next year, Smith brought Open Court to the fourteen schools in Anne Arundel County.[7] The year after that, he required the curriculum at the county's sixty other elementary schools too.

Shortly before the 2002–03 school year started, principals were asked to compose plans for implementing Open Court. Tina compromised: Tyler Heights' younger students would still get Literacy Collaborative, she wrote, and the older ones, Open Court. You don't get it, her boss said. Open Court was to be used in every class, every grade, every day.

◆ ◆ ◆

Although Tina didn't like that Open Court was introduced with no input from principals or teachers, she appreciated that students would learn phonics and that the program seemed to be comprehensive and methodical. The flow of each day was the same; each week too. A new reading selection—stories and poems, from biographies to fables, all adhering to the theme of the unit—would be introduced each Monday and reread and discussed every day until the test on Friday. Younger children would learn phonics, and word skills would be emphasized for older students in daily drills.

To ease the shock of the transition, Tyler Heights engaged in minor acts of subversion. Principals were supposed to insist that teachers discard their old language arts binders, but Tina couldn't bear to see some good ideas tossed into the trash and made sure they were stashed away. Not every teacher kept student desks in a U, even though the trainer from the county told them, "Dr. Smith will be looking for this." The Open Court consultant sent to Tyler Heights who helped teachers figure out how to use the program stuck around, but Tina got rid of the one who insisted every instruction be followed to the letter. ("The Gestapo," they called her.)

Generally, though, teachers jumped into a faithful administration of the new curriculum. At the front of their rooms they posted the forty-three illustrated "sound/spelling cards," which represent consonants, vowel sounds, and letter combinations. Teachers introduced children to the cards one by one with a poem tied to the letter's mnemonic device—"Carlos clicks his camera, kuh-kuh-kuh. The pictures come out crisp and clear, kuh-kuh-kuh"—and encouraged them to refer back to the cards when they had trouble figuring out a word. They read with their classes lists of words on the overhead projector and quickly identified what each line had in common. "Outside inside shiny dull beautiful ugly," Miss Johnson said with the class, and waited for somebody to offer "antonyms." "Board bored for four no know hole whole": homonyms.

The teaching of reading comprehension was conducted with a similar formality, according to the expectations of Open Court and reflecting a nationally popular approach. Each reading passage was deconstructed into the basic elements (title, characters, setting); main idea (something Tina wanted perpetually emphasized); message (quite often some version of "Never give up" or "You can't judge a book by its cover"); and always, always a problem and solution. Students were expected to identify whether the "author's purpose" was to persuade, entertain, or inform and often were encouraged to choose only one—even though many texts, like this one, can attempt to do all three.

Today, the norm in American elementary school classrooms is to parse a text using comprehension strategies, such as summarizing and predicting the events of a passage, without equally emphasizing the value of the content. Such an approach implies, according to the education theorist E. D. Hirsch Jr., that reading is "just a set of maneuvers that can be transferred," as if students were learning to type. This emphasis of structure over substance, he writes, is fundamentally anti-intellectual and shortchanges children from acquiring the actual knowledge they need to truly understand what they read.[8] In a classroom that focuses primarily on sounding out words and comprehension strategies, it can seem like reading is more of a basic arithmetic problem instead of a starting point for exploration or thought. Exploration is not absent from Open Court; the teacher's guides list many ways to launch children from the stories on the page into deeper understanding and creativity. But when it takes a class all its allotted time just to make it through the basics and their understanding is still tenuous, the paths to inquiry are the first to be closed off.

In a process called "Clues, Problems, and Wonderings," Tyler Heights students discussed each story before they read it. The children approached this enthusiastically, paging through and raising their hands. "Why would she keep a picture of someone in a box?" "She doesn't want to go outside because they're teasing her." "What is she dumping on her brother's hand on page thirty-eight?" "What is V-i-e-t-n-a-m?" Once done with the story, they loved to speculate about what they might do in the character's shoes. Each class also has a "concept/question board," the primary tool by which Open Court classrooms are supposed to encourage student investigation. The board, changed for each of the six or so unit themes, is a place to display students' thoughts about stories, magazine articles, and photos brought in from home, puppets and props from skits the class might put on about the theme. It is the one place children have some say in what's worth paying attention to, the main outlet for creativity and higher-level thinking. It is, the county trainer told Mrs. Facchine and Miss Milhoan at orientation, the way to "communicate and share what we are learning and the questions we have."

"In an ideal world," mumbled Mrs. Facchine, who had taught Open Court in Baltimore, "where we don't have to worry about MSA."

At Tyler Heights orientation Tina had said about the concept/question board, "There is tremendous room for exploration." The same day Miss Johnson told her colleagues, "We don't usually have time to do inquiry and investigation."

The questions children put up on the board at the beginning of a unit often went unaddressed, sometimes because they were unanswerable (*"Is mars a lifetime?"* from one fifth grader; *"I want to know why do friends care to much about us?"* from a third grader) but more often because the need to get through the material seemed more pressing than attempting to figure out *"Why do me and my friend always fight for hows the best player in vidogames?"* or *"Who made up the word Heritage?"* Puppet shows and skits? Unlikely.

Miss Johnson didn't ask her students to bring in examples from magazines because she figured they didn't subscribe to any. She didn't date items on the board, so visitors to the classroom couldn't tell how long they'd been up. For the first unit, on friendship, she did tell students they could bring in photos of themselves with their friends, and three did. For the duration of the unit, the board held just those photos, one of Miss Johnson and a friend, and the same Post-its kids wrote questions on the first day of school. She kept the board decorated: foreign currency for the Money unit, pictures of animals for City Wildlife, Picasso and Chagall reproductions for Imagination. But the board, like most of her colleagues', remained largely stagnant.

This concerned Tina. "It is a display," she told her Literacy Team. "There's no connection to what's happening with kids." She suggested a staff training session on the concept/question board, but that never happened. Ms. Prater, a reading teacher, suggested an award for the best board, but that didn't happen either.

At a staff meeting the principal commended the concept/question board in Miss Antes' fourth grade, which was always filled with newspaper articles the students commented on, little essays they wrote, advertisements. Relevant library books were propped on a table underneath. "The concept/question board is the way you help your students connect stories in the unit," Tina said. "We may as well just take them down if they're just decorating the room. Should you be referencing the concept/question board on a daily basis? Yes. Should you be talking about it thirty minutes a day? No. This is the place to encourage higher-level thinking. The questions on there should not be, 'Who is the man on page fifty-four?' One hundred percent of the questions on the MSA are above the literal level." For the kindergarten unit on wind, Tina suggested, "What is the wind? What causes it? Good! You could show the effects of the hurricane. Give me another theme. Second grade—camouflage—that's a big theme! Lots of animal stories, other kinds of camouflage."

"They're just animal stories," a teacher said.

"No other topics?"

"No. Just animals."

"You've gotta kinda force that connection."

◆ ◆ ◆

Most of the Tyler Heights teachers were happy their students were finally learning phonics properly, evidenced in their ability to sound out words: This was a big deal. And at the beginning of the year, many new teachers appreciated that Open Court laid out everything for them.

But in many ways their frustrations outweighed their relief. Some were quibbles, such as the way the sound/spelling cards had a picture of a dog on the "H" card ("hound") instead of on "D" and a horse's face on "N" ("nose") instead of on "H." Because everything had to be taught in order, kindergartners learned about the wind when it was too cold to go outside; reading curricula from other publishers scheduled butterflies and picnics for winter too.

Other concerns were more fundamental: the inanity of the "decodable" books used for phonics practice that made "Dick and Jane" look plot-thick. ("A bib. A bat. A bib.")[9] At the other end of the spectrum was a set of heavy stories in fifth grade, nearly all in astronomy and history, that the students didn't find any fun. In some ways the program moved too fast, in other ways, not fast enough. Talking about camouflage with seven-year-olds for a month and a half, wind with five-year-olds for a month and a half, not having the choice to swap out stories or assign an actual whole book, re-reading the same story five days in a row, every week: The strictures could feel stifling.

"I'm over this Open Court stuff," one kindergarten teacher said halfway through the year. "It's the same thing day after day after day."

The Open Court guide is not the Bible, Tina told me. "Any teacher worth her salt will not read every word as is. You can't respond to kids when you're reading a script." You can't respond to kids when you're rushed either. "What's going on here?" Miss Johnson asked one day of the fourth line of word study: *hung rehung take retake make remake.*

"Rehang?"

"Adverb?"

"Homograph?"

She called on reliable Tisha, who spurted out, "Prefix," and moved on.

Unlike Literacy Collaborative, where students read selections at their own reading levels, Open Court gave all students in a grade the same stories, and they had the same amount of time to master the material. Many Open Court proponents thought phonics instruction worked best in classrooms with a limited range of abilities. Teachers "cannot give the focus, the intensity, and the systematic instruction if they've got people from the fifth percentile to the ninetieth," Bush adviser Reid Lyon said at the Charlotte conference. But tracking classes by level is taboo in many school systems, so Open Court is taught in Anne Arundel County to classes with all levels of students, from those who plow through chapter books to those who can barely get through a paragraph. Open Court provides "reteach" and intervention lessons linked to the regular curriculum. Teachers are supposed to use the forty-five minutes of daily "workshop" time to address the differences of students in small groups, or by giving them materials to work on on their own. Workshop, though, was when most Tyler third graders got reading interventions unrelated to Open Court—to just get them to the level where they could understand at all. Those concerns notwithstanding, the percent of county students scoring proficient on MSA reading rose each year after Open Court was brought to all its schools. Dr. Smith's sweeping changes were chronicled in long, effusive articles in *Education Week* and the *Washington Post.*[10] Teachers were reluctant at first about Open Court, he told me years later, but after six months they began to see results, "and the attitude turned around."

Not exactly. Teachers and administrators never stopped resenting how he dropped this curriculum, as well as a new math curriculum, on them with little forewarning and, worse, no consultation.[11] More than once teachers worked-to-rule when they thought Smith's budget favored money for new programs—programs that increased their workload—over pay raises. Some board members, who were responsible for Smith's employment, thought he was heavy-handed too, on curriculum and other issues.

Figuring out the best way to teach children to read, Smith would tell me, "is a twenty-year research project. I've got to get going right now, make some rapid-fire decisions. If I think we have the strategies, I think we have the responsibility not to play with that—not to delay." The big-district superintendents of the twenty-first century do not delay. They make their mark with grand new initiatives, in the face of an audience (school board members, journalists, to some degree parents) that expects improvement, quantifiable and quick. Outsiders who tout such reforms rarely talk about how disruptive the collateral damage is—the costs not just in time and money but in emotion—if they even know.[12]

Smith did exactly what he was brought to Anne Arundel County to do: focus on the achievement gap and bring up scores. Anyone who had read the *Charlotte Observer* before hiring Smith would have expected the same actions and attitudes he displayed in his last job, the ones that would eventually be criticized as arrogant.[13] It didn't matter. As was the case with many "change agents" around the state and country, and for similar reasons, relationships went bad.[14]

By the time the 2005–06 school year started, three years into Smith's four-year contract, the Board of Education had lobbed several gripes at the superintendent: that his cabinet members received excessive raises and bonuses, that some employee records lacked proof of background checks, that he didn't include board members in his planning. Only one of the officials who had hired him was still in office. The teachers' union was preparing for a vote of no confidence. An endorsement over the summer from the county PTA was about the extent of Smith's official support. It was okay, Smith told me later, that a couple of board members "wanted me in jail." But once he felt they would block his academic programs, he decided it was time to leave.

So on September 6, the day Miss Johnson's class was doing "Clues, Problems, and Wonderings" for a story called "Angel Child, Dragon Child," kindergarten teachers prepared for their first full day with their students, and Ms. Panetta suggested at the staff meeting that teachers give pop quizzes on MSA terms with rewards like popcorn and Pop-Tarts, Eric Smith announced that he would be leaving his fourth superintendency, the one he'd hoped would take him to retirement. "While my focus has been on the success of the children of Anne Arundel County, recent public disputes have resulted in considerable distraction from the important work that I was brought here to do and that I love doing," he said in a statement. "I cannot allow these distractions to interfere with the exciting journey that our children have begun."

Smith would go on to a job as a senior vice president at the College Board, which administers the SAT and Advanced Placement. He would be replaced temporarily by a well-liked insider who had worked with Tina as an elementary school principal, and permanently by a former high school teacher who was best known for his amiability rather than any zeal for reform. The change agent among the three finalists was reportedly the board's last choice.

Before Smith departed in November, the teachers' union followed through on their promised vote of no confidence, nearly unanimously. The achievement gap hadn't closed, not even close, but MSA scores had gone up. So the same day as the union vote, the Board of Education approved a $17,000 bonus for Smith, for meeting some of his quantifiable academic goals.

◆ ◆ ◆

The most advanced readers in fifth grade bragged about devouring fantasy books, and three girls thanked Mrs. Williams for allowing them to free-read at school, because they'd started to do it at home too. There were always some kindergartners who chose to page through picture books during free time. A huge contingent turned up for cookies and milk at an evening event for children to read with their parents.[15] But many Tyler Heights students had an ambivalence about reading that was disturbing. Months after a school-wide book giveaway, Mrs. Williams watched a few kids dig the books from the recesses of their dirty desks on cleanup day and throw them away, unread. When a fourth-grade teacher named Ms. Huffman tried to match her students with novels they would like from her extensive classroom library, all they wanted were joke books and Captain Underpants books.

"I don't like chapter books," one boy said.

Ms. Huffman groaned. "Chapter books are not bad, people."

The world teachers talked about from four years before, when children ran to bookshelves, seemed very far away. There was a poem making the rounds of American reading teachers, in which a group of fictional second graders could comprehend a medical textbook, read aloud seamlessly, finish all their workbooks ahead of time . . . but hated to read.[16] At least Tyler Heights students were getting the phonics skills necessary to sound out the words on the page. But reading had begun to seem, to the third graders, merely a prelude to a BCR. They were given very little time to read for fun in school; few said their parents read for fun at home.[17] Miss Johnson, who revisits *To Kill a Mockingbird* every year and lives for the next Harry Potter, read her class a novel about a haunted house bit by bit over the course of a few months, and they loved the mystery of it. Next door Mrs. Facchine had worse luck with *The Little Prince, Charlie and the Chocolate Factory, Charlotte's Web.*

She started reading aloud one novel after another, but all she got in return were rolled eyes, fidgeting with notebooks, heads clonking on desks. The teachers despaired of ever getting their students to love books the way they did.

The school gave away many books, thanks to Reading Is Fundamental, other charities, and teachers themselves. The library was stocked with thousands of books, which Ms. Borinsky eagerly helped children sort through. A program was begun wherein students could earn points toward very fun prize activities—a pizza party, a "pirate cruise" in the harbor with a free book at the end from Barnes & Noble, a McDonald's breakfast served on blue tablecloths in the cafeteria—by reading books and taking five-question quizzes on the computer. During lunch and recess kids begged to come to the library for Accelerated Reader. For some it was an opportunity to rack up points by racing through the easiest books they could find. When I asked a whip-smart kindergartner named Isabel about all the books she'd been reading lately, she said, "It's for getting ice cream!" For others, though, it was a huge step: Miss Johnson's lowest readers were *begging* to look at books.

Tina told parents at the November awards assembly that Accelerated Reader "is just taking off at Tyler Heights, and we are so excited. I tell you, we're going to be some of the best readers in the city, the state, and in the world." To me she acknowledged that the children's enthusiasm might be based on the rewards, but she felt it was a step in the right direction. "I hope and pray that some of them are bitten by the bug and realize they love reading," she said. "You gotta start somewhere. You cannot build intrinsic motivation from nothing."

Twice a year Tyler Heights students, many of whom had never been to a real bookstore, could buy books from a temporary book fair provided by Scholastic. The younger children were big on *Barbie and the Magic of Pegasus*, a Spiderman coloring book, the Clifford books, a My Little Pony workbook—anything with a commercial tie. On the day Miss Johnson's class came to the library to create their wish lists, they ignored the Beverly Cleary and Judy Blume books on the dollar table, as well as *Holes* and Lemony Snicket and *Amelia Bedelia*. Instead they zoned in on a Pokemon book, posters, a little calculator, and activity kits—to create secret codes, do experiments with bubble gum, build tiny planes.

Miss Johnson was disappointed to see that the next day, when students returned with their money, only Manny and Lilia bought books: a story about a black Lab for him and a Holocaust novel for her. Jamila went home with a lanyard kit and erasers instead of the Junie B. Jones novel she'd written down; Elena bought coloring books. Malcolm had wanted a science fiction chapter book, but he didn't have enough money.

7

This Is Just Like the Real Test

By early October, the third graders at Tyler Heights had taken six assessments for Open Court and six assessments for Saxon Math. But they faced in short order their first big test: the county reading benchmark. Benchmarks, periodic exams that let schools know how students and teachers are doing in advance of the state test, are becoming more common. Eight in ten school systems were expected to give state-specific "formative" benchmarks over the 2005–06 school year, representing a 50 percent growth in sales over two years and revenue for the testing industry of more than three hundred million dollars.[1]

In Anne Arundel County elementary schools, benchmarks were given six times a year in math and three times in reading; they were modeled after the questions anticipated on the MSA. Although results were sent to the board, there were no cosmic consequences for the hour-long tests; they were supposed to be used by teachers to diagnose problems and adjust instruction. But at Tyler Heights benchmarks were seen as facsimiles of the MSA and treated with commensurate intensity.

The benchmarks are no secret, so Alia Johnson looked through the reading test—four written responses and thirty multiple-choice questions—on October 6, eight school days before her students were supposed to take it. She didn't remember the test making her this nervous last year. Back then, upon taking their seats each morning her students would work on math problems, phonics review, and the many word skills tested on the MSA and benchmarks but not covered in Open Court. Then Alia would review with them—forty-five minutes in all. This year character education had taken away most of those minutes—with little impact, as far as she could tell from the chaos of playground kickball. On the field the third graders would get so offended by an opponent reaching base or a teammate making an error that they would come unhinged, and the game was banned.

The benchmark included several topics Alia hadn't taught yet: the elements of a poem, words with multiple meanings, text features such as boldface type and numbered lists. Two poems on the test were supposed to be compared with each other, ostensibly because they both used metaphor. But metaphor hadn't showed up yet in the scheduled lessons, and the classes had only looked at one poem at a time. Teachers always hear that children in poverty come to school knowing thousands fewer words than their better-off peers, and Alia figured that among those were several on the vocabulary section of the benchmark, such as *construct* and *vanish*.

"I am very scared," she said.

◆ ◆ ◆

The next day, Alia brought her apprehensions to Tina and asked permission to put aside Open Court and daily interventions, for all but the total nonreaders, so the third grade could focus on skills specific to the test. They postponed the benchmark until the last possible day of the county's window, October 18.

For Mandi Milhoan and Nikki Facchine, this was the first taste of how their new school treated testing and the first day in a week and a half of walking the students through each skill that would be on the benchmark. "Quite honestly," Mandi said—"quite honestly" being something she starts lots of sentences with—"it makes me sick, what these kids have to do every day. It goes against everything I learned in school." Nikki was at the moment working toward a masters in leadership and math education, doing research on the achievement gap that warned against relying on too-frequent testing for children in poverty. More than anything she was annoyed that there was no time to demonstrate a skill, practice with the students, then let them apply it themselves; instead it was model, model, model some more. A few years ago Tyler Heights teachers didn't walk students through problems enough; kids had to fend for themselves. Now the opposite was the norm, part of the school's laser-sharp focus on improvement.

Back in Baltimore County Nikki dodged scissors, but at least she had time to teach more than BCRs. Most schools around the country use a similar format for writing answers: a topic sentence, a few supporting details, a sentence to sum up. At Tyler Heights the formula was called BATS and was explained in posters hung in every classroom: borrow from the question, answer the question, use text support, and stretch. "Stretch" means to give a "so I think" or "so I know" sentence—"kind of a bonus," Miss Johnson told her students, that might earn you an advanced score.

Students were taught to fill their paragraphs with what the school calls "hundred-dollar words" and underline them for emphasis. These included transitions, such as "because" or "so I think," and vocabulary from the state content standards, or MSA words, as they're called at Tyler Heights: "character trait," "graphic aids," "dialogue." The children were instructed to review these words on flashcards in their spare time—vastly more attention than was given to the real-world vocabulary from their Open Court stories. They would boast about how many hundred-dollar words they managed to include in each BCR. "$900!!!" a proud child would write at the bottom of his page.

Because the benchmark was going to ask the children to compare two poems, the third graders of Tyler Heights were guided through practice BCRs comparing sets of poems. Because the benchmark was going to ask how they knew a passage was a poem, they wrote practice BCRs about how they knew passages were poems. ("I know 'Smart' is a poem because it has stanzas and rhyme. I know the text has stanzas and not paragraphs because they didn't indent. . . .") Because the benchmark would ask students to choose which of several meanings of a given word best matched the example sentence, the third graders were walked through those types of problems, and because the benchmark would ask which of several words had the same sound as that underlined in the example word, they were walked through those questions too.

They had to learn how to fill in an answer sheet properly—writing *a, b, c,* or *d* instead of the actual word, writing on the answer sheet and not the test—and how to finish on time, a skill they didn't master. During the first of several practice tests, the timer beeped on Miss Johnson's students, who had only two questions of five complete.

"This is just like the real test," Miss Johnson said.

The children gasped.

The benchmark would ask, regarding a passage about making greeting cards, what text features made the instructions easy for third graders to follow—this strange construction was one the kids would see all year—so on the day before the real test, the students read a cookie recipe. Miss Milhoan asked, overhead pen at the ready, "What text features made the directions easy for third graders to follow?"

"Underline?" one boy asked. Nothing was underlined in the recipe.

"Stanza?"

"How to make sugar cookies?"

"Font size?"

Miss Milhoan drew a quick breath, and exhaled slowly. The kids had been drilling this stuff for days. She hated that, she hated this stupid question. Aren't there more important things for an eight-year-old to be able to explain than the importance of italics? Maybe they should actually make a set of directions, or use one? But the children were not yet able to explain what text features made a set of directions easy to follow, so she plowed ahead. "I want everyone in learning position. You will have a question exactly like this on the test tomorrow."

"It's too hard," Montell said.

"It's too hard," Ricky said. (Among the third graders, some version of "I can't do it" was almost as popular as "Can I eat with you?")

"What did I say about hearing one more peep from you about this being too hard? Maybe you should fail third grade and do it again so it will be easier for you next year. Montell, would you like to start now or do it at recess?"

His chin was down. "It's hard."

"Go to Mr. Al."

Sierra was picking her fingernails with her pencil; several others weren't starting either. Juan, the newcomer from Mexico, had not written a word. He knew the test was important and knew he wouldn't understand much of it, even though because of his language problem, Mrs. Davidson was going to read the test to him and write down the answers he dictated. If it were in Spanish, he told me, it would probably be a cinch.

"*This is easy for a third grader because,*" Sydney had written. Miss Milhoan said that was not a precise enough reformulation of the question.

"Okay, we need to stop, because there's only one person who got it right," she said, and had Emily read her beginning out loud.

"The text features that make it easy for third graders," Emily said in her raspy voice, and Miss Milhoan took it from there silently. She wrote on the overhead, and the kids copied, "*The text features that make it easy for third graders to read are font size, bold print, and numbering.*" She got someone to offer that the font size was to get the reader's attention, and she wrote, "*It was easy to read the directions because font size and bold print got my attention.*" She got someone to say that numbering "tells you what order," and she wrote, "*It was easy to read because the numbers told me what to do first, second, third, and fourth. So I know how to make sugar cookies.*"

"If they use bold print tomorrow, it's to get your attention," Miss Milhoan said as the children continued to copy. "If they use italics, it's to get your attention. If they underline, it's to get your attention. If they use font size, it's to get your attention."

Mr. Al brought Montell back into the room, and Miss Milhoan asked, "What's the game plan if he does this during the test tomorrow?"

"There *won't* be a problem tomorrow," Mr. Al said.

◆ ◆ ◆

Up until the third graders took the benchmark, almost every BCR they wrote was heavily guided by their teachers, and they were uneasy about doing them on their own—though, characteristic of their love-hate relationship with BCRs, they badly wanted to. On Tuesday morning, benchmark day, Manny, one of Miss Johnson's students, felt his tummy tighten and was certain the stress would make him do worse. "Sometimes I feel like I ain't going to go to fourth grade," he told me. "My heart says I can do good and my brain says I can't."

"I'm not going to pass. Those hard BCRs," David said. Borrow from the text, answer the question, give text support, stretch: "We gotta write all that. Some people get the B right, some people get the B and the A right, but nobody gets the S."

While Miss Johnson practiced with her class up to the last minute—working on how they knew "Smart" was a poem—three teachers came to take away the students who receive testing accommodations. As Mrs. Marshall arrived to help proctor, Lilia told Autumn, "You have a mustache." Miss Johnson, handing out the tests, explained that there might be a nicer way to let someone know they need to wipe milk off their face, and Autumn focused her glare on Lilia the whole time the instructions were being given.

With all the warmth of a proctor for the grad school boards, Miss Johnson told her students, "Your name should be on the answer book. The answer book and test book have a number on them—it should match. You need to put your name on it. You need to put the date on it—October 18, 2005. You will have an hour to do all five sections. Take your time, but don't sit there and do nothing. You need to work at a medium speed. I do not want to read BCRs that are garbage. I want to read BCRs where you used your brains. Don't ask me if it's right, if something is a hundred-dollar word, how to spell something. You may not get a dictionary or take out your MSA folder. Do your best, handwriting counts, stay in the box."

The room was filled with the murmuring of the students reading aloud as they tackled the multiple choice.

5. *Which word has the same sound?*
*sh*ovel
a. *coach*
b. *action*
c. *cheese*

10. With *rocket ships, it is possible to travel to <u>remote</u> places like the moon.*
    <u>Remote</u> places are—
    a. *small*
    b. *far*
    c. *lonely*
    d. *pleasant*

12. *In which sentence does the underlined word have the same meaning as*
    the example?
    James was stuck in a traffic <u>jam.</u>
    a. *Try to <u>jam</u> all your clothes into the closet.*
    b. *There was such a <u>jam</u> of people, I could not move.*
    c. *Blackberry <u>jam</u> is tasty.*
    d. *Did you <u>jam</u> your thumb playing baseball?*

Jamila heard "sh" in shovel but in "action," where she was supposed to, she only heard "ch." She knew "remote" turned on the TV and that the moon was small, far, and probably lonely too. Traffic jams are crowded; the closet and those people sounded like they were too. She was confused, but her attention did not waver, despite many distractions. In front of her, a boy kept checking the timer, racing through a question, then stopping cold to daydream. To her left, a boy alternately looked into space and beatboxed quietly but madly. To her right, a boy yawned, rubbed his eyes, and fetched a wad of Kleenex. "Do we do the BCR?" he asked. "Time is ticking away while you're blowing your nose," Miss Johnson said. "You still have four more stories to read and four more BCRs to write." A girl in the front raised her hand, confused at why there were no more questions to answer, not realizing she needed to turn the page. To Jamila's right a boy played with his glasses and green eraser. "*The poem The Rainbow,*" he wrote, then kept erasing and rewriting the "w."

On the other side of Jamila, Felicia was distracted by hiccups. "C'mon," Mrs. Marshall said. "You know that word. You're a smart girl. Skip it. Take a guess." Two minutes left on the timer for multiple choice: Felicia stretched her body out, every limb, and threw her head back. "If you could do the examples, there's no reason you shouldn't get all the answers done," Miss Johnson said. Jamila looked up, shook her head, and continued.

One multiple-choice question asked, *"In this poem the poet sounds . . ."* Instead of the poet's state of mind, which was "happy," Jamila was thinking back to the questions about letter sounds. She looked at the word *poet* and said to herself, "Pote. Pote. Poot. Pout." Because "pout" and "proud," one of the choices, had the same "ou" sound, she checked "proud."

Mr. Al passed by the door with one of Mrs. Facchine's students; she had gotten mad that a boy finished questions before her and refused to continue. Felicia picked at her elbow rash and then her wrist. "Miss Johnson, my arm's bleeding," she told her teacher, who was cutting out pictures for the concept/question board. Felicia pulled a paper towel from her desk to wipe her arm. This was the longest this year these students had sat working on one thing by themselves.

On the question about which text features made the greeting card instructions easy to follow, Roman wrote how to make a card. "I don't think that you answered the question," Miss Johnson said, and he started over: *"So text features to make the directions easy for al third grade is to . . ."* Miss Johnson said to Felicia, "Does that answer the question? Is that a BCR? That is a garbage BCR and you know it. You are much smarter than that." Without finishing, Felicia shut her answer book and moved on to her ankle, then her hangnails. The boy behind Jamila counted his money. Several BCRs were answered with only one sentence, and only four students were still working.

"Cyrus, you did one and a half BCRs. You have two minutes to do the rest of your test. I suggest you hurry up. Autumn, your job is to be proofing and polishing until I tell you to stop, not to play with your hair knockers. Put them away. Put them in your desk." Miss Johnson scolded Roman for circling instead of underlining his hundred-dollar words and for proofreading with a purple pen, the way they had in class, instead of with a pencil, as they were supposed to do on the actual test.

"You should be checkin', not chillin'," she told the class, then the timer beeped.

"I love my benchmark like it's my own child," Tisha said with a smile, as Miss Johnson collected the tests.

Tisha in a couple of weeks would be the only child in the room to make the first-quarter honor roll, all A's and B's. She often did the best work in class and was always Miss Johnson's go-to girl for the right answer during lessons. But Tisha's pride on the benchmarks was misplaced: She was one of the third of the grade who failed the BCRs, mostly because she didn't finish two of them. Half the third graders got the equivalent of C's and D's on their BCRs, and only one-fifth got A's and B's.

Jamila wrote one of the higher-scoring BCRs, which rated two out of three possible points. *"I know The Rainbow is a poem because it has rhyming words. In the poem the to words that rhyme is seas and these. So I know, that this is all about sailing."*

In grading the BCRs, it doesn't matter how jumbled the syntax is. So Miss Milhoan scored this one a two, also: *"The text features make the directions easy for third graders to understand to follow is nomberd. The text tells me that we need Leafe gleo and more thing. We need to put them numberd bedcause you need to know what comes first. So I know that we need to follow the descrison."*

"Compared to the rest of them, that's great," she said.

◆ ◆ ◆

It's common practice, and in some cases law, for schools to write annual improvement plans with measurable goals. Tyler Heights' goal for the MSA coming up in March was for at least 85 percent of students to score proficient, including 17 percent advanced. For third graders on the first benchmark, the goal was 65 percent proficient and 5 percent advanced. They didn't come close. At the staff meeting where each grade's scores were listed on the overhead, the third-grade teachers got to see that in math they were in good shape—86 percent of the kids passed—but in BCRs they had performed awfully. Especially when compared to fifth grade, where two-thirds of the kids wrote BCRs that rated A's and B's.

It wasn't an easy week for Tina. She was dealing with her mother's return to the hospital, her son's kidney stones (and possibly more), and her own nasty cold and infected foot. She'd been getting cortisone shots to forestall the bone removal surgery she needed because she couldn't fathom being off her feet for the prescribed six to eight weeks, and she hoped to buy herself the rest of the school year this way. She kept this to herself. To her teachers she reiterated the goals from the improvement plan. "It's not just wishful thinking," she said. "We're going to really see if we can put those kids in those columns. I have to sign my name in blood that we get to these scores. Who can tell me where we were last year? What were our scores last year? Reading?"

"Eighty-five point seven."

"Math?"

"Seventy-nine point six."

Last year when the school was fighting to get off the state watch list, making its way to the scores now chanted over and over, Tina was in Alia's classroom several times a week, and Tina's boss was in a lot too. Now Alia rarely got visits, and she thought her superiors' apparent lack of urgency was probably a mistake. "It feels like since we made AYP last year, they think they don't have to worry," she said. "But we should worry."

◆ ◆ ◆

Six third graders got all A's and B's in the first marking period, and nearly everyone got a medal around their neck for math at the awards ceremony, but it was risky to use classroom success to predict test scores. There was a big gap between the exams and what the structured curriculum covered and when. A topic that the MSA might include in March may not show up in Open Court until May. And Open Court's weekly reading tests assessed different skills than would appear on the standardized tests. "You can do really good on Open Court and bomb on MSA," McKnight told teachers.

So Tyler Heights staff created a many-page list of all the Maryland reading standards, which teachers could check off once taught. The Voluntary State Curriculum, or VSC, lists standards, which are broken down into indicators, which are broken down into objectives, which are broken down into "assessment limits": the specifics students might be tested on. Any of the assessment limits were fair game for MSA (lend-ing surreal humor to the word *voluntary*). But since teachers saw the test each year, and it didn't change much, they knew that some stan-dards were likely to appear and others weren't, and focused their atten-tions accordingly.

In September a county instructor displayed Arctic photos on a PowerPoint and told Nikki and Mandi to think of the Voluntary State Curriculum as "an ice floe we are going to climb." The assessment lim-its, they were told, "are your road map." One day in early December, with subs in their classrooms and another benchmark looming in a month, Tyler Heights' third-grade teachers met in the small conference room to see how far they'd made it up the ice. They had to find a way to get the rest of the assessment limits taught before March, regardless of the Open Court schedule and pacing guides.

"What date did you do drawing conclusions?" one teacher would ask, then they'd write down the date and run their highlighter pens through the item. In this way they checked off main idea, drawing con-clusions, making predictions, prefixes and suffixes. They marked no date for diaries, atlases, flyers, and journals, topics that weren't covered in Open Court and wouldn't be tested on MSA.

Articles?

"We did an article on sea turtles for text features," Alia said.

Websites?

"Definitely not done," Mandi said.

Science investigations?

"In media they investigated inventors—who invented what."

Chronological order?

"Does that go with the sugar cookie recipe?" Nikki asked.

Ms. McKnight came in as they got to "tone." "I do know you will be tested on tone," the principal said. "Do we have a text feature page in our MSA folder?"

"Yes, and we're going to make a poster of it."

"The third graders this year, you've got to overteach," McKnight said. "They've got to overlearn that."

McKnight looked over Johnson's shoulder at the checklist and said,

"I love this. I love this process. At the end of the day you can say, this is where we're going and this is where we need to go. When you are teaching, are you using the language of that objective? 'Today we're really talking about how the actions of the character affect the outcome of the story.' You can say it, then paraphrase it in kid language. I think they could get more higher-level. Be sure that kids know the language. The language of the objective should also be the language of our questioning."

"They don't need to understand the language of the VSC," Alia fumed after McKnight left. The night before she had learned, thanks to a newspaper article Frankie e-mailed her, that his cruiser was guarding the two biggest oil platforms in the Persian Gulf, accompanied by a contingent of inept Iraqi sailors who couldn't keep control of their AK-47s. It was hard to tell what infused her with more anxiety at this moment: the Iraqis or her students. "They need to understand what, why, who. They need to stop playing with their erasers, picking their scabs, and picking their nose. They need to know four minus three. I had a kid tell me today that 'one' isn't a word—it's a number. They thought the apostrophe in 'can't' was a question mark."

As for the ice floe: one hundred seventeen assessment limits down, eighty-five to go.

8

Market Discipline Is the Key

The Anne Arundel County school system wanted its educators to pick up the phone before the third ring, and smile when they did so. Messages were to be returned within twenty-four hours, calls transferred only when necessary, and the person on the other end of the line should never hear "She went home early." Employees would have to prove their customer service competence through a quiz. *"Think of a time when YOU were not treated with courtesy and respect. How did you feel?"* *"True or false—It is good practice to interrupt a customer while speaking if you missed part of what he/she has said."* Just like in retail, mystery shoppers might be employed for quality control.

When a school system official introduced the "Polishing the Apple" customer service initiative—via PowerPoint, of course—at a principals' meeting before the school year began, Tina McKnight was not the only one to roll her eyes. Later, reading teacher Stephanie Tabor represented Tyler Heights at the "Polishing the Apple" training and returned with a pile of suggestions from the county. Give out certificates that say, "Thank you for representing our school/office in such a positive manner." Put a Great Customer Service cookie in each staff's mailbox, with a card that says, "Ingredients for Great Customer Service: A teaspoon of kindness. A cup of concern. A bowl of knowledge." Reward the school's Customer Service Star of the Month with Starbursts or a sheet cake decorated with fireworks.

"I used to teach children to read," Mrs. Tabor said plaintively.

Schools today are expected to behave like businesses, and not just through phone manners. "'We're not corporate America'—that couldn't be further from the truth," the woman who introduced "Polishing the Apple" said. Lately, she's right. The more time you spend in school, the more you see the influence of business practices. There are the obvious touches: naming rights for sports fields and building wings, exclusive deals with soda companies, the relabeling of superintendents as Chief Academic Officers. The corporate bible *Good to Great* sits on the bookshelf of nearly every principal, and a lot of Stephen Covey gets quoted at education conferences. A growing love of jargon has resulted in not just a change in the way educators talk to one another, about "stakeholders gathering to align curriculum to content standards" and "authentic, outcome-based assessments," but in the way they talk to children, who do "selected-response" problems (multiple choice) and "decode text" (sound out words) during "Time to Care" (homeroom) in the "media center" (library) or "learning cottages" (trailers).[1]

More deep-seated are philosophical and management changes that indicate a new way of looking at teaching and learning. In July several Anne Arundel County administrators, including the superintendent, spent a week at Harvard Business School in a program designed to bring business thinking into the quest for academic achievement—a process evident in both the everyday workings and ideological debates of American education.[2] Like corporations, schools aim to meet growth targets and suffer consequences when they do not. Some advocates have pushed relentlessly for choice in the form of private school vouchers and public charter schools, in the belief that competition will force progress. The industrial efficiency expert has cropped up in schoolhouses in the form of a new breed of educational consultant, and the Malcolm Baldrige Total Quality Management approach to meta-analyzing "continuous improvement," once a tool for productivity in the manufacturing sector, has become equally popular in schools. (If your six-year-old seems queerly familiar with flow charts and plus/delta lists, her school has probably adopted Baldrige.) Not long ago a superintendent friend of mine, who knew I might want to teach one day, suggested I instead become a data analyst, a full-time position that many schools now employ. I told him I wanted to work with the children. He said without irony, "The data are the children." The data are the children, and the teachers, it seems too, as many states and districts have begun to tie worker compensation to results in the form of student test scores.

When you run a business, data stream constantly. How many units were sold—by state, by store, by clerk? Did profits increase after an advertising buy? What was the impact on the bottom line of an increase in health benefits, a new employee schedule, a four-second reduction in production time, a two-cent increase in production cost? Certainly a teacher who pays any decent amount of attention to his students has long had as much information to work with, and sees when his children have learned new letters, new vocabulary words, new math techniques. He knows when they read fast and when they read slow, when they ace a quiz and when they bomb it, when they write articulately and when they write poorly. Such information, however, does not always come in the quantified, standardized forms required to make the kind of institution-wide, analytical decisions that are expected of schools today. Tests have filled that gap. At Tyler Heights, in addition to the MSA and benchmarks, there were, of course, the kinds of classroom assessments teachers have always given, such as the weekly tests in Open Court (up to an hour) and Saxon Math (twenty minutes). A one-on-one literacy assessment was administered three times each year in kindergarten through second grade, and in the spring the second graders took the half-hour Naglieri intelligence test and the four-hour Stanford 10, which ranked them against other students across the country. (The intensity of preparation nearly matched the older grades' for the MSA, though the Stanford didn't count toward No Child Left Behind.) Students participating in reading interventions took status tests at the beginning, end, and often in the interim; ESOL students took English assessments twice a year, which had to be conducted one-on-one, meaning the ESOL teachers were out of commission for weeks.

"I'm not really sure why they need us to test so much," a fifth grader named Thomas told me over lunch one day, sipping his Capri Sun.

Truth is, Thomas had it easy compared to children in some other schools, where for language arts alone, there's the Test of Word Reading Efficiency, the Qualitative Reading Inventory, the Comprehensive Test of Phonological Processing, the Woodcock Reading Mastery, the Clinical Evaluation of Language Fundamentals, and the Gray Oral Reading Tests. Students at a sample of American schools take the National Assessment of Educational Progress, and in some districts, young children take a literacy assessment every week and the Foundational Reading Skills assessment three times a year, the data entered into Palm Pilots and zapped regularly to Central Office. I have even seen children given tests about the tests.

Several of these assessments require one-on-one sessions with students, for anywhere from five minutes to an hour. At schools with less staff than Tyler Heights, whose resource teachers can administer the assessments, that means dozens of hours the classroom teacher tries to get seven-year-olds to read aloud about turtles without a diversion into their past pets, while elsewhere emanate the sounds of idle scribbling, math facts shouted aloud, helpful pronunciations from across the room, and the occasional gross noise. That means dozens of hours of deflecting requests for help from the children being tested. ("Beautiful—is that right?" "Keep reading. I can't tell you.") That means dozens of hours a teacher can't teach.

All this results in an awful lot of data, which states are spending billions of dollars to track (funds often diverted from budgets originally planned for technology that students themselves would use).[3] Sometimes educators find these data helpful, like when last year's benchmark results caused Tina to break the fourth-grade classes in smaller groups for six weeks, or when this year's first reading benchmark caused her to put resource teachers in second grade, where nobody had passed. Alia could see when she broke down benchmark scores by item that students could not explain why they knew a poem was a poem, so they wrote that BCR dozens of times.

"How can you not be for testing?" President Bush said on one anniversary of No Child Left Behind. "If you can't know what a child—whether a child can read and write, how can you solve the problem?" But the information Tyler Heights teachers had received about individual children's performance on the MSA told them no more than the scale score of each in the broad categories of "reading" and "math."[4] The information had been available for two years for the school as a whole on the state website. Had teachers looked for the 2005 data, they might have found something to work with in math: The median scale score on "processes of math" for last year's third graders was relatively low, at 405, and highest in "number and relationship computation," at 442. But the median scores on the three reading categories ("general reading processes," "comprehension of informational text," and "comprehension of literary text") were nearly identical, ranging only from 417 to 420.

The following year, the county would provide teachers a database in which each student's score was broken down into three categories for reading and five for math. At Tyler Heights teachers didn't use the data much—they were never sure what constituted a good score in each category, and they didn't feel the divisions were detailed enough, particularly in reading, to help. How did the kids do on multiple-meaning words? Vocabulary? Nonfiction BCRs? Breaking the items down in such detail, a state official told me, would risk making them statistically insignificant.

As for data from the testing given more frequently, like benchmarks, teachers felt they didn't reveal much they didn't know from teaching class. The numbers don't do much good, one Anne Arundel County principal said at a meeting, when they show trends in contradictory directions, or when there is simply so much that it induces "paralysis by analysis." When Tyler's third-grade teachers filled out a grid on one of the three full days of the year they took time off class to analyze data, Miss Johnson could see that two-thirds of her kids failed the benchmark BCRs, including one student who had aced everything else all year; two of her lowest students, meanwhile, got A's and B's. Different kids faltered on different topics, but everyone fell short on something. Most did so on a few things. Seven failed the comprehension questions. Six failed context clues. Five failed word study. Four failed multiple choice, four others failed synonyms. One, Dantay, failed across the board. Add that to the columns of data about attendance, behavior referrals, reading fluency, Stanford scores from last year, and projected MSA scores, and what does it tell you?

That something was wrong with Dantay, but Miss Johnson knew that from the fact he had to sound out "it" and sometimes would write "10" as the answer to every addition problem on a page. That her kids were low in just about everything, but she knew that too.

◆ ◆ ◆

One day in February, Lisa Koennel, a math coordinator from the school system, visited Tyler Heights. "I've been thinking a lot about the data," she told Tina in her office, and started to page through a packet of charts she had brought.

When Superintendent Smith had arrived in Anne Arundel County, there was a math curriculum but no textbook. He mandated the Saxon Math program, published by Harcourt, for the same elementary schools that were the first to use Open Court and required a curriculum from Pearson Scott Foresman in the other schools. On first seeing Saxon Math, teachers were concerned and Tina "died inside," as she put it. The materials were numbingly devoid of color and illustrations. The structure, in which telling time might be taught on Monday and area of a rectangle on Tuesday and bar graphs on Wednesday and subtraction word problems on Thursday, and weeks later you'd get back to telling time again, seemed to have been designed by someone with attention-deficit disorder. The pacing left little time for hands-on activities.

Three years in, though, Tyler Heights was comfortable with Saxon. If kids forgot how to do a math skill, the spiraling structure meant it would come around again soon, either in a lesson or on a worksheet. Colored illustrations would have been distracting anyway, Tina figured. Saxon wasn't squishy math, like some programs out there—it was *math* math. And the school's math MSA scores were going up, way up.

The charts Koennel had compiled didn't show that. Instead, she had evaluated students' drop in math scores from fifth to sixth grade for the Saxon schools and a somewhat demographically similar group of Scott Foresman schools. Mean MSA scores fell across the board—standardized test scores are usually worse in middle schools—but more so in the Saxon schools, ten points compared to two.

You didn't have to have taken college statistics to know that this study was a little lame, like a lot of data being used to drive decision-making at schools across the country. Comparing the results in March of fifth grade to the March of sixth grade probably told you more about the middle schools these kids were attending than about their elementary school math. They were based on such a short time frame, just a year. And the mean scores in the fifth grade, when the kids were actually subject to the two curricula, were nearly the same for the two groups of schools. Tina was unconvinced, but here was the data and she had to respond.

"I have been around long enough to know there's a desire for county-wide adoption," Tina said. "I've also been here long enough to see pre- and post-Scott Foresman. There are features about Saxon—teachers and students like the recursive element, that it's not built around units and chapters. The constant review—if a program doesn't do those things, I don't think it will be successful at this school. I do believe this kind of breakdown . . ." She fingered the charts with her French-manicured hands and thought of a way to put it nicely. "There are problems with the comparisons."

Tina went on, about how spending three weeks on any topic the way Scott Foresman does is risky because her students don't hang on to information, how with nineteen nontenured teachers she doesn't want to switch out the one thing they like as is. Her personal goal was to hang on to 85 percent of the staff for next year, but eight teachers were engaged, two were having babies, and one was hoping to. "I can't control for those sorts of things," she told Koennel. "So I've got to put in their hands something that's going to make it easy to hit the ground running from day one. I do know that if Saxon went away, I have people here who would be absolutely livid. You'd be taking away something that works."

Koennel pointed out that if you want to get all of the state standards covered before the MSA, you have to jump around with Saxon, violating the integrity of the program. Then the weekly tests are screwed up, because they include topics you haven't covered yet. Scott Foresman, on the other hand, publishes Maryland-specific editions that correlate better with the state test. There's a difference, Tina said, between the program matching with the MSA and matching with the students.

"These kids don't have parents doing mental math with them at the grocery store or on a road trip," she said. "They don't have a car for a road trip. With Saxon, you might get parents to help kids with homework. When parents first saw it, they told us, 'It looks like math.'" Scott Foresman, with all its visual clutter, "it's too much distraction for our kids."

All this talk about pregnancy and road trips clearly wasn't what Koennel had expected. When Tina finally paused long enough for Koennel to respond, she did so gently. "I just wanted to share it," she said. "Any decision wouldn't be mine."

Once Koennel left, Tina shut her office door and held her head in her hands. That someone bothered to even make these charts meant her program's days were numbered. Saxon was already paid for for at least another year, she told herself. Then again, Literacy Collaborative had been paid for too.

◆ ◆ ◆

You may be forgiven if you can't imagine that the subject of the following passage is America's schools: "Results are not achieved by bureaucratic regulation. They are achieved by meeting customer requirements by rewards for success and penalties for failure. Market discipline is the key, the ultimate form of accountability."[5] This is from a 1994 book by Louis Gerstner, the former head of IBM who was one of the driving forces in the education reform movement, and this is the kind of talk that makes many great teachers cringe.

Schools are not businesses, and the techniques that work for corporate CEOs won't necessarily work for principals and superintendents. Jim Collins, the author of *Good to Great*, published a monograph after learning that so many educators and other social service providers were relying on his book. In *Good to Great and the Social Sectors: Why Business Thinking Is Not the Answer*, he clarified that while the fundamentals of leadership success translate throughout fields, people like principals not only are measured by standards other than profit, they also are restricted in decision-making in ways no corporate executives are. In 2002, an ice cream company chief named Jamie Robert Vollmer explained how he learned to stop criticizing schools for unbusinesslike behavior. Once he paid attention, he said, he learned that "schools are unable to control the quality of their raw material, they are dependent upon the vagaries of politics for a reliable revenue stream, and they are constantly mauled by a howling horde of disparate, competing customer groups that would send the best CEO screaming into the night."[6]

It's hard to imagine a business running efficiently with the level of bureaucracy educators face. When the speech therapist at Tyler Heights meets with each of twenty-seven students a week, she must log twenty-seven progress reports. Special education teachers must fill out so many Medicaid forms for their low-income students that they wind up cutting short the time they work with children. Tyler Heights has to document every parent attending every meeting and every event, every hour of reading intervention for every child. Just getting a translator from the neighborhood to help out, last-minute, with parent conferences requires fingerprinting for a background check. Not only does the school have to run all manner of safety drills (Code Red for an active shooter, Code White for toxins, Code Green for a fire drill with a silent walk two blocks away, etc., etc.), each one has to be timed and evaluated in writing.

State and local school boards are accountable to the public in a way business executives are not, as they are either elected or chosen by people who are elected. Schools not only have to satisfy their immediate customers (delivering both a pleasant phone manner and a decent education) but also produce productive, responsible citizens—a task both less quantifiable and potentially more complex than turning a profit.[7] How well educators do that is hard to measure in numbers. Certainly any principal and most parents can tell you who the good teachers are. Now many states and districts are trying to assess the same thing, using student test scores as a key measure.

"Pay for performance," the education world's version of commission, revolves around the idea that teachers should be compensated based on their effectiveness and not, as most are now, by how long they have been around. The U.S. Department of Education included in its 2006 budget request fifty million dollars in grants for states to set up "performance-based compensation systems"—which generally means pay based in large part on scores—and at least a dozen states have already implemented such plans or are actively considering them.

The idea is to reward "effective teachers," teachers "who get results," you hear in speeches. I agree that the best teachers should make the most money. And the current system of evaluation in many districts is lacking. ("I truly don't know these people," one principal said about evaluating teachers at another school, which is part of the process in Anne Arundel County. "So I find myself just checking boxes—satisfactory, satisfactory, satisfactory.") But to believe that pay should be linked to test scores is to accept two assumptions: that the bulk of a student's test score is attributable to the performance of the classroom teacher—*that year's* classroom teacher, in most versions of merit pay—and that the test tells you most of what you need to know about a child's progress.[8]

Florida governor Jeb Bush, whose state would begin to rank teachers on whether their students improve their test-score levels from the previous year, was quoted in the *Washington Post* as asking, "What's wrong about paying good teachers more for doing a better job?"[9] What's wrong is the unequivocal supposition that "better job" necessarily correlates with scores. Of course teachers matter, but which teacher? The typical struggling reader at Tyler Heights is taught not just by the classroom teacher but also by a special ed teacher, two resource teachers, and an after-school tutor. Do the people who favor these plans think it reflects on the teacher when a boy's father keeps him home forty school days and refuses to give him his medication, or when it takes months of effort to secure special ed services for a desperately needy child, or when a mentally ill, uncontrollable student misses lessons because his violence kept him out of the classroom—all situations with consequences on testing day?

Do the supporters of "pay for performance" realize that the superintendent and principal have a far greater role than Alia Johnson in what her third graders learn, and how, every day?

9

You Gotta Be Tough

Test scores are not the only numbers followed carefully in American schools. In early December at Tyler Heights, one highly scrutinized figure was 95 percent: the current attendance rate. Another was 34: the percentage of families that had attended at least two school events. And 119: the number of times children were referred to the principal for bad behavior or received formal warnings, called pre-referrals.

The attendance figure was short of the school's objective for improvement, but a point above the state requirement. The parent involvement number fell far short of the school's 80 percent target, and a third of the parents had yet to show up at all, but there were many months to remedy that.

As for the discipline data?

"Right now we are really not on target for meeting our goal," Tina told teachers at a staff meeting.

The school was aiming to reduce infractions by 10 percent, and at the beginning of the year Tina had been optimistic. Several of last year's worst offenders had graduated to middle school; referrals were low in September; there was a critical mass of kids who had lived with the same discipline system in the school for three years. "The students are already making those good choices," she said then.

There were many incentives, besides calm, to get the numbers down. The state had already warned Tina that more than fifty-five suspensions would label Tyler Heights an "unsafe school." The civil rights agreement promised to address the disparity between the number of black students in the school system and the number formally disciplined—in one year, 20 percent of the population yet 44 percent of expulsions. Suspended kids counted as absences, threatening that data too.

Then there was the fact that when children were misbehaving, they usually weren't learning.

◆ ◆ ◆

"So many people compliment me on our school climate," Tina told her Discipline Team at the beginning of the year. The school had indeed come a long way from the chaos of years past: Children walked the halls in single file, brawls were few, the kind of firefighting Jennifer Johnson remembered from years back, like the time six suspensions were doled out in forty-five minutes, simply didn't happen anymore. Every morning children pledged aloud to respect one another, and many did.

But you got a different picture if you happened to have been around when Cairo choked one of his pre-K classmates or shouted, "Get away from me, you niggers!" You got a different picture if you saw Eddy in third grade kick Mr. Al or Qantay in second grade throw pencils or Lamont in first grade bang on his desk when he didn't get his way, louder and louder and louder still. You got a different picture if you sat in Mrs. Facchine's third-grade classroom when she said no to yet another of Michelle's requests to go to the nurse. After Michelle defiantly paged through *Guinness World Records* during the math lesson, after she put her face in her teacher's and said, "*Ex*cuse me. My rash hurts. What if I die?," after she swung her book in front of the screen, blocking the problem on the overhead, after she hopped to the side of the room and ran the faucet, after the tension in the room had distracted the other children so much that Mrs. Facchine said, "I'll have to remove you," after which Michelle responded, "Go ahead. I'll have someone remove you too!"—only then was Michelle taken away and peace restored, to a degree.

Tyler staff call these children "high-flyers"—the students, about one per class, whose misbehaviors are so severe they make teaching and learning difficult nearly every day. Three-quarters of middle and high school teachers across the country say they would be far more effective if they didn't have to spend so much time dealing with disruptive students and that they face persistent troublemakers who should have been removed from the classroom.[1] In all types of schools, behavior and attitude problems that used to be indigenous to high schools and middle schools have infiltrated even the earliest grades. On the first day of kindergarten one boy came to Tyler Heights with a six-page behavior plan; another let out "bitch"; a third tore his name tag to bits and threw it all over the floor. The first half of the year, as many referrals were made for students in pre-K through first grade as in the intermediate grades. The librarian, Ms. Borinsky, appeared stunned one day after a futile attempt to tame three tussling little ones. "I don't think I've ever yelled at a kindergartner before," she said.

That these behaviors came just from a few students and not, as they used to, from the majority was a considerable improvement from when Tina McKnight first arrived. Those days it seemed most kids had a beef they carried to school from the housing complexes: They fought often; they yelled at teachers. "The climate was so angry you could cut it with a knife," Tina said. Her first year—a year without a Mr. Dillard or a Mr. Al, without a full-time guidance counselor, without much in the way of school-wide rules—there were four hundred suspensions. The following year, when Miss Johnson started, she was afraid to walk her first graders through the intermediate hallway, where she might see kids pinned against lockers and staff members caught in the middle. There were a hundred suspensions that year, more than 250 referrals to the office—"and that's just the ones we bothered with," Ms. McKnight said.

Many of the high-flyers who accounted for the vast majority of the school's suspensions and referrals had emotional disorders, a diagnosis that had multiplied at Tyler Heights the last few years. Many had troubled family lives. One boy's outbursts coincided with the mom's disappearing into drugs and the dad's getting a new girlfriend; another's occurred the week his fourteen-year-old sister gave birth. Support from home was sporadic. Parents often challenged the school's version of events or the sense of gravity. When Cairo hit two teachers in front of his mother, all she said was, "No McDonald's"; after a choking, the mom asked about the victim, "What did *she* do to him?" A parent might help in some ways but fail to follow through when the school recommended outside counseling and found therapists who would take the family's insurance.

At weekly meetings, the Discipline Team—Ms. Johnson, Ms. Benefield, Mr. Dillard, Mr. Al, and Ms. McKnight—discussed everything they knew about these children's lives that might be affecting their behavior: how one third grader was watching *Beloved* and *Laguna Beach* on TV, how she told Mr. Al that her mom had said she wished she was never born, how at Christmas the new baby got a closetful of presents but she didn't get to open all of hers as punishment for a suspension. Last year, the staff wrote on the school improvement plan that the children with the most behavior problems were frequently the ones failing the MSA.[2] The plan listed the root causes: *Need to be taught explicitly how to respond during social conflicts in school. Lack of appropriate models in home and community. Frustration with peers and rules. Lack of anger management.* Sometimes, students with emotional disorders are so disruptive they have to be removed from school and taught by school system employees at home. It is a terrible cycle, because these children need as much academic help as, and often more than, anyone else—and home is often the place that makes them the most miserable. Do you keep them in class, where then nobody can learn? Send them home and hope they follow through on a study program?

The amount of individual attention that goes into soothing the truly dysfunctional children and keeping them in class is extraordinary. Nearly every moment at Tyler Heights during the 2005–06 school year, an adult was trying to manage the anger of one of the high-flyers, occasionally through physical restraint or a police officer's visit but far more often through preventive strategies or gentle conversation, scheduled for some children daily. Discipline was designed to keep the focus on the positive. Behavior charts were tailored to each high-flyer, dividing the school day into chunks as small as twenty minutes and allowing children to accumulate points toward a hand-picked reward. The members of the Discipline Team constantly walked the halls, giving thumbs up to the kids they peeked in on or calling them out into the hall when there was something to defuse.

Felicia, a third grader who was nearing the lead in number of suspensions, visited the Respect Room regularly to talk with Mr. Dillard and Mr. Al. One day she composed a note to a classmate, as Mr. Al had ordered. *"I sorry I stepped on your shoe I was just sad will you exsept my apoligy,"* she wrote, then looked up at Mr. Al, who was writing *"The Principles of Good Sportsmanship"* on an easel, part of an attempt to reinstate kickball.

"At my old school nobody talked to me like this," Felicia told her tall, grown-up friend. "Except for the principal, saying how I'd be suspended."

◆ ◆ ◆

Managing a class means making a constant stream of decisions about which misbehaviors to address and which to ignore. In a class like Miss Johnson's, you simply can't address them all; you'd do little else. When two seatmates sniped back and forth all day, sometimes Miss Johnson ignored it, because they bothered only each other. Malcolm, on the other hand, had the potential to annoy everyone. He was bright but worked slowly; falling behind in class by a problem or two, he would panic, refuse to continue, fling things off his desk, go catatonic. Miss Johnson stroked his head to calm him, but that made the others laugh. She slowed her teaching pace so that he didn't yell or cry in frustration, but that held the others back. She asked the nurse to test his eyes, because he said he couldn't see the overhead right in front of him, and made sure he got free glasses from Sam's Club. Still, he needed greater help than she could give, and she wasn't sure how far he'd have to take his behavior—violence, maybe?—in order to get it. The last time someone from the county came to observe Malcolm, he was fine. Fifteen minutes later he melted down and refused to do anything, blocking the door so that nobody could leave the room without shoving him. Miss Johnson wished she wasn't the only one who saw what he could be like in class. His slowdowns occasionally decimated time for recess and science, and then the other students fumed through math.

The students in Miss Johnson's class, at least three-quarters of them, fumed a lot. In character education they were told over and over again to ignore people who annoyed them, but there was nothing these children could leave alone. Their psyches were threaded with anger, their voices dyed with disrespect. "You gotta be tough. The streets is tough," LaVell Smith told me one day, on a field trip bus to visit museums in Washington. LaVell, a big, charming guy whose son Avante was in Miss Johnson's class, had spent his life since graduating from Annapolis High School twenty years earlier between the neighborhood and prison—assaults, drugs, guns, theft.

Avante told me he preferred it when his father was away. When LaVell was around, he made Avante plod through biographies and chapter books because reading comprehension was his weakness and arithmetic workbooks because math was his strength. When Avante got a bad report card, his dad took away the Nintendo. LaVell knew his boy was smart, good not only at Madden NFL but helping to fix bikes. At the same time, he was teaching his son to embrace the anger that he had passed along, as he saw it, in the DNA. LaVell wasn't proud of the inheritance, but there was no other choice for a young black male, he said.

It was a little odd, then, to hear LaVell complaining about Avante's attitude, his misbehaving in class and tussling at the bus stop. "I see what the issue is," LaVell said. "He want to play. All the other kids sit back and enjoy the ride. He want to play. I gonna get in there—get on it. What I need to do is sit in class. He won't like that." The paradox wasn't lost on Avante. He got in trouble from his teachers because he got in fights because "my dad doesn't want me to be a punk"—meaning a wimp. At home toughness made him a man; at school it made him a miscreant.

This lack of vulnerability, a perpetual sense of always having to be on guard, not only seemed inappropriate for eight-year-olds but also pushed out room in the brain that could have been devoted to schoolwork. (The effect of anger on "student achievement": too difficult to quantify to make it into the scientifically based studies, but hugely important nonetheless.) The children in Miss Johnson's class were consistently mean to one another, so much so that it was hard to see them holding a job one day, no matter how much reading and math they learned. Any perceived slight was occasion to suck teeth, glare, shoot nasty remarks across the room, seethe. When Avante knew an answer but Miss Johnson called on someone else, he was filled with rage. When someone bugged Roman, no matter how slightly: "I just wanna be so mad I wanna get somebody together," he said. While practicing times tables for speed, they trash-talked: "This is my tenth time." "This is my eleventh time." It could be passed off as mere boasting, but David told me that when someone outpaced him, he couldn't concentrate for the rest of the lesson.

The third graders' difficulty in following even the simplest of instructions sucked away time every day. "Take out your spelling list. Take out your spelling list. Take out your spelling list," Miss Johnson would say as Autumn studied the lunch menu and Avante played with his ruler and Roman did whatever Roman does inside his brain whenever instructions are being given. "You need to follow directions the first five hundred times they're given," Miss Johnson would say, and Roman's round face would break out in his hallmark smirk, which unnerved her even more. Roman knew the smirk was obnoxious but told me, "I just can't control me."

This was a particularly difficult group, but not anomalous. Most teachers, and in fact most parents, blame parents for not teaching discipline at home.[3] "We're trying to get them to adhere to a whole different set of norms," Jennifer Johnson said. For children living in the rough world of the Annapolis projects, the ways to get ahead at school often conflicted with what secured survival at home. Lying, aggression, and detachment got you in trouble by day, saved your ass at night. The kids were only partly aware they were being nasty; as they explained it, being mean in response to meanness or even passing on someone else's mean comments didn't count. One third-grade girl told me, "Some people think you're ugly." That wasn't nice to say, I replied, and she huffed, "*I* didn't say it."

Plenty of children told me their parents yelled far more than they talked. "Don't make me smack you!" was a phrase I heard several times from parents, as students reached for a toy or ran ahead, in excitement, at a museum. When a six-year-old arrived at school on the first day and told his teacher, "I hate white people" and "You've got X's on your eyes," the teacher couldn't help but wonder what kinds of messages he got at home. Children were quick to remind teachers of their rights, something they'd surely heard at home. As is increasingly true across the country, many parents often believed their children before they believed teachers, knowledge the students carried to school with them as weapons.[4]

A lot of research links attention problems to risk factors from the early years: teenage motherhood, substance abuse during pregnancy, low birth weight, malnourishment, lead poisoning, even excessive - television-watching. The special education teachers at Tyler Heights were convinced of the connection in many of their students. Some analyses of why children in high-poverty, high-minority schools have more problems with academics and behavior than their middle-class peers blame teachers for not being sensitive enough to the cultural and academic needs of their students. Sitting in third grade every day, watching children who thought it was okay to sass their teachers, who refused to or couldn't follow the rules of a simple game of checkers, who failed to quiet down even when the principal appeared, whose innate desire to please adults seemed to have died shortly after kindergarten, I asked myself if the Teacher of the Year could have done better. Could even she have brought order and purpose to children who felt unwanted, who every day were bombarded on the screen with images of things they could not have, who went home to see very little evidence, no matter what their teachers said over and over, that school would take them somewhere worthwhile?

◆ ◆ ◆

In her third year at Tyler Heights, Tina initiated a comprehensive behavior plan. The staff would proact as much as react. All students would be indoctrinated with the rules and high expectations, consequences would be consistent, and good behavior would be rewarded. Students would be instructed that the power to do well was in their hands. "Make good choices," the mantra went. The plan was based on the Positive Behavioral Intervention System, which encourages a schoolwide, systemic approach to discipline. One requirement is a formal display in each classroom of how students are behaving. At Tyler

Heights, students are "on green" by default—designated by markers labeled by name and clipped to a poster. If a child misbehaves, his marker is moved to yellow and then red, colors that are supposed to be accompanied by specific, consistent consequences, such as a call home or a lost recess. The student fills out a "Think Sheet":

This is the rule I broke:
____ *respect self*
____ *respect others*
____ *respect learning*
____ *respect property.*

Who was disturbed or bothered by my behavior?
____ *teacher*
____ *students*
____ *others.*

When I return to class I will _____.

Before Thanksgiving I saw, on a first-grade classroom door, a decorated turkey that read, "We are thankful for great behavior!" The turkey summed up just how much attention schools like Tyler Heights pay to keeping order, far more than in middle-class communities. "These kids need structure," I heard again and again.[5] The idea was that students with unpredictable home lives, attention deficits, and innate antagonisms needed rigid structure at school in order to thrive. Miss Johnson felt she could best condition her students for a cold world by being strict instead of "cute and fluffy," as she put it.

The pursuit of decorum was understandable but too often took a disappointing form, in which the failure to raise a hand was seen as a disruption of order, in which opportunities for engagement—the kind that brought busy murmurs to classrooms—were missed. Because they might snap at one another, Miss Johnson almost never let her students solve problems together, and she rarely had them do "Ask and Answer," the process Ms. McKnight loved so much, in which a lower student quizzes a higher one and then they switch roles with the same question.

Because they fought over spaces on Miss Johnson's rug the way siblings fight over the backseat on a long car trip, they almost never left their desks during the course of instruction.

"You can't handle going to the carpet," Miss Johnson said when they begged.

As might have been expected, then, children constantly needed to sharpen pencils and requested visits to the bathroom and the nurse. Recess was the only time of the day the students got to interact freely and learn social skills and cooperation—not through a character education course, but just by being. Even at lunch, the normal volume of 150 children in conversation often was too much for the cafeteria monitors to bear. "Signal!" one would shout, upon which the children fell into silence and raised a hand. If the response wasn't adequate, students had to obey "silent lunch" for the rest of the period.

◆ ◆ ◆

In response to the distressing discipline data and a bad beginning of December, McKnight suggested that kids who behaved the last week of school before winter break be given a reward. In particular she worried about the high-flyers who might not have a Christmas present at home to look forward to, so she suggested teachers make a positive phone call home every day they behave. "And why not take them to a party?" she said. "I know it's a little bit bleeding-heart."

McKnight heard once that you should give six positive reinforcements for every negative one. So the school was awash in positive reinforcements, mostly of the edible kind. If students did their Code of Conduct homework every night the first week of school, they got a Popsicle. If they returned their library books at the end of the year, they got candy. The character education program funded by Chick-fil-A awarded well-behaved students free kids' meals at Chick-fil-A. Classes with high turnout at parent-teacher conferences got coupons to Old Country Buffet. The class with the most days of perfect attendance each month got potato chips or candy canes at lunch, and students who returned a signed calendar saying they read at home every night got to do a special activity, with a treat, once a month. Summer school students who showed up sixteen of the eighteen days were rewarded with several free field trips, including a Baltimore Orioles game. Every quarter, there was a small festival of sorts for children who had no more than two prereferrals: soccer and football, cheerleading, karaoke, bingo, musical chairs. At an awards assembly every quarter, students were given not just an unending series of certificates and medals for good grades and attendance but also golden dollars, supplied by the Navy credit union, for doing homework every day. "Hard work does pay off here at Tyler Heights," Ms. McKnight said at one ceremony.

Reading was commoditized through Accelerated Reader, and of course there were the ubiquitous Scholar Dollars, payable for a whole stash of goods piled up for "shopping" in Mr. Dillard's office. Three hundred Scholar Dollars got you a button maker or a Lego kit; fifty bought a Tigger water bottle and twenty-five a My Little Pony; Pop Rocks and pencils could be had for far less. Early in the year Miss Johnson explained to her class that learning was their job and that Scholar Dollars were their pay. So when one student sprawled across her desk as the tape of *The Legend of Damon and Pythias* played, Miss Johnson said, "Autumn, you're not earning your money." When another kept getting out of his chair, she told him, "If you want to get paid today for doing your job, I suggest you stop."

Ms. McKnight thought it was over the top that some schools and districts award cars, rent money, and Disneyland trips for perfect attendance.[6] She wished Tyler Heights didn't have to give as many prizes as it did. The way she saw it, though, brains don't fully develop till young adulthood. Children are "still developing their moral fiber," she told me, and need help to "make good choices." Most Tyler Heights teachers loathed what they saw as bribes and hated the way kids responded to them. Practically every time Casey Dunleavy gave her second graders a Scholar Dollar, she'd be asked, "Why didn't I get two?" The entitlement made Alia Johnson crazy. Her dad died when she was in second grade, her mom had worked three jobs, she had to get by without plentiful food at home, and she still showed up to school and did her work and behaved without the promise of potato chips and parties. "We give them clothes, food, snacks, presents, prizes, cheap-ass field trips, these great experiences," she said to her teammates one day. "We're basically saying to their parents, 'You don't have to be a parent.'"

"Soon we're going to be giving them candy if they wipe their butts," Mandi Milhoan said.

At the staff meeting last June when McKnight announced the 2005 test scores, she had brought up the idea of hiring a consultant to improve behavior without so many incentives. "The fact that we did not improve on the data made me think we might need to try something new," McKnight said at the time. "Students shouldn't always be rewarded to do what they are expected to do." Alia had heard that from her principal often, but it was followed, as always, with, "We can't stop cold turkey."

She wondered why not. After all, coming to school is the law. Doing your work is the rule. Her students recently had gotten dictionaries to keep in their desks. This was very exciting to them. Miss Johnson made up a scavenger hunt game to get them familiar with the books, and they loved it. She did too, until someone asked, "What do you win?"

"You win getting smarter," she said, wishing that meant as much to them as a Popsicle did.

10

What Gets Taught Is
What Gets Tested

Jamila spent a lot of time eyeing the plastic science bins stacked in the back of Miss Johnson's room. "There's a lot of things in the boxes," she said, eyes big, and indeed there were: chalk and clay, calcite and mica, Petri dishes, funnels, thermometers, lightbulbs. "I'd like to make inventions and experiments," Roman said. "I want to see stuff—bubbles and all."

"After the MSA," Autumn said wistfully, "we can do social studies and science."

There was a lot of talk about how important science was. The local banker who addressed the school system conference over the summer warned that the country was falling behind in health, engineering, and technology. The cover story of a *Time* magazine that floated around the teachers' lounge for a month asked, "Is America Flunking Science?" At orientation, third-grade teachers had been told to devote forty-five minutes every other day to a science curriculum that would include the very basics of motion and cell structure, nutrition, and plate tectonics. They were told that science was a stepping stone to all sorts of learning and how much students loved it.

True. I never saw the students of Tyler Heights more rapt than during an assembly when a young woman showed how to use common household materials to send objects up in flames. (Ms. McKnight stood dazed at the side of the multipurpose room, fearing nascent pyromania and thinking she'd like her three hundred bucks back.) In class Miss Johnson would bring up something like the life cycle of salmon because it appeared in a reading passage, and students kept the questions going forever. Miss Johnson loved these rare exchanges. I loved watching them, because as far as I could tell, she could explain everything about the universe.

But when McKnight had happily told her teachers in September that for once they would have everything they needed to teach science, that they wouldn't have to run out to Giant for supplies, she forgot to mention one necessity they would lack: time. As it was, the third-grade teachers only slated twenty minutes, not the recommended forty-five, for science and social studies. And because time for reading, math, lunch, and specials was held sacred, science and social studies were the first things a teacher cut when MSA approached, when a day grew busy, when the kids earned extra recess for being good. It was a sacrifice being made at all levels: At the high school Tyler Heights children would one day attend, the "at-risk" students—who for the first time had to pass a state exam in order to graduate—were being given as many as three math periods and three English periods each day, leaving no time for electives.

At orientation, McKnight voiced an often-hushed reality affecting schools around the country, particularly those teetering on the edge of proficiency. "I'm a realist," she told the teachers. "What gets taught is what gets tested." The rest—even if it is part of the state standards—gets left behind. So I saw very little science in the third grade at Tyler Heights. The kits in Miss Johnson's room would be opened to roll marbles one time early in the year and later to make goo and sculpt a landform and compare seeds and pebbles in a Petri dish. This was only a tiny fraction of the experiments inside, and at any rate, those projects were presented in class severely abridged—no hypotheses, no data. Mostly students read from the textbook and did worksheets. The only full pass through the scientific method was made after MSA, in the days spent preparing for the science fair.

Because I so rarely saw the third graders do projects, I was excited one day to watch Mrs. Facchine's students conduct an experiment in motion. They were excited too, because they had heard they were going to get to run down the hall. At 1:58 p.m., after they reviewed map terms for a quiz but shortly before they would have to pack up for the day, the students were supposed to get ready for the experiment. In their enthusiasm, they couldn't stop talking. Mrs. Facchine waited. The talking didn't stop. "Forget it," she said. "Put your head down." Fervent shushing grew as loud as the talking, and Mrs. Facchine began passing out clean sheets of paper. "Write your name and date at the top of the paper," she said. "You're going to write a letter home saying why you were not allowed to do your science experiment." *"We did not do are science experiment because people cep on talking,"* they wrote, denied the one thing that might make them unfidgety and unbored.

◆ ◆ ◆

When it came to the accountability movement, Ms. McKnight epitomized the ambivalence of most educators I've met: She was supportive of standards and testing in theory but painfully aware of the unintended consequences. She was passionate about the subject she used to teach, social studies, and particularly geography, but when it came down to it, social studies fared no better than science.

Tyler Heights' third graders got only the most cursory introduction to economics and Native Americans, and much of the curriculum was skipped altogether. The students were geographically ignorant. Approaching the Naval Academy after a three-mile bus ride, several shouted, "Look, it's New York!" The third graders had heard Africa mentioned a lot but were not sure if it was a city, country, or state. (They never suggested "continent.") At the end of the year, each child in Miss Johnson's class was asked to name all the states they could. Cyrus knew the most: three. He couldn't name any countries, though, and when asked about cities, he thrust his finger in the air triumphantly. "Howard County!"

"Please don't say outside this building, 'Tina McKnight said don't emphasize social studies,' " the principal told teachers at orientation. At least, she said, use the map to show kids the places that pop up during reading. Every time Miss Johnson introduced a new story, she'd say something like, "This takes place in New Zealand, which is *not* in the United States, which is *not* in North America," or, "This is Massachusetts, which is in the United States but is *not* Maryland." Frankie was at the moment between Africa and Spain, Miss Johnson said one day, pulling down the map. "It's very far away. He has to go all the way across the ocean."

Neither No Child Left Behind nor any other reform of the accountability movement disallows schools from teaching science, social studies, or creative writing. The law does not prevent children from giving oral presentations, learning computer skills and personal finance, and solving geometric proofs, just because those things may be absent from state tests. The law does not bar children from racing around the playground at recess. When somebody blames No Child Left Behind for breakouts of head lice (schools need to make the attendance numbers whether or not children's scalps are infected) or peed pants (students mustn't leave the room during mandated reading time) or canceled spelling bees (having one winner inevitably leaves others behind), clearly these are lousy interpretations of policy.[1]

But it is a fact: Educators around the country say the intense focus from above and outside on reading and math test scores is why they have pared away elsewhere.[2] For a while the American public only noticed when "elsewhere" meant the arts and recess. Tyler Heights students still have three and a half hours of specials each week, unlike districts around the country that have cut art, music, PE, and library. McKnight suspects that the school system would have liked to reduce those too, had classroom teachers not been guaranteed in their contracts that much time away from their students to plan lessons. As it was, recess had been halved to fifteen minutes a day. Former Atlanta superintendent Benjamin Canada got a lot of attention when he eliminated recess in that city, saying kids don't learn "hanging on monkey bars" and claiming the change increased test scores.[3] Every elementary school teacher I've met thinks children are more attentive if they get occasional breaks, but if there are nonbelievers, plenty of research exists that might convince them.[4] The National PTA and the Cartoon Network, under advisement from the Centers for Disease Control and Prevention and others, launched a "Rescuing Recess" campaign in March 2006.

Can we hope for a "Rescuing Learning" campaign to follow? Education researchers have long warned, in journals no average citizen reads, that schools would narrow their curricula amid such a strong focus on standardized testing.[5] In 2006 the voices got louder, including a front-page article in the *New York Times* based on a national study that received some attention in the education world.[6] The National Council on History Education and its who's who of Pulitzer winners declared the situation a crisis, urging at the very least that reading textbooks include biography and history. The Maryland schools superintendent appointed a social studies task force to look into the issue. One Arizona social studies teacher told *Education Week* that the lack of basic knowledge now is "simply shocking. Not only do they not remember, but more often they have never even heard of some of the most important people and events in American history."[7] Miss Milhoan, who had made sure her students in Akron researched John Glenn and Goodyear and Ohio facts, said, "How are we going to have informed citizens if they never learn social studies?"

Maryland used to test social studies, science, and writing. Despite a deep concern that those subjects wouldn't be taught anymore, they were dropped from the test when the state's accountability system was overhauled in 2002. Why? "The law made it easy," deputy superintendent Ron Peiffer told me. And the climate makes it easy to drop them from the school day too. Tyler Heights was not explicitly ordered to deemphasize topics that are not tested; then again, nobody from the school district, and nobody who lauded the school for its scores, bothered to make sure the whole curriculum was taught. Even educated, involved parents were surprised when I talked with them about what their kids *weren't* doing. I knew of only one parent who brought it up on her own, after listening to Miss Milhoan at Back to School night. "I'm hearing all this about reading and math," said the mother of a bright girl named Sydney. "What about science and social studies?"

Subjects like science and social studies and creative writing are often the hook it takes to get students low in math and reading skills to care about school at all, to understand that reading has a purpose beyond being able to write a BCR that identifies the main idea. Superintendent Smith had told teachers when he popped in the door during the county science training, "You're going to teach your students to read through science. You're going to teach them to write through science." In reality, teachers are now expected to do it the other way around. The common phrase is "reading in the content area"—the idea that social studies and science can be taught primarily through text. Reading in the content area, however, has serious limitations as the route to deep understanding and fails to engage students the way hands-on activities and true problem-solving do. McKnight asked teachers to give students passages on social studies and science topics for supplemental reading lessons in preparation for MSA. But the passages the third graders read touched on random knowledge—Billie Holiday's alcoholism, female Arctic explorers—and breezed by quickly. They were hard to understand on the fly when the children had had such little exposure, at school and at home, to history, culture, and the natural world.[8]

The county trainer had told teachers, "Science is not reading. Science is doing." She had urged them to take their students outside as often as they could, to read only after they explored. She gave them a copy of the Anne Arundel County Philosophy of Science Education, which said, "Students learn science by describing objects and events, and asking questions. Students learn science by acquiring knowledge, and constructing explanations of natural phenomena. Students learn science by testing those explanations many different ways, and communicating their ideas to others." She gave them a document that listed thirty-one best practices in science—collaborating in teams, collecting data, making tables and diagrams—before it ever mentioned, almost as an afterthought, multiple-choice questions and BCRs.

A few teachers at Tyler Heights, less panicked about their students passing MSA, did not cede as much social studies and writing and science time to test prep. Miss Antes in fourth grade, asked her favorite subject by students writing a newspaper in an afterschool club, said, "Put this down: Anne Arundel County does not give enough time to teach social studies and science," and took it upon herself to do so anyway. Antes talked with her students about Hurricane Katrina and posted biographies of Sandra Day O'Connor and Martin Luther King; she had them make fake passports for "trips" to Kenya and Japan and reenact Maryland's Civil War battles and put together a collage on

African animals. The fifth graders learned a little bit about the American Revolution and astronomy, mainly because those subjects were two of the year's five Open Court units. Mrs. Williams, who loved social studies, led her students on various tangents, discussing the importance of historical documents and where you might find them, how immigration might be changing the English language, why certain names might be historically accurate for the American Revolution (Thomas, Elizabeth) and others not (Brianna). In the library, Ms. Borinsky showed fifth graders how to search the Internet for nineteenth-century history and gave the third graders Baggies of foreign coins to inspect during their Open Court unit on money.

But corners were still cut, leaving questions about how prepared students would be for the required classwork in middle and high school. Mrs. Williams brought in crustaceans to her classroom, and in every spare moment the kids headed to the little habitat where the "dinosaur eggs" waited to hatch. These eleven-year-olds insisted these were actual dinosaurs. The sixth-grade science teacher, I kept thinking, was about to receive students who thought dinosaurs weren't extinct, who couldn't use basic scientific instruments, who lacked so much basic knowledge. However, once these kids did arrive in sixth grade, their science teacher pointed out to me that at least she no longer received children who could not sound out words.

Those fighting to preserve subjects in the crush of testing (and tight budgets) have begun to defend their fields not on their own merits but by emphasizing that whatever they teach will help raise scores in reading and math—a side effect of the belief that unless "achievement" in a given area can be, and *is*, quantified, the learning taking place does not have value. At a recent congressional hearing on No Child Left Behind, a gym teacher told lawmakers that "physical education is the ideal vehicle for reinforcing academic standards." (His students demonstrated the bizarre "sport" of speed-stacking, in which plastic cups on a table are quickly unstacked and restacked, the brain allegedly developing all the while.) A representative from the Maryland State Department of Education cited studies saying that teaching arts helps math scores, and Representative Vernon Ehlers, a Michigan Republican and nuclear physicist, said that teaching science improves reading skills.[9] Supporters of disciplines besides math and reading are actually hoping for *more* testing, presuming that if their subjects are added to the federal calculations of progress, they will have won a golden ticket to relevance. Four-fifths of Americans said in 2005 that testing should go beyond reading and math, in order to give a fairer picture of whether a school needs improvement.[10] Some school systems and nine states have begun the complex endeavor of requiring standardized tests even in the arts.[11]

Science, at least, is guaranteed somewhat of a future: No Child Left Behind requires that the subject be tested three times over a student's schooling, beginning in 2006–07. Even though states won't have to include the scores in calculations of adequate yearly progress, and there is no requirement to go beyond the kind of content knowledge that can be acquired only through textbooks, the mere existence of a state test is certain to restore at least some classroom time. Tradeoffs, of course, endure: McKnight knew this meant that what little time was spent on social studies would be "obliterated." That pained her, but, she said, "What can I do?"

◆ ◆ ◆

Tisha wrote a story in October for the Friendship unit, called "The Fight." The five students who stayed with Miss Johnson during workshop time, the ones who did not need reading intervention, each wrote about a friendship experience, then typed their stories in the computer lab.

Tisha, who had little keyboard experience, typed slowly:

> One day a little boy was teasing me so we started to fight. Then Raychelle got all up in it so we all started to fight and she scratched my lip. Then my mother went to her mother and said "your daughter scratched the top of my daughters lip." Then her mother said "It's not like she planned to then my mom said forget about this. Then we went to her house and we argue.

This story was disturbing not for its subject matter—though Tisha did tell me it was nonfiction. The problem, rather, was that this was the only story Tisha would write all year, even though the county calls for forty-five minutes of writing twice a week. What Tisha did write, several times a day, were BCRs. At a conference on assessment in November, Kathy Volk, a reading specialist from the Maryland State Department of Education, told teachers and principals desperate to unlock the secrets of the MSA that BCRs are not tests of writing skills at all, but of reading. "I'm not saying kids shouldn't write well-developed paragraphs," she told the standing-room-only crowd. "But that's not what we're worried about on this test."

"You could bullet it, list key phrases, and you could get the same number of points as someone who wrote a well-crafted answer," Ms. McKnight said. The formula is a helpful scaffold, she said, but "if the only thing you're teaching is BCRs, your kids are not learning to write."

The third graders at Tyler Heights, then, did not learn to write. They learned, thanks to a timer broadcast on the overhead projector, to fill in the box of eight lines in seven to nine minutes. They learned to "proof and polish" with a special purple pen, and whisper their paragraphs to themselves through C-shaped sections of PVC pipe held to their ears— what they called "whisper-phoning," a strategy good for detecting if your answer makes sense. They learned to adhere to the BATS formula, in BCRs like the one Miss Johnson led her students through one day:

> Damon and Pythias is a play _because_ it has the _elements of a play._ Some elements of a play are that plays have _stage directions. Also,_ there is a _narrator._ This play also has a lot of _characters. So I know_ this play has all the features it needs.

The BCRs tended to repeat themselves, responses to a limited range of questions teachers knew would be on the county benchmark tests and suspected would be on the MSA. The fifth graders were usually asked how illustrations made information easier to read, how an author set a certain tone, or how the setting influenced a character's actions. The third graders answered again and again what traits described the main character of a story. They wrote the _"I know this is a play because"_ BCR about ten times but never got to take the parts of characters and act a play out loud. They wrote _"I know this is a fairy tale because"_ and _"I know this is a fable because"_ but never tried their hand at creating either. About a fake brochure they wrote, _"The text features that make this easy_ *for a third grader to understand are italics, numbering, and underline."* But they never made their own brochures with their own text features; the only thing they underlined were hundred-dollar words. They wrote about fifty times, *"I know this is a poem because it has rhyme, rhythm, and stanzas,"* Miss Johnson estimated, but they only wrote three poems: During the Friendship unit they wrote an acrostic, a poem composed of character traits starting with each letter of a friend's name; after MSA they wrote an acrostic about spring and a nature haiku.

Even if the students were going to write a paragraph instead of a poem, why couldn't they have been given anything interesting to write, to stretch their minds? One week the Open Court reading passage told the story of a hallucinating cat who burst into verse upon sleeping in catnip and took strange medicine from a witch—the tale was so kooky Miss Johnson could barely keep a straight face—and all the BCR asked was, *"How do you know this is a poem?"*

The Open Court unit was Imagination.

This is not just an elementary school problem. High school students, even those in honors classes at some of the country's most competitive high schools, also write according to formulas, or rubrics, later found on the tests—their answers are just longer, five paragraphs instead of five sentences. Maryland teachers cited in a June 2005 report by a national think tank said that as these writing styles have seeped into instruction, larger assignments have disappeared.[12] The National Council of Teachers of English has complained that state tests, along with the new SAT, which includes a writing portion, have hurt students' writing—ideally an individualistic endeavor—by standardizing the skill.[13] University officials complain about not just formulaic writing on application essays, but many freshmen's need for remedial writing despite increasing scores on state tests.

I learned the paragraph formula in elementary school too. But my classmates and I also wrote science fiction stories, book reports, poems, and plays. Even when we wrote formulaic paragraphs in class, everyone's was different. In Maryland students write BCRs in math too, explaining how they got their answer, and practically every BCR the Tyler third graders wrote about probability started, *"I know prob-*

ability is the likelihood of an event." "Tell me in your own words," Mrs. Facchine sometimes said, but after so much coaching her students were unable to.

At Tyler Heights, summaries of reading passages had their own formula: main idea, detail, detail, detail. One time, when it had been a while since the fifth graders had done such a BCR, Thomas, one of the brightest kids, said, "I don't remember how to write a summary." It wasn't that Thomas couldn't sum up what the story was about if you asked him to. He just couldn't remember the formula.

"The top kids we're shortchanging," Mrs. Williams told me, "because they're learning to do the formula and forgetting how to think."

In crafting BCRs with her class, Miss Johnson always looked for a very specific construction. One day the prompt was, *"Brer Rabbit is a tricky fellow. Give examples from the play that prove this."* "You're going to do this by yourself," Miss Johnson said, but she got them started. "How can I restate this? How can I turn this and form my 'B'? Autumn?"

"Brer Rabbit tricked—"

"No. Cyrus?"

"Brer Rabbit is a tricky fellow because . . ."

Miss Johnson wrote on the overhead, *"Brer Rabbit is a tricky fellow,"* and I wondered why Autumn's answer couldn't also have been the start of a good BCR.

On nearly every BCR I saw the third graders do throughout the year, the teacher sat at the overhead, prompted the answers she was looking for, wrote them down, and the children copied. The students begged to be able to write BCRs all on their own, but Miss Johnson figured too many of them would get it wrong, and the "modeling" was encouraged from above.[14] The children had lots of good ideas when playing "I'm Thinking of a Word" and worked eagerly and well when they would design their own story problems—I had five friends at my Build-a-Bear party and one more came late; I had four gum balls and my dad bought me two more. The math curriculum too, however, relied heavily on guided practice, emphasis on the "guided."

Ms. McKnight was a big fan of conceptual, hands-on math but said there was no time for anything beyond the fundamentalist Saxon Math curriculum. She talked to me and to her Literacy Team about how the skills and knowledge tested on MSA should be only the minimum of what kids learn, and she had high regard for what she called "higher-level questions." But when it came down to it, she rarely pushed class-room teachers in any meaningful way to stretch past the basics.[15]

The children were often able to give the right answer when the question came in a format they recalled. But when they had to deduce independently, they had trouble, or thought narrowly. When the third graders were asked how a character in a story felt, they could only come up with "happy" or "sad." Miss Johnson's class could recite the "Thirty days hath September" poem but five minutes later be unable to tell you how many days were in a given month. When Mrs. Facchine drew a number line on the board and asked the kids to round to the nearest ten, they couldn't, despite the Skittles and Scholar Dollars being offered. Frustrated, she shut her teacher's guide and arranged the students in a human number line. "Are you closer to twenty or thirty?" she asked. "Five or above, give it a shove," she said. For a while they got it. But when they were back in their seats, she asked, "Where do you round forty-one to, Demetrius?"

"Fifty-one?"

"Dena, seventy-nine."

"Seventy?"

"Is seventy-nine more than seventy-five? Would you rather have seventy-five dollars or seventy-nine?"

"Seventy-five."

As troubling as the achievement gap is what I call the "imagination gap." The smaller the universe of a person's experiences, the more limited her curiosity about how the world works in general—you're a lot less likely to wonder how a plane flies if you've never gotten to see one—and what might be possible personally. Teachers of low-income children will tell you that the stories their students make up, in writing or orally, usually center on characters and situations they've seen on the screen—a universe they sometimes have trouble understanding is fictional. Several of Miss Johnson's eight-year-olds, because of a commercial they saw, actually believed the color of their milk was linked to the color of the cow. At this Miss Johnson shook her head and said, "If it's on that big giant screen up there, nine chances out of ten it's not real. That's the TV. Things on TV are fake, unless it's the news, or a biography. Cartoons are fake. *That's So Raven*, it's fake." More detrimental to everyday instruction was the difficulty the children had going beyond the literal. Teachers had to walk their students through the process of creating mental pictures, whether of a number line or a story they were reading. "Close your eyes for just a second," Ms. Huffman told her fourth graders. "We have reviewed the story 'Mrs. Frisby and the Crow.' The cat was named Dragon. When you hear that description, what's the first thing that comes to mind?"

"A dragon."

"What kind of cat are you visualizing?"

"A big, fire-breathing, sharp-teeth, long-tailed dragon."

A descriptive sentence, but still, the boy couldn't see a mean cat—only a dragon.

Peeking into fifth grade one day, Tina watched Mrs. Williams introduce the Heritage unit with a photo of a boy on a motorcycle toting a woven basket on his back. McKnight was hoping the teacher would ask her students what in the photo showed a contrast of cultures. Instead, Williams told them. "She's stuck in the literal," McKnight said after we left the room. "We're still teaching kids on such a literal level that they don't have to make that leap to use their brains."

The kind of problem-solving and interpretation that would help these children beyond the MSA and beyond elementary school, a type of instruction they need more than anyone, doesn't occur nearly enough in schools primarily focused on testing. The same official who at the assessment conference said that the state wasn't looking for well-written paragraphs on its BCRs bemoaned students' inability to think critically, connecting details and attaching personal thoughts that are actually relevant. "If all of our instruction is at the literal level," she said, "they'll never get to a three," the highest score.

A three, though, seemed possible without great depth. Often teachers walked their students through examples of BCRs that I knew would merit a three but were not, by any definition, exemplars of writing or critical thinking. When Miss Johnson sat with her highest students at a small table and asked for comparisons of Lakota and Iroquois dwellings, the students were productive and attentive. But there was no push for more interesting and thoughtful examples, as long as they had enough. Longhouses and tipis "were both villages," Manny offered.

"They were both houses," Savannah said.

"They both had people in them," Manny added.

The resulting BCR, which they each copied down, read, *"The homes of the Iroquois and Lakota are the same because they both have people living in them and they are both villages. They both have types of houses. Their homes are different because they are made from different materials."* The students boxed the hundred-dollar words, *same* and *different* and *because,* and whisper-phoned the final product to themselves to make sure there were no mistakes.

◆ ◆ ◆

When Bush adviser and reading guru Reid Lyon talked to Anne Arundel teachers over the summer, he defended direct, scripted instruction. "If you're having a tumor removed from your squash, how creative do you want your neurosurgeon to be?"[16] Most people, I'd venture to guess, would want their neurosurgeons to be creative. They'd certainly want the person trying to cure their brain disease in the first place to be creative. And if teachers aren't creative thinkers, what chance do their students have?

"None," said Yolie Marshall, a resource teacher who had spent nearly thirty years at Tyler Heights. "We don't get to be creative anymore, and neither do they."

The Tyler Heights staff talked a lot about a former second-grade teacher who last year didn't stick with the program and taught over her students' heads. Students themselves, and the parents, talked about how much they loved this teacher. "There's not enough time for creativity *and* the basics," McKnight told me about her. "That's why third graders are so behind."

The best teachers, of course, do both. Proponents of a stripped-down, structured focus suggest that it is better than what used to happen, that before the accountability movement, schools like Tyler Heights were filled with desperately arrested students and completely inept teachers. Of course, the reality was more complex. Critics on the other side complain about teaching that sees children as merely vessels to be filled.

Frankly, I wish the vessels in the third grade of Tyler Heights would have been filled higher, with the United States map and parts of speech and details of life outside the Annapolis Neck peninsula and enough math facts so that they didn't have to add on their fingers. But if in the process of filling the vessel students are given little chance to explore, to solve, to think, education has failed. Child development experts frequently stress that learning to solve problems is the keystone of successful intellectual development. Working in groups, asking questions, and seeking answers is possible for even the youngest students, when given the chance and the guidance. This takes time, this often cannot be scripted, this runs the risk of a classroom that is not quiet. But it is worth it—especially for children who don't learn these kinds of skills outside the classroom.

One study found recently that engagement, to teachers, mostly meant keeping students occupied physically though not necessarily intellectually.[17] A depressing thought, as good teaching is not simply a matter of staving off boredom and detachment. It is about teaching students to think. "The research is crystal clear," the sociologist Kathy Hirsh-Pasek told me. "We're making kids more passive."

The teachers I followed at Tyler Heights knew that this was a problem but were either unwilling or unable to veer from the program—they felt they were not allowed. One day in the teachers lounge, two former teachers who were now an aide and a mentor reminisced about the days when third graders read novels and did chemistry experiments and worked in groups to design versions of the thirteen colonies and did writing, real writing. Mandy Panetta, a resource teacher who was an active part of the school's laser-sharp focus over the last few years, had begun to question her own role. She listened to the veterans and added her two cents. "While our scores were really good last year, can I tell you our kids are any smarter? I don't know."

11

I Didn't Even Know
That Was an Option

While the third graders at Tyler Heights stayed a course bound by a direct interpretation of the curriculum guides and deep concern for the MSA, their counterparts at Crofton Elementary School fourteen miles away created fairy tales on the computer, posted staff biographies on the school's website, and wrote ten persuasive letters (*"I strongly believe I should get 'The Revenge of the Shadow King' . . ."*). Sitting in a circle on the carpet, Sandra Krainer's students discussed what they read, and they proofread one another's work. Every day they filled their journals with five sentences, an illustration, and no evidence of BATS, except for the kind that shows up in passages like this one: *"The tiny little Mouse crept into a Dark Deep CASTEL."*

At Crofton, the fifth graders made paper cubes printed on each side with the biographies and stances of political candidates, and they helped run an actual bank branch, where students maintained savings accounts. The fourth graders gave speeches on Olympic sports and, during an Open Court unit on money, held a craft fair. In preparation they created business plans on PowerPoint, business cards on Microsoft Publisher, budgets on Excel, as well as the paper snowflakes and greeting cards and picture frames they sold to their classmates. The second graders learned hieroglyphics, and even the kindergartners made research posters, about animals.

Each day Crofton teachers fit in the full forty-five minutes of science or social studies—plenty of time to maintain a compost pile for the garden in front of the school, make tortilla teepees and sugar cube igloos, create brochures about Native Americans and pictograph stories on faux animal hides, and work their way through every object in the science bins. When the curriculum called for the study of Anne Arundel politics, students asked questions of a county official who visited the school.

The town of Crofton is a planned community, centered on a looped roadway lined with flowering trees. Household income is well above the state average, and college degrees are twice as common as in the state as a whole. While Crofton Elementary is nearly two and a half times the size of Tyler Heights, it has one-eighth the number of children living in poverty and one-fourth the children with limited English. Blacks and Hispanics make up less than 10 percent of the student body. Family life, at least by the numbers, is more stable: Crofton students are as much as four times less likely than Tyler Heights children to switch schools midyear, and single-parent families are uncommon—factors that contribute to academic success.[1] One Crofton teacher told me that nine in ten of her students lived with both their parents at home; in the third grade at Tyler Heights, the teachers calculated, one-fifth did.

Tyler Heights Elementary and Crofton Elementary are both part of the Anne Arundel County Public Schools, the entity Eric Smith called "not a system of schools, but a school system." As such they are subject to the same curriculum and pacing guides. Students take the same benchmark assessments throughout the year, the same big state test in March. In reality, however, the children at Tyler and Crofton get two different educations.

That children from well-off families and children from poor ones have divergent school experiences is nothing new. What is significant is that the disparity continues in spite of (and in some ways because of) a movement designed to stop it. The practice of focusing on the tested subjects of reading and math at the expense of a well-rounded curriculum is far

more prevalent where children are poor and minority.[2] "You're not going to be a scientist if you can't read," a superintendent once told me in
defense of a school's pared-down curriculum. Well, you can't be a
scientist—one of the most common career goals of Tyler Heights'
graduating fifth graders—if you never learn science either. You can't be
a lawyer if you never learn to think critically, you can't be a computer
programmer if you never learn to solve problems, you can't be a politician if you never learn to speak in front of a group, you can't be a professor if you never learn to research, and you can't be an author if you
don't learn how to write.

Besides, plenty of children at these schools *can* read. It is one thing
to give students who lack basic skills an intense dosage of them; doing
that at the expense of engaging the most dynamic parts of their brains,
and letting that drive instruction for everyone, is another matter. In the
case of Tyler Heights, Tina McKnight felt she was laying the ground-
work for a future in which the students consistently score well enough
on the MSA that scrutiny might ebb and more active learning, in all
subjects, could be encouraged. I hope this is the case. President Bush, in
introducing No Child Left Behind, vowed to banish the "soft bigotry of
low expectations" for the nation's disadvantaged children. To condemn
them to a rudimentary education in the name of improvement is bigotry too.

◆ ◆ ◆

From the day they arrive at kindergarten, buoyed by the advantages of a
middle-class life, most Crofton students know their letters, they know
their numbers, and many can already read. It's not just that educated parents are more likely to read to their children, though that matters. Without realizing it they engage in the kind of activities and conversation, rich
with logic and analysis, that stimulate the brain and saturate children
with learning strategies.[3] (Many children at Tyler Heights told me their
conversations with adults at home were usually brief, centered around
whether or not they were doing what they were supposed to.) Middle-
class parents are more likely than poor parents to provide their children
with computers and the Internet and more likely to keep television out of
their children's bedrooms, both of which directly aid education.[4]

Well-off children are less likely to have brains compromised by pre-natal substance abuse, lead poisoning, and malnutrition. The amount of brain space for learning is shrunk by worry, so students free from the concerns of poverty, family instability, fathers who may or may not return, and drug dealers in the front yard are at an advantage when it comes to memory, attention span, and motivation.[5] Middle-class students see every day how schooling relates positively to the riches of everyday life. They see this through their parents' jobs. (That they even know their parents' occupations gives them a leg up over the third graders of Tyler Heights, many of whom have no idea what their parents do for a living.) They see this through travel and cultural exposure that extends beyond the Chuck E. Cheese's–shopping mall–television circuit that narrowly bounds the experiences of many children at Tyler Heights.[6] This exposure fuels motivation, which is why a school like Tyler Heights gave its students layers and layers of rewards if they did their work while Crofton didn't give any. Every quarter, children at Tyler Heights were commended in awards ceremonies; Crofton didn't even have an honor roll. Principal Wayne Bark got complaints about this but stood firm: "Everybody would get honor roll," he said.

Disparities in the knowledge children bring to school sharply affect the classroom experience. Take the Open Court story called "What Ever Happened to the Baxter Place?" The story, which runs twenty-two pages, tells about a farming family struggling to keep its land in the midst of suburban sprawl. Several of its concepts (mortgages, crop rotation, leasing, milking machines) and many of its vocabulary words (*barley, realty, livelihood, boutique*) were either already known to Mrs. Krainer's kids or fairly easy for her to explain, given their realm of knowledge. Miss Johnson's students? On a test one day, Avante thought that "automobile" meant the same as "bicycle." David thought "claw" was a synonym for "beak." Roman thought a cow's udders were a nest to make her sleep comfortably. With patience, conversation, and an awful lot of time, I believe these children were sufficiently smart that they might be taught enough of this material to truly understand the story, even though they were eight- and nine-year-olds living in rentals on the sketchy fringe of a small city. But the pacing requirements didn't leave time for catching students up in all the words and concepts they'd need to grasp the story.[7] They didn't account for the fact that everything took longer to teach in a school where even the brightest fifth graders asked, "What's a dome?" and "What's a boast?"

The Crofton students who had gone to the Winter Olympics in Turin surely would have had a better shot at answering the following question, which Miss Johnson's class faced one day:

Which of these would be most like a cartwheel because it requires practice?

> *a. Eating breakfast*
> *b. Watching a movie*
> *c. Learning to ski*

Before Miss Johnson's students could answer, she had to tell them that "skiing is when you put the long boards on your feet and go down a mountain in the snow." In one benchmark passage, siblings came home from school and found a note instructing them to pack a sweatshirt, flashlight, hiking boots, and sleeping bag. The BCR question asked where the children were going. Few in Miss Johnson's class knew. Of another passage, about a boy walking in the woods, Miss Johnson asked, "What is he doing?"

"Skiing," Malcolm said, remembering the explanation of the other day.

"Running," Savannah said.

"Walking," Manny said.

"Jogging," Avante said.

Miss Johnson interjected. "There's an 'H' word that means walking in the woods."

"Hunting," David said, and finally Lilia offered "Hiking! I did that in Salvador!"

No matter their MSA scores, the students of Tyler Heights can truly push ahead academically only if they are exposed to the world. The achievement gap is slave to the imagination gap and what author E. D. Hirsch Jr. calls the "knowledge gap"; the first cannot be closed as long as the other two yawn large. It is not just because knowledge will motivate children, though that is a factor. It is because, as Hirsch points out, reading is meaningless without knowledge beyond the scope of what students might be able to decode in text.[8] You could answer the cartwheel question without knowing about skiing, since you'd know the other choices don't require practice, and anything that starts with "learning to" probably does. You could explain that a boy was walking in the woods even if you had never done so yourself, or even heard of it, if the reading passage were explicit enough. Someone "surpassed" someone else in the fifty-yard dash: Even though Tyler Heights third graders had never heard of the fifty-yard dash when they saw this standardized test question, the cleverest among them might have deciphered the meaning anyway, by looking at the root "passed." But, clearly, a child who is even remotely worldly holds the advantage, in time and facility and lack of frustration, when answering a series of these questions.

And those who have a head start gain further advantages more efficiently, in sort of a winner-takes-all scenario. As cognitive scientist Keith Stanovich explains what reading researchers call the Matthew Effect, "The very good children who are reading well and who have good vocabularies will read more, learn more word meanings, and hence read even better. Children with inadequate vocabularies—who read slowly and without enjoyment—read less, and as a result have slower development of vocabulary knowledge, which inhibits further growth in reading ability."[9]

◆　◆　◆

With such advantages, it was no surprise that Mrs. Krainer's students could do the weekly Open Court exam in half the time it took Miss Johnson's class. When Miss Johnson's students were skimming through "Baxter Place," the Crofton kids were choosing from an array of enrichment activities: making a diorama, writing a newspaper article about farm life, inventing a breakfast cereal made from ingredients cultivated on farms. One Crofton teacher complained to me that the new structured curricula and test preparation left her time to do hands-on activities only every other day; Tyler Heights third graders did few hands-on activities of any kind. At the beginning of the year, Ms. Huffman told her fourth graders at Tyler Heights that they would write in journals every day, about anything they wanted, and she'd write back. But within the first week, she realized she couldn't fit that in.

A big reason behind the time crunch at Tyler Heights—a pressure that existed even though classes were about ten students smaller than at Crofton—was the massive amount of time devoted to test preparation. When Miss Johnson's class finally got to the farm unit, they were behind because they had shelved Open Court for a month in order to prepare for MSA. Every benchmark test was preceded by days of practice, and the MSA followed eight formal mock exams and many prep sessions. Crofton third graders, in comparison, prepared explicitly for the MSA only a few times, using practice software in the computer lab twice for reading and twice for math.

Crofton's MSA scores have always been high—in 2005 96 percent of the third graders passed reading and 98 percent passed math, compared to 90 percent and 80 percent at Tyler Heights. It's not that the principal didn't feel pressure to keep scores up. The superintendent had set a goal of 85 percent proficiency throughout the county by 2007, and nationally all schools were supposed to be at 100 percent by 2014. Schools like Crofton were expected to get there sooner.[10]

The culture of competition at the highest echelons of American schooling is a new, prominently publicized fact of life, in which parents hire private tutors for their perfectly able kindergartners and high schoolers pile up a tower of Advanced Placement courses and dissect microscopic fluctuations in SAT scores. When your scores are in the high nineties, it is no small challenge to push them higher—a reality lost to those who would phone Wayne Bark's office after test-score day. "If we drop two-tenths of a percent," the Crofton principal said, "I get calls—'What happened?'"

The school was not in danger of failing, but even if it did, there would not be a federal penalty, because schools that don't have enough poor children to receive Title I funding are not subject to the adequate yearly progress sanctions laid out in No Child Left Behind. Free from those requirements, they have more leeway. In some of Maryland's top high schools, scientific exploration was a staple of a curriculum on steroids: Teenagers extracted DNA and toyed with thermodynamics in world-class labs. These programs are no doubt ensured a long future.

As the bar rises for proficiency, though, and public pressure increases, educators even in schools like Crofton foresee a future in which test prep may trump the education they think is best for children.

◆ ◆ ◆

The entrances of housing projects often face away from the street. This keeps stoop life hidden from passersby but, in a sprawling, poorly lit complex like Harbour House, it also makes it terribly inconvenient to find street numbers. On the winter night I visited Jamila, in fact every evening I came to Harbour House, men gathered in small groups; women and children stayed inside. Outside Jamila's apartment, a crutch lay on the sidewalk, and brown-bagged bottles dotted the grass. Inside, graffiti in the hallway screamed *BLOOD SPORT.*

About half the students at Tyler Heights live at Harbour House or Eastport Terrace, adjacent public housing complexes that together house nearly a thousand residents. Rents range from fifty dollars to nearly seven hundred, depending on income. I was not surprised that the Tyler Heights teachers cautioned me against visiting the projects; most of them never would. I was surprised, however, by the children's warnings. No white people come there, they told me. I was crazy to come at night, they told me. "There's shootings there!" Jamila said. Jamila's mom, Vicky, was hesitant too: happy to talk with me but embarrassed about her environment. I'd been working as a journalist for years, venturing alone into far worse areas, but I'd never seen this degree of wariness at the idea of a white person visiting a black neighborhood.

Vicky filled her pleasant two-bedroom apartment with lots of plants, an aquarium, G-rated videos, and a green velvet living room set. Still, Jamila, like her classmates, told me often how much she hated Harbour House. "The moms beating their children," she said. "The men, they hang out behind the Dumpsters. They urinate in front of small children. They sell drugs. They rape children." I asked her what rape meant. "If a grown-up rapes, it means kill," Jamila told me, her voice dropping to a whisper. "If a child rapes, it means—" With her eyes, she indicated sex. Jamila slept poorly at night because the tenants below her had nightly "barbecues," she called them, with music, yelling, and laughing. In her fantasy apartment, "it's noisy in the day and quiet at night. That's not how it is in Eastport. It's noisy in the day and it's noisy in the night, and I can't stand it."

Jamila was the kind of girl who, when you asked what she'd do with a million dollars, would pay off her mom's bills before treating herself to imaginary indulgences, and, while her behavior was not flawless, she was the only one of Miss Johnson's students I ever saw try to stop a classmate from being nasty to another one. When Jamila wasn't chatting with whoever sat next to her, she tried hard in school, but she had trouble understanding what she read. So she didn't like to read. Still, she was one of the more curious children in Miss Johnson's class and was fond of new words, even as she mangled them. "Do you have more plungerines?" she asked for months after she tried my dried nectarines at lunch. "Pauve and muce!" she would say each time she saw me the week after we looked up shades of purple in the dictionary.

Jamila's mother worked at a moving company for a woman named Alice, whose son attended a county school demographically identical to Crofton. "I'm just amazed at the stuff they do at her kid's school," Vicky said. Her boss would talk about all her son's field trips and research projects, leaving Vicky wondering why the Tyler Heights kids didn't have those opportunities too. Vicky went to Tyler Heights back in the day, and through Jamila's eyes she viewed the school as boring as ever. "They don't do anything to broaden their minds, so the kids tend to get restless early on," she told me. "Not much has changed. Not much has changed at all." Her daughter's cultural experiences were limited—because of lack of money, unsafe surroundings—to the Disney Channel and ad hoc dance practices on the playground; the waiting list for Big Sisters was long; and Vicky had hoped the school would show her daughter the world in a way she couldn't. "I'm like, what is going on?" she said. "I'm knowing a lot more could be going on to pique their interest and get them involved."

What Vicky envied most was how Alice's son's teacher e-mailed parents that week's curriculum, how Alice could check assignments and grades online, how she bought the Open Court book to keep at home. "I didn't even know that was an option," Vicky said. Vicky went on field trips when she could, pushed the swings and sat with her daughter when other parents hung back. She knew to ask Jamila if she'd finished her homework, and she thought to make cards with the MSA words on one side and the definitions on the other, for Jamila to practice with. But Jamila would lie about homework. Or she would struggle with an assignment while her mom watched her at the round kitchen table, unsure how to be of use. When Vicky checked the Tyler Heights website, looking for guidance, she found only a series of staff photos that were out of date by a year and a brief list of school activities that was older than that.

It seemed to her that the Tyler Heights teachers assumed the worst about parents—that they wouldn't look online if the school had an informative website, that they wouldn't help their kids if given the opportunity. Certainly at upper-middle-class schools there is often closer communication between teachers and parents. At Crofton nearly all the parents, at least through third grade, attended Back to School night; classes had room mothers; there was an informal competition among moms to elaborately decorate teachers' doors. The PTA had four officers and eighteen committee chairs and a budget triple that of Tyler Heights. While Miss Johnson crossed her fingers that permission slips would come back to school and even held on to kids' eyeglasses at day's end for fear they would never return, Mrs. Krainer had no qualms sending her students home with the class turtle and hamster.

Alice helped Vicky compose a letter to send to Miss Johnson, asking that she be able to check up on schoolwork online and get copies of the Open Court stories so she could help with homework. Vicky wanted to know why her boss's son seemed to learn such different things in math. One day a little later, she ran into Miss Johnson at school. The teacher told her that online assignment tracking was not part of the math curriculum Tyler Heights used, unlike the one at her boss's son's school. The answer was good enough for Vicky.

12

Where's the Sand Table?

In Sheila McDermott's kindergarten classroom at Tyler Heights one autumn day, a bright-eyed girl named Isabel bent her head, her French braid mussy, and sounded out as she wrote. "My brothers' friends came—c-c-c-came toooo toooo ourrr. House." *"My Brd frns Km to R hos. And dy wr bod."* "And they were bad." Next to her, a serious boy named Lucas drew in detail the surgery he had recently undergone. Crayoned Lucas lay in a hospital bed in a green gown, attached to an IV by a squiggly tube and attended by a doctor wearing a mask and brimless cap. *"I yate to the HAPADO A LoA tAe A go,"* Lucas wrote. "I went to the hospital a long time ago."

At another table, Lamont drew what he said was a person but looked like the head-on view of a strange fish: a circle with random lines sticking out and dots for eyes. Where he was supposed to have written letters, he had scrawled three misshapen triangles. With help from an aide, a boy named William wrote with difficulty, *"A M i M A."*

Before setting them off on their thirty minutes of journal writing, Ms. McDermott had demonstrated at the easel. "On Saturday I went to the Halloween store," said McDermott, who was wearing a kicky ensemble from Petite Sophisticate and a dark blond ponytail. "Hmm, how do I write that? On. Onnnn. I hear an N. Saturday. Where can I find that in my resources?" She pointed to the calendar. "To—that's a pre-K buzzword. The—that's on our word wall." The final product: *"n Saturday I wt to the hln store."* The aim was not perfection but rather general proximity of letters and sounds. No problem for some students, beyond the range of others. And not even attempted in Mrs. Weaver's kindergarten next door, where nobody arrived knowing the alphabet, where a few children knew no English, where even the highest-skilled students were less knowledgeable than nearly any of McDermott's.[1]

Vast gaps in abilities exist not just between communities like Tyler Heights and Crofton but within any given school. The gaps were easy to predict even before the children showed up.[2] In parent conferences before school started, Isabel's mother told McDermott how the girl was jealous of her older brother's homework, so she made up her own from a big stack of workbooks. Lucas's mom, a teacher, wrote on a form that she wanted her son to learn high-level questioning techniques, Spanish, and computers. When William's mom filled out the same form, she wrote in Spanish that she'd like her son to learn colors, shapes, and letters—he didn't know any. Lamont's mom didn't show up at all, although she sent the boy, whom Mr. Al had to drive home when she wouldn't come get him.

Some of the children seemed to their teachers like little adults, while some seemed to have very little going on in their minds. Ms. McDermott was not surprised to find out that Lucas could read, and Isabel was on her way. Big-grinning Lamont—who had attended only a few days of kindergarten the year before and was enrolled this year only after Jennifer Johnson had spotted him in the housing project ("You're tall," the counselor had said. "Where's your mother?")—knew his colors but no letters. William, a chunk of a kid with a dimpled chin and a belly that made buttoning his denim shorts impossible, floated through the day in a sort of contented haze, unable to give coherent answers to even the simplest questions.

Like one-third of American children entering kindergarten, William had no prior school experience. Tyler Heights offered pre-kindergarten for forty children; that these two boys sat home all year when they could have been in school amazed McDermott. "They have had the opportunity to go to full-day pre-K. It's free. You get watched. You get fed—twice."

Also, you learn.

Catch-up began immediately. Ms. Dove, McDermott's teaching assistant, worked with Lamont every day, running his finger along the letters of his name and spelling it out with a puffy glitter pen. After a month those six letters still took him three minutes, even with guidance, and he couldn't tell you L was for Lamont. "I don't know what's with him," McDermott said. Was it vision problems? Was it phonemics? Was William autistic? McDermott is the kind of educator colleagues call a "master teacher," an opinion formalized in the fall when she won National Board Certified status, an honor bestowed by a nonprofit organization on only 1 percent of American educators. But no special designation was going to win her what she wanted most: the chance to get behind those boys' eyeballs and see what they saw.

◆ ◆ ◆

Back when kindergarten was considered a place to learn to get along, tie your shoes, and acquaint yourself with the alphabet, it didn't matter so much if five-year-olds arrived with few skills and advanced at their own pace. But now kindergarten is all about academics—not just ABCs but main ideas and number sentences. In Maryland, according to the state standards, kindergartners will, among other things, "algebraically represent, model, analyze, or solve mathematical or real-world problems involving patterns or functional relationships" and "use scientific skills and processes to explain the composition, structure, and interactions of matter in order to support the predictability of structure and energy transformations." On the checklist Tyler Heights kindergarten teachers filled out for each child several times a year, they were supposed to evaluate not only whether the student "holds book correctly" and "talks with peers" but also "uses upper emergent writing forms for a purpose" and "uses manipulative and oral story problems to make sums to ten." Students' skills are tested and their scores monitored regularly long before they are federally subject to the state assessment in third grade. Stragglers are identified and targeted, lest they fall even farther behind in a world where academic expectations are higher than ever.

With no time to waste, more children, like those at Tyler Heights, spend a full day in kindergarten, where they focus on academics. "Where's the sand table?" a puzzled new teacher, a transplant from private schools, once asked Ms. McKnight on her first day. McDermott and her colleagues fought successfully to preserve a half hour of playtime when the school expanded to all-day kindergarten, but in Anne Arundel County, like many other places around the country, play was not a given and naps were history. "The time is very precious," Dr. Smith said when he nixed rest time. "It's nonsense, as limited as our time and resources are, to pay teachers and teacher assistants to say, 'At one thirty, we're going to turn off the lights and you're going to lie down and sleep for thirty minutes.' "[3]

Smith once said of his county's kindergartners, "I don't care if those kids come out and can't do anything but read and read well," and in fact nearly everything these children did was centered around letters and words. On the first day, kindergartners jumped right into the daily calendar task, identifying the month and day and establishing that there was a period at the end of the sentence, "Today is September 1, 2005." Ms. McDermott read a poem called "Getting Ready" and a story about the Gingerbread Man and deflected in her firm and friendly voice every time—and there were many—that a girl named Rosie asked, "It is time for playing?"

Learning was snuck into every crevice of the day. Before lining up to leave the classroom, students had to identify a letter or a word's initial sound or the color of their clothing. Journal writing, years ago a weekly activity, was now done daily. McDermott even introduced MSA terms—she called them "big-kid words"—on illustrated strips of paper. By November Lucas could tell you that when words are in boldface "your voice gets a little loud"; Ebony could tell you that "playground" is a "pompound word"; Kojo knew that dialogue is bound by "quoquation marks." McDermott prepped kindergartners for a future of BCRs by making sure they used phrases from a question in their answers—"A character trait of the Gingerbread Man is . . ."—and whenever they failed to respond with complete sentences, she would ask, "Are there babies in here?" Tyler Heights kindergartners learned that the stories they read always had a problem and a solution. They decided that a book called *I Am an Apple* was in first person because the apple talked and was nonfiction because its explanation of the apple tree's life cycle was true. After a correct answer McDermott would say, "Kiss your brain," and the child so commended would kiss his hand and smack his forehead.

◆ ◆ ◆

"All the letters," mumbled a boy named Leo one day, puffing in a desperate attempt to write his name. Deja hung her head over her phonics mistakes and cried several times over, "I am dumb." Marquis wrote in his journal, *"I hat my sof Be cus I Dw Not No how to Rit."* Moments like these fuel a concern that a strong academic push is inappropriate for very young children. Some studies show that the pressure of highly academic programs increases anxiety and harms self-esteem in very young children, without any commensurate long-term benefit.[4]

Certainly I can imagine that effect in well-off, normally progressing toddlers who are being funneled into academic tutoring, in a sort of rat race of upper-class parental anxiety.[5] And the stress of high academic expectations was definitely evident by the time Tyler Heights' first graders were expected to write paragraphs with topic sentences, supporting details, and conclusions, a task so far over many of their heads that all they wanted to do was roll around on the floor. For most kids, though, "the expectation that they'll be beginning reading and writing by the end of the year is realistic," Ms. McDermott said. (Indeed, elsewhere in Marquis's journal he proclaimed, *"I thac I can rit so gd."*) To fail to give kindergartners the background they need to succeed in school every year thereafter seems unjust.

One September day Mrs. Weaver noticed a kindergartner paralyzed in front of the bookshelf.

"DeShay," the teacher said, "why don't you pick out a book to look at?"

"I don't know how to read," he said.

That DeShay thought you couldn't look at books if you didn't know how to read them said a lot about his household—at best aliterate and at worst illiterate. Compare this to children in a kindergarten class I visited at Crofton Elementary School. Rooms at the two schools had the same display of numbers wrapping around the walls, representing how many school days had elapsed. They had the same Open Court units, the same sound-spelling cards. But the Crofton children noticed upon entering the room that their teacher would be introducing a new letter—"She flipped over the camera card!"—and when it came time to write words with K sounds, they sat at their tables and came up with dozens: caddy, creature, Caroline, kangaroo, carnival, koala, caveman. Every child except for one signed their papers with their full names, and most wrote their middle names too. In math, while Tyler Heights students were still learning to write numbers, the children at Crofton figured out which sets of beads in front of them might total nine—four plus two plus three, for example—and then wrote the corresponding number sentences.

The Crofton children had stories read to them since infancy, letters and numbers pointed out to them since toddlerhood. So why shouldn't DeShay get a good push at age five? Making preschool available to everyone who wants it and giving kindergartners solid basics should not be defended on the grounds, which one hears often, that this will keep children out of jail or improve their odds of law school admission two decades hence.[6] Rather, this approach says: You have potential. That potential can probably be better tapped at school than anywhere else many of these children spend their time; failing to do so would only exacerbate their disadvantages.

Children do need to play, so it's nice to see that at Tyler Heights, the kindergarten teachers not only insisted on free time for their students but also provided the early academic focus in an environment that's hardly like cram school. Ms. McDermott, a woman who drags her fiancé to Pixar films, could not imagine kindergarten without the chance to inhale the salty, delicious essence of Play-Doh; she could not imagine kindergarten without singing. Play-Doh and songs were not listed in the chalkboard objectives "the students will" do each day:

TSW review the letters of the alphabet.
TSW identify syllables in multisyllable words.
TSW blend syllables to make words.
TSW learn the importance of letter order in words.

TSW identify thoughts and feelings of characters in a story.
TSW retell the sequence of events in a story.
MSA vocab: Clarifying.

But there was nothing that couldn't be sung in Ms. McDermott's classroom. Learning numbers, the students sang, "Down around, put on a hat, to make the number five. Slant on down and give it a curl, to make the number six." Her library of cassette tapes included "Who Let the Sounds Out," in which the students each hung a letter around their neck and stood to dance when theirs was called. To spell two-letter words they used the tune of "Happy and You Know It": "If you want to spell *me* say M-E." For three-letter words they used "Three Blind Mice": "Y-O-U, that spells *you*." Four-letter words were mashed somewhat awkwardly into "Clementine": "W-I-L-L, W-I-L-L, W-I-L-L spells *will*." After an intense discussion about nonfiction, McDermott would lighten the air with a round of "No More Monkeys Jumping on the Bed."

During the hour devoted to independent language arts work each day, children copied their names the regular way, but they also drew letters on Magna Doodles and stamped them from Play-Doh, no penalty if they stopped to mush it around a little. They learned color patterns using little plastic teddy bears; they did a weekly art project so they could master scissors.

The kindergarten teachers were supposed to adhere to the Open Court theme, which was easy to do with School but not so much when it was Stick to It or Shadows. McDermott brought the kids outside at different times to look at their shadows; they experimented with flashlights and shadow puppets in the classroom. Well before the required twenty lessons on the topic were completed, though, McDermott knew she would have to deviate—"There are only so many things you can do with a shadow"—and didn't hesitate to do so. Lacking a looming state test and the attendant scrutiny, the kindergarten teachers were far more likely than anyone else in the building to adapt the structured curriculum to what they thought their children needed, and wanted. They were not supposed to cover holidays but they discussed them anyway. McDermott's children fussed with a class hamster named Princess. She read them Junie B. Jones books, which had nothing to do with shadows or anything else official, to calm them down before recess.

"I feel like in kindergarten there's more leeway," McDermott said. "It's the one place you can sneak that stuff in."

◆ ◆ ◆

Marveen Sharps, one of the resource teachers at Tyler Heights, was trying to suppress the giggles. At the desk in her small office, she had been testing kindergartners all morning, one after the other.

For one of the test's four components, children were told a word and had to use it in a sentence. Leo didn't yet know what a sentence was. When Mrs. Sharps said, "Tell me something about a rabbit," he could, sort of: "A rabbit can walk and say meow." But asked for the word *rabbit* in a sentence, Leo said, "Rabbit mabbit." He continued like that for every word Mrs. Sharps gave him, thoughtfully and confidently and adorably. "Blue glue," he said. "Happy yappy. Open jopen. Alone abone. Listen jisten."

Asked what sound the word *letters* began with on another part of the test, Leo said, "They're in the mail." Shown a page of pictures, he was able to identify that the "duh" sound belonged to the doughnut and "sk" the skateboard, but when Mrs. Sharps asked, "What sound does 'plate' begin with?" he pointed to the tomato.

"What sound does 'insect' begin with?"

"Errrrrr! It wants to make noise."

"It sure does. You are so right," Mrs. Sharps said, as she marked the score sheet. "Which begins with S?"

"Stranger."

"What sound does 'mule' make?"

"Chicken."

"Leo, you need a tissue."

"No, it was boogers. I got them out." As he wiped his hands with a tissue Mrs. Sharps handed him, he asked about a photograph on her bulletin board, "Those your sons?"

"No. And they're girls."

"They go to school here?"

"Yes. That's Danelle and Danay."

"Danay my friend?"

Leo went on to point to the doctor for the "buh" sound and the pliers for the "pluh" sound (good guess). "What sound does quilt start with?" Mrs. Sharp asked, and Leo was confused, because blankets don't make noise.

The Dynamic Indicators of Basic Early Literacy Skills assessment, called DIBELS, is one of the most commonly used tools for evaluating the literacy skills of children in the early grades. The test is cheap— about a dollar per student to track the data—and relatively easy to administer. Nearly two million children since the late 1990s have been tested with DIBELS, including those attending most of the schools funded by federal Reading First grants, as DIBELS is a favorite of the current administration.[7] Kindergartners in Anne Arundel County were DIBELed, as teachers say, three times a year, and their scores supposedly correlated to whether they'd pass the MSA three years later. (First and second graders were DIBELed too.) The quality of DIBELS is backed up by scientific research. But watching it administered to about thirty children over the year, I could see why many early-childhood experts advise not to read too much into the results of standardized tests for kindergartners—and not just because they are easily distracted by boogers and photos.

At Tyler Heights I heard even the most able kindergartners ask "What's that?" to pictures of a mop, a pie, a button, and a pear. DIBELS is not supposed to test the students' vocabulary, just their prereading skills, but the items chosen for the test made vocabulary absolutely an issue—in sometimes strange ways. Whether or not these kids knew their letters or their sounds, they almost never knew beetle, rooster, or mule, pictures they were supposed to point to when they heard "buh," "ruh" and "muh." On one administration of the test, for the "buh" sound they were marked incorrect if they pointed to the bear (that was "cuh" for "cub") or the bug ("i" for "insect"); the correct answer, peculiarly, was the two cars crashing: "buh" for "bump," as in bumper cars, which judging from their reactions was not something the children of Tyler Heights had had much experience with.

Unless students were directly drilled in the format of the test, they had trouble catching on to what was asked of them, and the strictures of the test prevented teachers in many cases from rewording the instructions midstream. Mrs. Sharps kept quiet and marked off zeroes each of the many times students identified a lower-case L as "one." She kept quiet and marked off zeroes when capable children started out stretching words into individual sounds, as required, but then began to smush everything together; she kept quiet when they started out using the word in a sentence but then began to repeat everything she said.

"What about *open?*"

"What about open!"

DIBELS is based on speed—how many letters you can identify in one minute, how many words you can use in one minute to summarize a passage you heard—and sometimes less-skilled children, because they guessed so quickly, scored misleadingly high. In a way, better-reading kids could be penalized. On the section where students had to sound out as many nonsense words as possible in a set amount of time, those who actually knew how to read sometimes took forever sounding out the words, trying over and over again to get what they read to make sense, just like Ms. McDermott had taught them to do. If they pronounced "zek" with a long E instead of a short one, they were marked off a point, because kindergartners were only supposed to know short vowel sounds.

Ms. McDermott starting throwing nonsense words into her lessons, "as much as I hate to teach to the test," explaining to her children that the examiner would try to trick them. It was time she would have preferred to spend on real words, which her children needed urgently to learn.

◆   ◆   ◆

Well into fall, William could not yet recognize his name. Ms. McDermott stuck a picture of an apple on his locker so it would stand out, and still he would freeze in the hallway, unsure which was his. William had random moments of clarity. After I told him about the health benefits of water over juice, hoping to spare him from yet another gold tooth, whenever he spied me in the cafeteria he held up his bottle and announced, "Look, water!" But overall he was a cipher. During "Head, Shoulders, Knees, and Toes," he did knees when everyone else did toes, head when they did shoulders. When he spoke at all, his syntax was strange. "We saw fishing in the bucket!" he said about an outing with his dad.

William participated in all sorts of small-group interventions. "There are seven days in the week," Ms. Dove would say to children at her table, following the script for a program called Language for Learning. "How many days are there in the week? Is this the front of the cat? Touch the box. Touch the house. Touch the car." In another program called Early Reading Intervention, she would point to pictures on the page and say, "Toe. What is it?"

"Toe."

"Lock. What is it?"

"Lock."

"Astronaut. What is it?"

"Astronaut."

"Alligator. What is it?"

"Alligator."

The teachers began to document their concerns about specific kids in September, knowing that even in the best of circumstances they might not be able to acquire special help until March. Part of this was because of an attitude, outdated in this era of high expectations, that "they're just in kindergarten"; assessments to qualify for services set an old-fashionedly low bar for what a five-year-old should be expected to do and know. But most of the delay was caused by the intransigence of educational bureaucracy. Teachers were told that the county team that approved special ed testing would not look right away at kids who had never before been in school. Before teachers were allowed to seek outside judgment, they had to try several strategies in the classroom and see them fail. They had to discuss the child at a meeting with other kindergarten teachers, fill out a form listing every technique they'd attempted, notify parents, request a spot on the agenda at the monthly "KidTalk" meeting, discuss the situation again, set goals that could be measured with data, and chart improvement over time.

Ms. McDermott attempted to track William's ability to follow directions, an abstruse endeavor. She suggested William be added to the list of students learning English as a second language, to secure him special attention, although his parents both spoke English at home. Some sort of disability should be diagnosed, she knew, but as policy was interpreted, that wouldn't happen unless there was a gap between what he demonstrated and his apparent potential. If William was just low in everything, he wouldn't qualify.

And Ms. McKnight was wary of going there, given the pressure to keep the numbers of minorities down in special ed—part of the NAACP agreement and a general concern around the country. "You really don't want to jump the gun in identifying special ed," she told Ms. McDermott. "That comes from the county."

◆ ◆ ◆

Heading into winter break, Sheila McDermott put her faith in the Turkey Rule: After Christmas, once kids have eaten turkey twice, many come back with brains that have magically clicked. Indeed, in January, it was evident that while the higher students were not as curious as McDermott's kids used to be—five years ago Isabel's brother and his friends used to write complex descriptions of dinosaurs in their journals and eat up chapter books—many were making great progress. Isabel's journal was thoroughly understandable by anyone with a rudimentary vibe for kid writing: *"I Lk Go to the Bej. I swm with my mom and De."* Her L's were at a perfect right angle, and as she drew, she had a look of slightly haughty boredom. Her people had hair that hung normally, hand-sized hands, and pupils in their eyes. Lucas could always be counted on to know "i-n-g" endings and tricky spellings and he too wrote better than ever. The two of them copied words out of the picture dictionary and read with Ms. McDermott on the carpet.

"What does a good reader do if he doesn't know the word?" Ms. McDermott said, legs tucked under her brown flowered skirt.

"Look at the picture," they said. "Sound out the first letter."

Isabel read aloud easily. "I like hot dogs. I like sandwiches. I do not like . . ."

"Get your mouth ready."

"Balloons!"

"Look at the picture. See if it matches." And it did.

Many of the lower kids were making evident progress too. A couple of children got eyeglasses and started buzzing along. One student of Mrs. Weaver's who had arrived speaking no English now couldn't stop. "Can we color now, Mrs. Weaver?" he asked during workshop. "It tells you when to do things," he explained of the word *schedule*. DeShay, the boy who had been afraid to pick out a book, now scrambled to the shelves, grabbing the green fuzzy teddy and plopping on the blue bean-bag. He paged through *Stellaluna*, through *Sports Illustrated for Kids*, through a book called *Friends*.

"I found an A!" he said to Mrs. Weaver.

"What is 'the' doing there?" he said to me.

As for Lamont, it seemed turkey did him good. Although the only word he knew by sight was *the*, and his letters slanted all wrong, he had learned his numbers and most of the alphabet; he could identify the characters in a book or the mistake in a pattern of shapes. William, though, was regressing. Some days he knew twenty-four letters, some days he knew eighteen, and the ones he missed weren't necessarily the same. He didn't stand when his reading group lined up at the door, he didn't interact with his classmates except on the few occasions when he pretended to shoot them with a gun. He never raised his hand. When Ms. McDermott asked, "Did you play this weekend? Did you watch TV this weekend?" he always answered, "No." Once she asked if he had something to share, and he said, "Reindeer."

"What about reindeer?"

"Reindeer. Home."

"You have a reindeer at home?"

"Yes."

Yet when the speech pathologist assessed him, he did fine: identifying two of five shapes, following two-step directions, pointing to top and bottom and in and out. Ms. McDermott wanted to know what kind of science fiction novel she was living in, in which this boy could communicate only with those who arrived to formally assess him.

A week later, the class got a new student, a child with an eager atti-tude, blue pants that exposed her entire bottom when she sat, and a Dora the Explorer backpack filled only with the butt end of a fat orange Crayola.

"I am a girl," Lina told her teacher. "I have an L in my name."

L was not the only letter Lina knew—she could list them all, her numbers too. But she couldn't identify one of the thirty-three words kindergartners were, by now, supposed to know by sight. The rate at which students move in and out of schools like Tyler Heights is troubling; by the time Lina arrived McDermott had already lost four of her students and gotten a six-and-a-half-year-old whose mother hadn't bothered to send him to kindergarten when he was five and who tried to kiss all the women. Often new children arrived in a cloud of mystery, as Lina did: Her mother, who spoke no English, told the community liaison that the girl had had two years of preschool, but she couldn't remember where. On the record from the school Lina had attended in the fall, the teacher had marked every category "still developing." *"Needs one-on-one attention to stay out of trouble,"* she wrote. *"Has trouble following directions."*

"Of course," Ms. McDermott said with equal doses of sarcasm and hope, "November was a long time ago, so we may have improved."

13

I'm Giving Him Everything He Can Get

Down the hall from kindergarten, past the office, around the corner, and all the way at the other end of the L that makes up Tyler Heights Elementary School, Laurie Williams's fifth graders comprised a group no less varied in their abilities than Ms. McDermott's kindergartners. Thomas and Gregory came back from summer break each year with reading logs topping a hundred books and constantly waved their hands to provide correct answers in class, as if they were trying to stay afloat in choppy seas. Close behind them were a set of girls for whom A's and B's didn't seem to be too much of an effort. Several students in the class received special services—for attention deficit disorder, English as a second language, speech impairment, lousy memory—though you could not necessarily tell by listening to them in class. More obviously needy were two transplants from other schools: Jada, who couldn't remember two times seven even when Mrs. Williams quizzed her on it every day for a month, and Nicole, who was such a poor reader, about four years behind, that she couldn't pick out her friend's name on the ballot for class president.

And then there was Mateo Eduardo Martinez Contreras, as he liked to sign his name, who arrived at Tyler Heights just as the last school year was ending. The sparklingly handsome boy was put in Mrs.

Williams's class in May and kept there in the fall, because after ten years in Mexico and eight months in America—half in Houston and half elsewhere in Annapolis—he could not speak English.

Part of every day, Mateo joined a few other students in Evelyn Davidson's classroom trailer for English as a second language. Watching a lesson there one day, Ms. McKnight said, "They are really so much more relaxed and engaged than they are in their classrooms." This was certainly true for Mateo, who enjoyed straightforward English lessons and the way Mrs. Davidson greeted correct answers with effusive praise. She didn't know what grade level Mateo read on in Spanish— probably not fifth—but she could tell he was smart. He would page through the picture dictionary whenever he had the chance, and during a lesson on family terms he scrawled intently on his palm, "*Gruendader*→ *nieta. Wouif*→ *esposa.*" When Mrs. Davidson allowed him to write in Spanish, for experiment's sake, he did fine. "*I think that if I won Respect King,*" a translation of his contest entry went, "*I'd try to win the respect of teachers and students, and I'd try to be respectful of my friends. I'd try not to get into other people's business.*"

When it was time to go back to the regular classroom, Mateo would beg, "No. No, please." (This he could do in English.) He would walk from the trailer to the building toe-to-heel, taking the smallest steps possible. He'd invariably arrive back in Mrs. Williams's room toward the end of a lesson, tuning out the incomprehensible snippets of something or another. "More than half the stars that we can see are binary stars," the soothing voice said one day on the Open Court cassette, as Mateo slunk into his seat and paged through an Autobús Mágico book. "There is a different kind of star cluster called a globular cluster."

When Mrs. Davidson began to feel she had to teach her students less about understanding English, which Mateo needed desperately, and more about writing BCRs and keeping up with Open Court, his light dimmed more.[1] His experiences in fifth grade, along with his classmates', made up a Technicolor display of the dissonance between two of American education's prime directives: that all children should be taught in the way that suits them best, and that all students should master the same material in the same amount of time.

At Tyler Heights, children with language issues, learning disabilities, emotional problems, and reading difficulties receive lots of attention. Every day three of Mrs. Williams's students were pulled out of class an hour a day for special education with Mrs. Rogers-Payne. Mateo and another boy were pulled out an hour for ESOL. Two boys were pulled out a half hour twice a week for speech therapy, and Jada and Nicole were pulled out an hour each day for SpellRead, which provided readings at their levels and drilled them in letter series they may or may not ever see in real words (aws, eeth, oysh, awth).

Specialized support was provided inside classrooms too. An occupational therapist might visit to make sure a developmentally delayed child had the proper pencil grip. During workshop, as other students filled out worksheets or practiced spelling or wrote final drafts of an essay, a resource teacher might gather a small group in the back of Mrs. Williams's room and work through BCRs step by step. In the winter, when Mrs. Davidson suspected her ESOL kids were relying on random answers and calculators to scrape by on increasingly difficult math, she sat with them in the back of the classroom and supplemented the teacher's lessons with whispered translations and gentle nudges. It was hard to keep up. "Two-eighths, *reducir.* You know 'reduce'?" Mrs. Davidson would say, but the teacher had moved on to averaging three numbers. "Mateo, you know 'average'? You know this word?" but the teacher had moved on to dividing 110 minutes into hours. By the time the group in the back started to turn minutes into hours, the teacher was handing out a quiz.

Special education, ESOL, resource teachers: all this staff to give struggling children the best education possible. But what about another group of kids with special needs? Educators across the country complain that challenges for gifted students have been sacrificed in a prioritization that focuses on weaker ones, the children least likely to pass state tests. In Mrs. Williams's class, Thomas and Gregory were smart enough to sense this too.[2] They resented lower students who didn't seem to pay attention, because they slowed down class. (Obnoxiously, the two clapped when a classmate got an answer correct.) At the same time, they envied them. "We never get to go anywhere, except around the corner for recess and lunch," Gregory told me over lunch. "We never get to be part of a study group. Anyway, it's the same thing every year."

Thomas chimed in. " 'Let's review. Let's review.' Even when we remember the stuff we're reviewing."

The only parent comment about Tyler Heights on the school rating
website greatschools.net read "Do not have programs in place to challenge those students that are above the average student." Thomas's
mom had this nagging worry his intellect was not being stimulated
enough, but she could never be sure if that was the case or if the boys
said they were bored in school because, well, they were boys, and they
were ten. Their principal knew it, though. "I'm getting kids over the
line and holding back kids who, we don't know how far they could go,"
Ms. McKnight said.

When the advanced kids were given extra work, it felt like more of
the same—less a challenge than a punishment. Some fifth graders were
so unstimulated—one girl spent her days counting paragraphs in the
textbook and reading a book stashed in her desk—that they had begun
to misbehave. "We used to do *projects*," the girl had said. "If I've got it,
why should I have to do it over and over and over again?"

At a Literacy Team meeting in December, Ms. Panetta said, "There's
a group of seven or eight kids who don't have to do a BCR for fifteen
minutes."

"The kids miss having a TD," Mrs. Marshall said. While the school
had at least ten staff members focusing on students who were lower
than the rest in various ways, the school would not have a "talent development" teacher for the gifted until January, despite Ms. McKnight's
attempts to hire one. "We still have time," McKnight said. "We have
lots of time before the test. We have lots of time before the end of the
year."

"The kids who are causing the most trouble are the brightest kids. I
don't think they think anybody trusts them," Ms. Panetta said.

"If they are not challenged and don't feel good about themselves, we'll
be in trouble in March," when MSA rolls around, Mrs. Marshall said.

"We shouldn't settle for proficient," McKnight said. She wanted to
ensure that a good number of kids would score at MSA's highest level,
advanced, at least in math. "So the plan is to—"

"Jack 'em up!" Mrs. Marshall said, and everyone laughed.

The talent development teacher who finally arrived after winter break had little experience with gifted children and no experience with the curriculum. McKnight had her pull small groups for math, since so few students had scored advanced on MSA math the previous year. The idea was for the teacher to devote most of the class periods to challenging extensions to the regular math curriculum, but in the end the main way the new teacher jacked 'em up was to teach the same lessons everyone else got, just faster.

◆ ◆ ◆

The classroom teachers tried on their own to adapt their lessons to students' needs—to "differentiate instruction," as it is called. During workshop Mrs. Williams would sit with a student who was having trouble matching literary concepts like onomatopoeia with examples. When Miss Milhoan gave her class articles to summarize, she would give Emily, her top student, extra. But differentiating instruction in a classroom of children of such varied abilities is something most teachers are ill-prepared to do. To Mrs. Williams, who was in her fourth year teaching, accommodating everyone was a quandary: The choices, as she saw it, were to teach class at a pace directed at the slowest students and lose the high ones, or leave the low ones behind.

Why did these seem to be her only two options? Partly because nobody taught her otherwise. Partly because the math and reading curricula were designed to be taught to the whole class at the same time, and what few accommodations they made for differentiation were difficult to implement in real life, in real time. Partly because getting each child to the same place in class and the same level on MSA, when some of them could not speak English or read, would have required an army of teachers so large even Tyler's budget could not afford it.

At the end of 2005, I had watched as Miss Johnson sat with a mentally retarded girl named Whitney, ready to transcribe a BCR about the "Baxter Place" story. While the other students worked on their own, Miss Johnson asked, "How did the farm change? What happened to the land?"

Whitney said nothing.

"What does the word *change* mean?"

"It became different."

"How did it become different? Let's think. How did it change from the beginning of the story to the end of the story? What was there in the end of the story that wasn't there in the beginning? What was built on the land that wasn't there before?"

"A house. The furniture?"

"What about the house?"

"The market. The woods?"

"What about the woods?"

Silence.

"Why would they need to sell the cows?"

Silence.

"What do you get if you sell something?"

Silence.

"If you go to the store and buy something, what do you give the person who is selling it?" Silence again. Miss Johnson looked up and said, "The rest of you should be underlining your hundred-dollar words."

Even without the burden of a whole class to tend to, teaching Whitney Open Court was still challenging. The following year, when she was in fourth grade, Mrs. Rogers-Payne, the special education teacher, walked her through a lesson on metaphors and similes. Explaining the words *bottomless* and *pit* took ten minutes alone; another ten went to explaining that Ms. McKnight was the *glue* that held Tyler Heights together. When Mrs. Rogers-Payne tried to teach homonyms, she had to explain *grate* at length before telling Whitney it was a homonym of *great*; same with *dew* and *due*.

"All children can learn," politicians like to say, and it is true. The problem wasn't that Whitney couldn't learn. It was that a girl who barely knew how to sound out words and possessed a paltry vocabulary couldn't learn third-grade material in third grade and couldn't learn fourth-grade material in fourth grade—even though in the new world of school, she was expected to. Seventy-five percent of public school parents think special education students should not necessarily be required to meet the same academic standards as other children, and Mrs. Rogers-Payne and all of Whitney's teachers agreed.[3] They thought it silly that instead of rewinding and learning fundamentals she had to dissect a complex story about a failing farm, she had to do the exact same Open Court worksheets as everyone else, she had to be prepared to sit down to a state test in March to see if she was proficient in fourth-grade material, when everyone knew she wasn't.

"They need more realistic goals," Mrs. Rogers-Payne said of her students.

The education researcher Mary Kennedy wrote in 2005, "Rarely do reformers think seriously about the array of real students and situations that teachers face in their classrooms."[4] I desperately wanted the people who write today's education laws and make judgments about schools to watch Whitney in class. It's one thing to expect teachers to challenge each child, and expect the kids to do their best. It's another to expect that the best will be the same for everyone.[5]

Mrs. Rogers-Payne couldn't stand making her students keep up with Open Court; she was trained to teach each child according to his own strengths. About three of Mrs. Facchine's third graders, she said in December, "I'm teaching them grade-level stories with accommodations, but I really need to get back to teaching them to read."

"Hopefully after the MSA," Mrs. Facchine said.

When a mentally retarded and autistic fourth grader named Alvin put aside the reading flashcards after MSA and built a circuit for the science fair, he won second place. When the special ed third graders put aside BCRs and told stories into a tape recorder, Mrs. Rogers-Payne was impressed with their imaginations. But when she kept up with the pacing guide, her students wound up just doing the same thing they'd do in regular class, albeit in a small group. Even when they could answer verbal questions about a story, they couldn't come close to formulating them on their own in a way that would get an acceptable score on a BCR. Because these tasks were over their heads, and because the children were in special ed for such different deficiencies, she often wound up dragging them through lessons and just telling them what to write.

One day the fifth graders had to write a BCR answering, "Explain how the setting in 'Sudden Trouble' influenced Chris's actions in the story."

"He was scared?" said Ellen.

"The setting of 'Sudden Trouble' influenced Chris's actions—I need a sharpened pencil," said Zavier.

Mrs. Rogers-Payne backed up. "What is the setting?"

"It's on a lake."

"Remember, I've told you a hundred times. You guys have to tell me what to write. I have to control myself from giving you prompts. Also in the setting it says—"

"The sky turns gray," Ellen said.

"The text says the sky turns gray?"

"Yes."

"You know, 'text' is a hundred-dollar word. What else?"

"He was blowing the whistle on the lake," Zavier said.

"Why did Chris blow the whistle?"

"So he could call the fishes."

"No, after that."

"To get help," Ellen said.

Mrs. Rogers-Payne narrated as she wrote on the overhead, and the kids copied slowly. "The wind began to blow hard. The setting influenced Chris's actions—'influenced' is a hundred-dollar word— because he blew his whistle to send a SOS to get help. I'm trying to make this sound like kid language but it still has to sound right. Oh lord. So this means Chris and his brother enjoyed the ride out on the lake? No. So this means Chris and his brother and sister were in danger?"

"They could get pieces of wood and tie it up and drag it to help them," Zavier said.

"But did they?"

"No."

"What did they have with them?"

"A whistle."

"So they made a choice to get help," the teacher wrote. When the students went back to Mrs. Williams's room, they brought with them identical BCRs, as they often did.

♦ ♦ ♦

After school, in the mostly Hispanic garden apartment complex that neighbored the mostly black Harbour House, Mateo changed quickly into shorts and played soccer with friends in the dirt. When the boys tired of running, they crowded into the urine-tinged stairways to talk and laugh. In quieter times, Mateo drew aliens and griffins and Frankenstein in his notebooks and imagined the jungle animals he hoped to see in Africa one day.

Though Mateo was shy when he arrived at Tyler Heights in May of 2005, Mrs. Williams could tell he was enthusiastic to learn, especially math. He was talkative in ESOL. Mateo's classmates liked him, not just because they loved to touch his carefully gelled hair but because he had a perfect smile for everyone. He was happy to attend a school where the blacks and Latinos got along, unlike his rough school in Houston. But after returning from summer break, Mateo played the outsider. He'd disappear to the bathroom for five minutes at a time. When he was given a test he didn't understand, he would burrow his arms inside his T-shirt and chew on the neck band. Was it laziness? Lack of confidence? Fear? Mrs. Williams suspected bad influences. "I blame myself for Mateo," she said more than once. When he first arrived, she paired him with a buddy named Harry, because he spoke Spanish too. She suspected that Harry, who had since moved on to middle school, encouraged Mateo to coast, ignore his work, and answer all questions with "I can't understand," because if you don't try, you can't fail.

"People must think I'm dumb," a dejected Mateo told me in Spanish one day after a test, his thumb idly running back and forth across an eraser. "I can't understand. I can't understand."

Mrs. Williams knew Mateo was not dumb but didn't really know how to help him show that, beyond using her few Spanish words and pointing a lot. During workshop, when she'd tell him to finish his vocabulary for ESOL, he would say, "I'm done." She made a book for him, in which he'd hunt for words that began with a certain letter. She gave him a puzzle with Spanish on one side and English on the other, but when she told him to use the English side, he lost interest. Mateo's inability to communicate in English meant he was never really integrated into the class. When the rest of the students wrote reports based on interviews with their relatives—about slaughtering lambs in Pakistan, slaughtering chickens in Mexico, and washing clothes by hand in the Philippines—Mateo didn't participate, though he was very interested in different cultures. When Mrs. Williams called on students, Mateo never raised his hand. When his classmates marched to the front of the auditorium to receive certificates during awards ceremonies, Mateo was left in his seat, hunched in his jean jacket.

Mateo occasionally understood more than he let on but didn't have the words to respond. Two doors down, in Miss Milhoan's third-grade class, another child had no such problems. Mateo's brother, Juan, who tackled homework before soccer and lacked his brother's inhibitions, sped ahead in math, inhaled English, and began to shout instead of talk, so eager was he to show off his skills.

As Mateo grew distant, Mrs. Davidson sought out his mother, Bertha. Bertha, who brought her boys to America illegally from Oaxaca, worked as a line cook at a restaurant to pay her share of the two-bedroom apartment she lived in with the boys and four other people. *"Prometo ayudarles en casa con su trabajo,"* she signed on the school pledge at the beginning of the year—*"I promise to help with homework"*—but without any English she wasn't sure how. Mateo needs structure, Mrs. Davidson told her, in a forty-five minute conversation in the Tyler Heights hallway. Make sure he does his work, because he is smart.

She said the same to Mateo: Work harder and start thinking about college.

"What's the use of college if I don't have my papers?" Mateo replied.

◆ ◆ ◆

No Child Left Behind requires that tests be given "to the extent practicable" in a "language and form most likely to yield accurate data on what students know and can do." But only a few states give children exams in their native languages, and Maryland is not one of them.[6] Some states simplify the language so that the English is more understandable for ESOL students, but Maryland doesn't do that either. "I really think that's something that as a school district and community, we're going to have to do," Ms. McKnight said. It seemed to her that Mateo's score on the MSA (which would count, since he arrived in Maryland before September 30) would measure neither math nor reading, only how well he'd learned English—a skill tested separately by the state, at any rate.

The vast majority of special education students, no matter their disability, were subject to the MSA too. While 14 percent of the nation's public school students are in special education, only 3 percent of any state's proficient scores used to calculate adequate yearly progress may come from tests adapted to the skill levels of the disabled, according to a federal rule.[7] Everyone else must take the state's regular test. For many children in special education and ESOL, being held to the same expectations as their classmates is not a problem, as long as they receive the proper accommodations during testing. One day in December, Mrs. Davidson and Ms. Prater met in the computer lab to decide what accommodations each ESOL student would get in March and on the practice tests until then. Some children would have the whole test read to them verbatim, some part of it ("selected reading"), and in some cases a teacher would transcribe answers as students dictated. Students could be given more time to take the test, or pulled into smaller groups that remove the distraction of the classroom.

"Munir," Ms. Prater said. "Small group, verbatim reading. Bilingual dictionary."

"I have an Urdu dictionary, but it won't do any good because he can't read Urdu," Mrs. Davidson said.

"Hmm. Eddy?"

"He gets selected reading."

"Alison. All she got last time was extended time and small group. Let's look at her benchmark score. She got a basic on her SRs, and she got a proficient on her BCRs. She's okay. So let's just say for her small group, extended time, frequent breaks?"

"Yeah, I'm giving those," Mrs. Davidson said.

"What do you want to add to that? Do you want to add a read-aloud?"

"I guess so."

"How about Paz? She was basic—should she be scribed for?"

"No," Mrs. Davidson said. "She shouldn't be scribed for if she is doing fourth-grade work in class."

"What about Elena? She takes a long time processing spelling, so she can be read to."

"I don't think she should be scribed."

"But if she takes a long time spelling, even though spelling doesn't count, it might get her frustrated and muddle up her ideas for her BCR," Ms. Prater said.

"I've seen her write BCRs better than fifth graders," Mrs. Davidson said. The ESOL teacher felt uncomfortable layering on all sorts of accommodations just because a kid was in danger of scoring low. Children who got accommodations often scored higher on practice tests than their skills seemed to merit, boosted by proctors who could not help but nudge them along. A child who was read to was really being evaluated on listening comprehension, not reading comprehension. And those who were scribed for often got lazy, blurting out the first answer that came to mind without realizing it was lame, because they didn't have the deliberate thinking time that the act of writing engenders. Ms. McKnight agreed that it was silly, in a way, giving ESOL students all these accommodations as if they were special ed. But, she said, when children are read to they understand two grade levels above when they're reading by themselves. "We would be crazy not to give them all the accommodations they're entitled to," Ms. McKnight said.

So Mrs. Davidson agreed to the accommodations, including for one of her favorite students. "Mateo," she said, "I'm giving him everything he can get."

◆ ◆ ◆

On a brutal winter Friday, Mateo carried a pencil and his whisper-phone to the annex for his weekly practice MSA. On benchmark after benchmark, practice test after practice test, Mateo took the same random stabs at the multiple-choice questions, mumbling as he ran his finger under dozens of words he didn't understand. He didn't know if "uproar" was a fib, exercise, commotion, or mixture. The electronic translator Mrs. Davidson had gotten him, thinking he'd be more likely to use it than an uncool dictionary, told him "alboroto," but he didn't know that either. He didn't know if "frothy" meant cold, foamy, wet, or tasty; he didn't know if "colonization" was an armed invasion, peaceful revolution, settling of new land, or control of goods. Mateo didn't know if "press" in the sentence "Don't press me about that now" was the same as in a basketball full-court press, a tailor pressing your shirt, a press agent—what fifth grader knows what a press agent is?—or pressing for a quick answer.

At least the passage Ms. Panetta read aloud on this day's test was about animals—better than that inscrutable benchmark about skating figure eights on a pond ringed with crabapples and cattails, or when he had to explain how the setting influenced Lisa's actions in "On the Trail," to which he could only answer, "Lisa had friendly. The ducks is like the pond." This BCR, a question the state had made public from an old MSA, was a summary of a story. Students were given the beginning: "Rabbit heard Elephant and Whale deciding to rule the land and the sea. . . ."

Mateo thought and offered, "The rabbit helping to . . ."

"What?" Ms. Panetta said as she wrote.

Mateo pointed to a picture of the whale. "Write it," he said.

"Oh, whale."

"Whale and elephant," Mateo said, then fell quiet. The heater hummed. After a long pause he asked Ms. Panetta what a word meant. She said she was sorry but she couldn't help. He asked me, "How do you say —?" I said I was sorry but I couldn't help. "Just try your best, Mateo," Ms. Panetta said.

Mateo hadn't taken off his blue parka. His elbows sat on the table and his fists pushed into his shoulders. "Um. Okay." He looked at the text and made little sounds—not quite whimpers, but close.

"The. The elephant . . ." He motioned to Ms. Panetta to erase what she was writing.

"Is this okay here?" she asked him. "Should I erase?"

"The elephant said to the whale, 'Hello.' "

Mateo looked at the top of the story. Each time he was given a standardized test, Mateo would ask, "No puede leer en español?"—"You can't read it in Spanish?"—to which the answer was always no. "Why not?" he would say, and there was never an answer. "At least try," Mrs. Davidson would tell him, "so they can know more or less where you are right now."

Where he was right now, more or less? More: Free to use Spanish with me, Mateo would talk all about bird flu, animals eating people (crocodiles and sharks), and people eating animals (dogs and snakes). In the library he always chose books and magazines about geography and studied the country facts. He taught me how to clean and filet a fish and asked me often about different religions.

Less: Because he couldn't write about the whale and the elephant in English, he was nowhere. "Mmm," he said, obviously troubled, and typed some more into his translator. "And powerful."

Ms. Panetta stifled a yawn. Mateo took the paper from her and wrote on his own, some phrases from his brain and some right from the text, for the next eleven minutes: *"The rabbit looked at the whale. Helped. All the animal that walk and all the birds that fly. The Rabbit that walk why I've come to you with my small problem. The elephant is happy to the whale. It was as help and found the elephant."*

Mateo sniffled, cleared his sore throat, and reached for a tissue. He pulled his whisper-phone from its Ziploc bag and used it to murmur to himself. Ms. Panetta stuck stars on his paper indicating that he proof-read and used his time wisely. It was time for lunch, nobody any wiser about how well Mateo could read.

14

I See Motivation All Over This

Forty-two school days until MSA, loud synthesizer music greeted students entering the cafeteria. On the stage, an air mattress was covered with a sports-themed comforter. The kids didn't know what to expect as they took their seats this January morning; the only clue in Miss Johnson's classroom had been the objective on the board. *"*Assembly— *We will be motivated to take the MSA test."*

As the music faded out, Ms. McKnight greeted the students.

"What are we having?!" she shouted.

"MSA!" the third, fourth, and fifth graders shouted back.

"Are we going to be ready for the MSA?"

There were yes's, and a smattering of no's.

"Are we going to be ready for the MSA?"

"Yes!"

"Does anybody know how many days till the MSA?"

"Forty-two!"

"Are we going to be worried about that?"

"No!"

"We're going to be . . ."

"Ready!"

To make sure of that, Tyler Heights was banking on a bell-shaped, seven-foot Muppet clone whose website promised an "Ace Your Test" program that, for five hundred dollars, "will definitely help your students be well prepared, confident, and energized to put forth their best effort."

"YoJo has a terrible attitude toward taking tests," said his sidekick, Scout, a man filled with the zippy energy characteristic of those who give school assemblies for a living. "He needs you to help and encourage him. Here's . . . YoJo!"

YoJo peeked into the room and then scurried away.

"Here's . . . YoJo!"

YoJo pushed Mr. Al in, and raced out again.

"Here's . . . YoJo!"

At this, YoJo—whose creator five years before lived inside the Baltimore Oriole instead of this coat of blue fur, thatch of red hair, and spare-tire belly—came in and smothered Ms. McKnight with a kiss. He sat on kids, danced with Ms. Borinsky, and enveloped Mr. Summey, the PE teacher, in his extra-extra-large T-shirt. "We're going to get you ready!" Scout said. "We're going to make you confident! We're going to make you king of the world—make you feel like you can do everything! Today's the day you step up and take an MSA challenge in front of everybody."

YoJo ran away.

"You don't think you can handle that?"

YoJo swayed to the ground. Over the course of the presentation his confidence would surge, though. With the help of Scout and the "Test-O-Matic 3000," rigged from what looked like a Dustbuster and two Lite-Brites, YoJo learned about the process of elimination. He learned to fill in circles properly, guess if he had no idea, and give supporting details in BCRs. (Clearly the duo had done their research on the MSA: YoJo explained the author's purpose in writing a poem.) He learned the importance of a good night's sleep, a good breakfast, and good penmanship.

After forty-five minutes of YoJo's pratfalls and test tips, Ms. McKnight took the mike. "Are you going to ace your MSA?" she asked.

"Yes!"

"Did you enjoy YoJo and Scout?"

"Yes!"

Ms. McKnight asked the children to stand for "Soaring High Like an Eagle," the school song. She sang into the mike—"a closet diva," Miss Johnson murmured—and tried to get the kids to sway along. YoJo had cracked them up, and at lunch they'd still be talking about whether his giant pencil could really write, but by now they had lost interest. Back in class, Miss Johnson had them write a BCR about three things YoJo taught them.

◆ ◆ ◆

Forty-one days until MSA, Jennifer Johnson asked Mrs. Facchine's students, "Who knows how many days until we take the MSA?"

"Forty-three!"

"Forty-two!"

"Forty-one!"

"We're getting closer to the MSA," the counselor said. "Today you're going to do a little practice. Does anyone know why we have to take the MSA? Because Mrs. Facchine wants you to take a big ol' test? Why, Estela?"

" 'Cause it's the, it's the . . ."

" 'Cause it's what?"

"Nothing."

"Andrea?"

" 'Cause we need to get—we're taking the MSA because. Because. To get us ready?"

"Estela?"

"Because . . . it's the . . ."

"We have to take the MSA so they can assess our performance. It's the way that they're measuring student performance in all those schools. Schools have different programs. We have Open Court, Saxon Math. Other schools have different programs. It's the only way they can tell those programs are working. It's the only chance we get to show everybody what we know. I say let's do our best, so everybody will be so proud of us."

"Remember that day Ms. McKnight was dancing in the hallway?" Gardell asked.

"Oh yes, I sure do!"

On the overhead Ms. Johnson put a transparency of a bear shaped like a star and wearing sunglasses. At each point of the star was an icon that indicated one "Star Strategy" for taking the MSA: money for hundred-dollar words, a bat for BATS, a woman looking at a paper for proofreading, a clock and a book for perseverance (the rule was to work until time is called), and sunglasses to indicate Mr. Trickster, the school's term for the process of elimination. Tricksters, to be noted systematically with tiny pencil marks, are the multiple-choice answers you know are wrong. The top of the page read:

YOU
Can be a
MSA
Star!

"These are ways to ensure that our answers are better than anyone else's answers," Ms. Johnson said. If your teacher sees you using the strategies, she said, she will give you a star. Enough stars and you win a prize. "If you finish early," she said, "you will not close your book. We're checkin', not chillin'. We don't have the scores we get by chillin'."

The class began the first of eight practice MSAs they would take over the next weeks. Everyone scribbled away except for Reggie, who sat slumped, his round head hung down toward his jean jacket, which was buttoned to the top. He had gone to four schools for first grade and arrived at Tyler at the end of second grade; in third grade, it hadn't taken long for Mrs. Facchine to realize three things: Reggie aced math. He had a broad vocabulary he showed off in his high-pitched voice at any chance. And he could barely read. In September Mrs. Facchine had recommended the special ed process be started, but first, various strategies had to be exhausted. Corrective Reading with Mrs. Marshall helped some, and a behavior plan kept him in line, but still he was only reading on a first-grade level as he sat facing a third-grade test he couldn't decipher. On his last benchmark, he scored six out of thirty-two.

When the practice test started and three students left the room with the special ed teacher who would give them accommodations, Reggie asked, "Why do they get help?" A meeting had been scheduled for the following week to seek permission to test him for services. For now, Mrs. Facchine and Ms. Johnson watched from the side of the room as he scratched the back of his neck with the whisper-phone, then bonked his head with it. With YoJo and Ms. Johnson and Ms. McKnight and everyone else acting like the MSA was the most important thing in the universe, Reggie felt like a huge loser—and his teacher felt helpless.

"It's so frustrating," Mrs. Facchine said. "I just wish to hell he could have been tested at the beginning of the year."

Ms. Johnson added, "How do I tell a nine-year-old, 'The federal law says we can help *those* kids but not you'? That's what good teachers do. They help."

Proficiency for Reggie on MSA was not her goal—he would likely score basic. What she wanted was for him to be able to take the test without trauma. Right now he was banging his head on the desk, not hard enough to hurt himself but hard enough to break her heart. She took Reggie's lousy report card from Mrs. Facchine and headed down the hall to photocopy it. "I hope that with forty-one days we can expedite the process," she said. "I think I'm getting a headache." Ms. Johnson opened the gym door, because she needed a smile. Mr. Summey was balancing a ball on a spoon and telling the gaggle of giggly kindergartners, "Nondominant hand! Repeat after me. Nondominant hand!"

"Nondominant hand!"

◆ ◆ ◆

Thirty-five days until MSA, Miss Johnson was not sure which upset her more about that day's benchmark: that her students answered the multiple-choice questions without first reading the accompanying passage, or that Roman sat grinning, happy with himself for finishing first, when he had missed a big chunk.

"You didn't tell me I had to turn the page," he said.

When she graded the tests later that day, the scores made her want to throw up. "I work my ass off," she said, "and they do this?" Very few students passed. One was Malcolm, who might have been written off as basic at the beginning of the year but was scoring high on practice tests with accommodations and was managing to walk away from confrontations without incident—a new high. Jamila, who of late had been giving "what" answers to "why" questions, missed by one point. Tisha, the one who was predicted to score advanced on MSA, did poorly yet again—she simply could not finish her BCRs in time. Nobody in school thinks you're dumb, Miss Johnson would tell the kids later, "but that is what you're showing."

Then, during math, Miss Johnson spent a whole lesson reviewing how you borrow during subtraction. "Let's go next door to borrow ten," she said. "Hey, Mr. Seven, can I borrow ten?" Leaning over Savannah's desk later to help her with a problem step by step, she asked the girl—one of the few children who passed the benchmark that day—what she borrowed.

"Sugar?" Savannah said. She wasn't kidding.

"Do you mean that?"

Savannah could see from the look on her face that Miss Johnson wasn't kidding either.

After school Alia broke down crying in Mrs. Sharps's office. She occasionally cried when she was angry, maybe on the phone to her mom, but never at school, never in front of people. One colleague after another came in.

"Are you okay?"

"Are you okay?"

"Are you okay?"

"No, I'm not okay. This is not okay."

Here it was, January, and she had done everything she thought was expected of her. From day one she'd been teaching the Star Strategies, from day two she'd been teaching BCRs. Every morning since December instead of math meeting the kids had been filling out MSA workbooks, and if they pulled out a free reading book instead, she set them back on track. She made sure they quizzed one another on MSA words in their spare time. She set a timer to get their BCRs down from twelve or fifteen minutes to the necessary eight.

"At the beginning of the year," she said, "you wonder, Why don't they know this? By now, you've had them for close to a hundred days. I don't think you can any longer point the finger at someone else. If the scores aren't good, will the fingers be pointed at me?"

Alia brainstormed ideas with the other third-grade teachers and brought them to Ms. McKnight. They would reintroduce the basics of phonics using the sound-spelling cards. Ms. McKnight would eat lunch with a group of students every day in her office, and she'd teach a lesson to each class. "Because the kids are very into themselves," Alia said, the teachers would make a bulletin board with photos of those who used their MSA strategies during practice tests ("Stars") and those who did all their homework each week ("Smarties"). The kids who made it on the Stars board would win potato chips; the homework board would earn them candy.

"I love it," Tina said.

The teachers would try to stimulate attention by reading aloud and using hands-on "manipulatives" for math. Maybe, just maybe, they'd stop having students write three BCRs a day, assigning one for homework instead. They'd glue text feature terms onto pages of actual text features.

"I see motivation all over this," Tina said.

"It's kind of going back to how we would have taught, back in the day," Alia said.

"I think the more things change, the more they come back to the same thing."

"We're trying to come up with ways to make this fun."

"Fun's good," Tina said.

But how fun would it be when, starting February 13, they began a schedule of all test prep, all the time? Despite intentions, the number of BCRs didn't decrease, especially when the after-school tutors were told to assign two each session. (And teachers were to refrain from helping students with their answers, because, as Alia put it, "They need to get into the habit of nobody telling them jack.") Each week was an opportunity to give a mock MSA, each day a quest to check off more items from the Voluntary State Curriculum. A typical schedule for third graders looked like this:

8:45–10 Mock MSA

10–11:40 Identify tone in a poem. Identify the importance of advertise-
ments. Review parts of speech.

11:40–12:30 Lunch and recess

12:30–1:50 Language arts

1:50–2:25 Summary of a fiction text

"We could just give it to them intravenously," Tracy Prater cracked. "It would be easier."

Some experts say it is unethical to focus so directly on what you suspect will be on the test; others say it is unethical not to.[1] Either way, the laser-sharp focus didn't sit well with the teachers. The county's seven hundred new teachers were told at orientation before school started, "Ask yourself every day, Is this the kind of instruction I would want for my child?" Hardly, Nikki thought. "I'm teaching, but I'm not feeling like I'm making a difference."

Alia was trying to make the best of it, picking stories and poems that fit with the skill being taught but were still entertaining. Because teachers were no longer pretending to cover anything but reading and math, Tina said they should also choose passages about science and social studies. "There's more than one way to skin a cat," she told Alia, as a half-eaten apple browned in her hand. She understood the pressure Alia felt—not the least of which was her worry that if the students didn't pass, colleagues would blame her for losing their bonuses. The results wouldn't come back broken down by teacher, but still, it was no secret which grade was most in danger.

Tina urged Alia to pack away her doubts.

"Every year you hit the testing wall and think, 'Oh god, are we going to be able to do it?' . . . You need to be a cheerleader. Let them know, 'You're going to be an MSA superstar.' Let them know that you know that they can do it. Let's lighten the mood. Even if you don't believe it, you say it."

◆　◆　◆

Thirty days until MSA, Tina was unusually wired for a day of meetings that began in the library. The day before, Sunday, she had watched her mom for hours after a seizure and didn't go to bed until two a.m. That wasn't unusual—the middle of the night was her favorite time for watching Oprah on the treadmill or cleaning the house—so she suspected all that 4:30 a.m. green tea. In a voice that dazed teachers with its intensity, Tina said that the new school uniforms were on track for next year and did anyone know of a spare washer and dryer, she said teachers could put in their names to learn Spanish in Mexico over the summer, she said Dr. Smith mentioned Tyler Heights in *Annapolis* magazine, and she said the mayor ran into Mr. Dillard and told him how much the city loved the school. Then the latest benchmark scores were presented.

The following day in his State of the Union address, President Bush would say, "Under the No Child Left Behind Act, standards are higher, test scores are on the rise, and we're closing the achievement gap for minority students." Despite his enthusiasm and assertions, though, across the country some scores were on the rise and some were declining—just like at Tyler Heights. According to the data placed on the overhead one grade at a time, from the first to the second reading benchmark, the fourth and fifth grades had mixed results. The third-grade picture was clearer, and bleaker: The number of students failing had increased to 43 percent. Kindergarten and first-grade test scores were headed upward, and in second grade, the share of students passing the benchmark went from 25 percent to 78. "I'm so proud of my girls," Tracy Prater said to the second-grade teachers, whom she had been coaching. A round of applause followed, during which Miss Johnson's arms were folded and her face was blank. Ms. Prater looked at Alia with a little smile. "Sometimes you get upset," she said. "Everybody sees you working every single day. You're going to get there."

To get there, Tina said, Tyler Heights would push back the national celebration of Dr. Seuss's birthday, Read Across America Day, from March 2 until after the MSA. Teachers who weren't making full use of the concept/question board and higher-level questioning needed to emulate the ones who were. The 23 percent of students with at least six absences, particularly the forty who had ten or more, would be targeted with phone calls and maybe home visits. Tina recommended that the art, music, and PE teachers give students a multiple-choice question at the end of each class, as some other schools did. "That's a way to get another bit of practice in," she said. "Bombard, bombard, bombard those children with the kinds of questions they'll have on the test. You want the students at a level of automaticity with reading those testlike questions."

The discipline data was off target, with year-to-date referrals up to sixty-six, compared to forty-eight the previous year, and twenty-one in January alone. "This month, the lid came off for some reason. I'm not sure why," Tina said. She suggested putting a stress relief box in every classroom for the kids who needed it. Alia shared that she rubbed lotion on one boy's arms to calm him; another teacher said one student liked being stroked with a nail brush; one kindergartner was given a small sandbag to hold on her lap for comfort. "Some of these students will not respond to rational sorts of things," Tina said. "It's not that the kids have gotten so much worse. It's just that we're not giving some of them the right treatment." She had a hunch that the sensory stuff would help, "but it won't be a schoolwide effort this year, because now the focus is on MSA."

"It's going to be focusing on individual students we can boost in the next thirty days," Tina said. "Thirty days is a lot of time. We're going to be okay. We're going to be okay. MSA, that is our end of the year." As the meeting ended, the principal gave every staff member a matching bobblehead pen and notepad printed with the slogan ATTITUDE IS EVERYTHING.

◆ ◆ ◆

Twenty-three days until MSA, at the second-quarter awards ceremony, the fourth graders got up on the risers and sang, "Go ahead and test me because I am ready! Let me show you I am ready! Let me show you what I know!" Tina had the urge to make this a school anthem and have everyone learn it, but to the teachers' relief, she suppressed it.

◆ ◆ ◆

Twenty-two days until MSA, Ms. McKnight passed around the hand sanitizer to Savannah, Tisha, and Summer and from the head of her conference table, which she had covered with a plastic blue tablecloth, she divvied up cake left over from the dinner theater the night before.

"Did you like the magic show last night?" she asked. "What did you like about it?"

"In the beginning when he made the bird come out," Tisha said.

"My favorite was when the rag was dancing," Savannah said.

"Can I tell you my favorite part?" Summer asked. "The rings. I don't think it was real but—"

"How do you think that worked?" Ms. McKnight asked.

"Magic!" said Tisha, digging up forkfuls of frosting.

"The blue on the cake is making everyone have a blue tongue," Ms. McKnight said. "Who did you take?"

"My mom," Tisha said.

"Did she enjoy it?"

"She didn't see it."

"She didn't see it?"

"She stayed in the car."

"It was cold outside," Ms. McKnight said.

"How about we do a black history play?" Savannah said.

"We doing a play," Tisha said.

"Is this in the Open Court book?"

"No, in the Girls' Club," Tisha said. "If we had scripts and could bring them home, I'd practice every day."

"We practice cheers at recess," Savannah said.

Tisha raised her hand. "I have something to share. I'm gonna be a cheerleader next year."

"With who?"

"Powell."

"My mother says it's a lot of money," Savannah said.

"How do you get really, really, really good?" the principal asked, shifting the conversation.

"Practice," Summer said.

"Practice," Savannah said.

"Do you know how many days till MSA?"

"Twenty-two days," they all said.

"I'm scared. Are you?" Summer asked.

"I am," Tisha said.

"What are you scared about?" Ms. McKnight said.

"That I'll get it wrong."

"Some questions might be really hard. Some will be easy-breezy. How are you getting ready?"

"Listen to tips," Savannah said.

"Like what?"

"Something of elimination."

"What does that mean?"

"You pick one choice, not all of them. Do Mr. Trickster."

"They're going to try to trick you," Ms. McKnight said. "Two choices will be really close. You've got Mr. Trickster to help you. I'd be scared. Whenever I was in school I tried really hard and used my strategies. I know you're probably a little nervous, and that's okay."

"That's called anxiety," Tisha said.

"What are you going to do about it?"

"Calm down."

"What can you do to calm down?"

"Take five breaths," Savannah said.

"You can think about good thoughts," Tisha said.

"I have to tell you something about the MSA benchmarks," Summer said. "When we was in class, everyone complained because Miss Johnson was doing Malcolm's test. She told us she has to write everything for him."

"That's called a scribe. Different students have what we call accommodations to help them get their best answers on the page."

"Some people think it's not fair. They huff and puff. She says, 'Try your best,'" Summer said.

"It's not fair for us," Tisha said.

"It's just his words," Summer said.

"Maybe it's because he writes sloppy," Tisha said.

Ms. McKnight said it was as if she didn't have her glasses with her and asked somebody to read something to her.

"When we came in from recess outside Miss Johnson said, 'Everyone finish your BCR. I don't even want to look at you,'" Summer said.

"Sometimes teachers are strict," Ms. McKnight said.

"My mom, she yell at you but she trying to tell you the right thing to do," Savannah said.

Ms. McKnight asked about their MSA strategies.

"Whisper-phones."

"Trickster."

"Process of elimination."

"What else?"

"Work till time is called."

"Why is that important?"

"You have to check it over so you know your answer's right."

"Hundred-dollar words," Summer said. "BATS."

"If you keep reading, what will happen?" Ms. McKnight asked.

"You will get smarter," Savannah said.

"And the pirate thing!" Summer said.

"Can you girls make a promise? That you will use all those strategies?"

"Yes, ma'am."

"Can we shake on this?" the principal asked, and they did.

◆ ◆ ◆

Eighteen days until MSA, Ms. McKnight asked Miss Johnson's third graders, "The characters in a story are?" She was teaching a lesson about writing a fiction summary, partly to motivate the students and partly to gain insight into their poor performance.

"Three little pigs," Roman said.

"Ms. McKnight," Summer said.

"The characters in *any* story," Ms. McKnight said, looking for the definition of the word *character*.

"Junie B. Jones."

"Author."

"The characters in *any* story. I'm getting lost here. David?"

"The people."

"Good. What is a summary?"

"Beginning, middle, and end."

"Why are we reading this?"

"So we can find information?"

"Find information so we can what?"

"Write our BCR."

"And this BCR is?"

"Summary."

That night, parents and a few children from twenty-four families gathered around tables in the library. Jamila's mom, Vicky, paid close attention to a PowerPoint presentation called "Soaring to Higher Heights on the MSA." She learned about Mr. Trickster and BATS and Star Strategies and YoJo and www.mdk12.org, where sample questions were posted. She learned that some students would get accommodations and all students would get water bottles and snacks and peppermints.

"We're going to give them every possible edge we can," Ms. McKnight said.

"When is this test?" Cyrus's dad asked his boy, who was taking notes.

Cyrus shrugged. "I think it's in June. March. April. May."

There's no doubt that parents would rather test scores go up than down: The positive impact on house prices shows this, as does the ovation Tyler Heights parents gave when Ms. McKnight announced last year's scores.[2] They care about their children learning, and of course when there is a consequence attached to the test—promotion to the next grade, for example—they tend to pay close attention. But many parents believe the Maryland State Department of Education's guide for parents when it says that the MSA isn't the whole story.[3]

"Personally, they're just numbers to me," Jamila's mom, Vicky, said. "It's just one test." Kids might do better than they should because the data hides problems, she said; they might do worse because, under pressure, they freeze up. Parents of the two highest-scoring students in third grade didn't put much stock in official measures. Emily's mom liked to hear Tina's enthusiasm more than anything. Of whether or not teachers met the formal qualifications required by No Child Left Behind, Gardell's mom said, "I work with people who have the whole alphabet after their name and that doesn't tell me if they're good at their job." Of the MSA, she said, "They're motivating, but they're not a good indicator. The most important thing to me is that Tyler Heights is intimate, the good feeling you get when you go in there." Indeed, that so few parents transfer their children when low scores allow it—only six at Tyler Heights in 2003, including two who returned, and 3 percent of those eligible nationwide—shows a concern beyond test data. Parents care about class size, extracurricular programs, logistics, and safety.[4] They care about their children being in school with their friends.

Vicky did want Jamila to do as well as possible. She planned to heed Ms. McKnight's advice that students get rest, do their homework, and arrive on time for testing day. Talk to your children about how they are feeling about the test, the principal said. "The frame of mind your children come to school in has a big impact on how they do. If you get up, it's a rushed morning, you're yelling at them and they're yelling at you because they can't wear what they want, and when they get to school they're still thinking about being yelled at, and being tired, do you think they can do their best? The part of the brain that should be focused on the test is worried about your argument."

"Don't yell," a third grader said to her dad, touching his arm.

"You can make the difference between basic and proficient," Ms. McKnight said. "You can even make the difference between proficient and advanced. When you send them off to school, give a hug, give a smile. Make that morning the best morning you can possibly have."

Cyrus knelt at the table and prayed.

◆ ◆ ◆

Fourteen days until MSA, teachers handed out tiny Dixie cups of water to the third graders crowding into the library. At Jennifer Johnson's command, with massage-table music playing from a boom box, the children put their fingers on their earlobes and caressed from top to bottom—"to clear your head," the guidance counselor said. "Look—I can drink my water without making a sound. Get your brain hydrated."

This was the start of a comical ritual Tyler Heights students would perform every week before a practice MSA. Mrs. Rogers-Payne had explained the purpose of the "educational kinesiology" the students were about to experience with the help of a model she had made, a mannequin head topped with Play-Doh-like brain sections, each labeled with a little flag. To juice up your brain and "get into PACE," she said—an acronym for "positive, active, clear, energetic," developed by a company called Brain Gym whose training she, Jennifer, and Tina had attended—you first have to drink water. "You've just activated your brain. Ninety percent of the brain is water. This activates the frontal lobe, which controls clarity and organization." Next the students rubbed themselves with their left hands on their belly buttons and their right hands on their collarbones. "Caress right here. The brain button is located in the occipital portion of the brain. That has to do with visual, seeing the print and reading. You have activated the brain button. The second step is the cross crawl." They touched their elbow to their opposite knee ten times, then switched. "The cerebellum—that's where hand-eye balance is and the ability to move." They clasped their hands together up high and lowered them slowly. "The tongue is on the roof of the mouth during our hook-ups, so our energy keeps flowing," Ms. Johnson said. "Hook-ups are here in the parietal lobe, and that's where the body's movements are coordinated. It's at the top part of the brain," Mrs. Rogers-Payne said.

Ms. Johnson then moved on to meditation. "Calm," she said in an uncharacteristically low voice. "Calm," the students repeated.

"Relaxed."

"Relaxed."

"Confident."

"Confident."

Some children appeared to be concentrating; others were having a hard time taking this seriously. Sydney asked why teachers were passing out Pep-O-Mints from big bags.

"The reason, Sydney, is there is research in these big fat books that mints help us to calm and relax ourselves. We're going to open our mints and put them in our mouths and listen to what Ms. Johnson is saying. I want you to turn and face the table. I want you to put your hands on the table. You need to close your eyes."

"Manny, close your eyes," Alia Johnson said. "Close your eyes."

"Calm, deep breaths. Deep breaths."

Dena spit her mint into the trash can and stayed bent over for a full minute, waiting for the last of her saliva to drop.

Ms. Johnson read from a book called *Ready . . . Set . . . R.E.L.A.X: A Research Based Program of Relaxation, Learning and Self Esteem for Children.* "Let the feel of the music calm you. Feel your muscles relax. Say to yourself, 'I am calm and relaxed.' Take another deep breath. Imagine today is the day for you to take the MSA. You are confident and look forward to the challenge."

David mimicked a yogi; this calmed him.

"Imagine your teacher passing out the test books. Watch the test come to your desk. The book is passed to you and you feel more relaxed. You can feel tension drain from your body. As you relax, you gain more confidence."

Alex couldn't stop laughing.

"The test book is on your desk. You turn to the page and you follow the instructions. You do the easiest questions first and come back to the harder ones. Take a deep breath and blow it out. When you notice yourself getting worried and anxious, say these words to yourself: *calm* and *relaxed*. Now the test is over. You are proud of yourself for doing the best that you could do. Take a deep breath. Open your eyes."

Teachers rushed three more kids over to the trash can to spit out their mints, then everyone headed back to class for the practice test.

15

Some People Are Selling Snake Oil

Observers come in and out of Tyler Heights all the time, so Miss Johnson and her students didn't give much thought to the woman with the blue writing pad and the Louise Brooks bob. Jackie Brown had come from California to evaluate teaching and learning at Tyler Heights. She did so by visiting each classroom for twenty minutes and marking on a Scantron form which strategies she saw in action during each of sixty-four five-minute increments—"articulating objectives," "facilitating discussion," "high-level questioning," and so on. Tina had heard about Pacific Learning, the company that employed Jackie, at a conference on assessment that she had attended in the fall. The principal of Ridgely Elementary, a school on Maryland's Eastern Shore, had presented a session on how much the process had helped her staff. The Pacific Learning website, which promised a tool to "Address AYP Mandates and Accountability," echoed this. "The Case Study shows how reading proficiency increased from 46.5% to 88.9% in one year!" the company crowed on the site.[1]

At Tyler Heights, Jackie watched fifth graders read "The Journal of Wong Ming-Chung" and first graders goof and fart their way through math meeting. A second-grade teacher helped her students replace nouns with pronouns ("Fred goes to the store. *He* goes to the store.")

and distinguish common from proper nouns: *dog* versus *Smokey, school* versus *Tyler Heights, boy* versus *Justin.* In another second-grade classroom, children did literacy center activities all over the room—at desks, at tables, on the floor—while the custodian came in to mop up one boy's pee.

Who would have guessed that Jackie would find the day's greatest calm in Alia Johnson's class? "Are some of her kids out?" Jackie asked when she saw how small the class was. No, they were all there, taking a spelling pretest and looking up *hastily* in the dictionary and searching for "The Cobbler's Song" in the table of contents and talking about money.

"My uncle has money from Vermont," Cyrus said.

"Kids in different states have our money on the board," David said.

"All the states in the United States use the same money," Miss Johnson explained, and then it was time for the consultant to move on.

Three weeks later Jackie, a former reading teacher, would return, having calculated the percentage of time good teaching strategies were in use at Tyler Heights and synthesized the information on an "Instructional Assessment Tool data report." On the positive side, she saw very few students reading out loud (apparently they shouldn't) but lots of oral responding, few teachers interrogating or giving direct explanations, and plenty of student work on display. On the negative side, 70 percent of the five-minute segments included low-level questioning but only 12 percent included high-level questioning. Jackie saw no conferencing, facilitating discussion, self-assessing, articulating objectives, talking about books, or small-group learning. She saw a decent amount of "modeling/demonstrating" but little "coaching/scaffolding/cueing" (whatever the difference was). Even if students made connections with what they read, under the Pacific Learning protocol that didn't count unless the teacher used the proper language: "Yes, you made a connection, which is a good comprehension strategy." They hadn't, as far as Jackie saw. All in all, the report had enough zeroes on it that Tina wanted Jackie to share it with the Literacy Team in her office before it was presented to the full staff.

"You have a beautiful school," Jackie started out. "Tina has shared some of the struggles you have with children, but that's not evident.

You have polite children. Everyone's working together—that's great. Remember: This is just two days out of all the days you were here." The strategies tallied, she said, are "research-based practices that are good for children and achievement." Mainly, she said, "to get more, you need more of the how and why."

"Give me a capsulized ideal sort of student performance scenario," Tina said.

"You'd want reading, writing going on, hands-on tasks, student-led discussion. Are the students reflecting on the work they're doing? You want to see children not reading out loud; that's not a research-based strategy. You'd want the teacher to be doing that scaffolding piece at a higher level. And cooperative groupings. A lot of desks paired up. What you're trying to build here are critical thinkers who can think for themselves and back up what they're doing. Teachers should be thinking, Is what I'm doing helping children to become independent readers and writers?" (If it is not, Pacific Learning could help on that score: The company sells a whole line of reading programs.)

Tina felt the judgments on the whole were fair, but she responded with a roaming analysis that silenced the consultant. "Kids come to us without background knowledge. The causes of the Civil War, and they don't know about northern states and southern states. They can't do critical thinking if they don't have something to think about. We have a pacing guide and assessments. How do we make it all fit? If we're just developing kids to get through assessments, we're not doing much good." Tina mentioned a magazine article she just read in which test scores in one state increased for black students, but increased faster for whites. "It doesn't look like a closing of the gap anymore," she said. "It just knocked my socks off. The data meant so many different things. We should not lose sight of what's important. We do need our kids reading more leveled books. We've got to begin looking at differentiation taking place *inside* the classroom. In the seventeen years I taught, no one ever left my classroom for intervention. Never."

Jackie listened as Tina continued.

"At the last principals' meeting, we talked about maybe redoing lesson assessments. The Open Court assessments are not appropriate. The vocabulary/word study piece is valid, but we should write our own BCRs tied to comprehension strategies. It could be a half hour and not all morning, with a score for mechanics, general spelling, which we don't know about. The new superintendent says he's going to be more of an open, collaborative leader. I'd like to see more independent reading and writing with choice. First grade, it was like giving them candy when they were writing with choice. There used to be too many choices in Anne Arundel County—then the pendulum swung the other way, and the second teacher could finish the sentence the first teacher was saying. That isn't where you want to be either. There are other purposes for writing that aren't BCRs, and there should be time to do that. I wanna know how staff is going to receive this," Tina said, touching Jackie's report.

"Not good," Yolie Marshall said. "It was two days. A lot of stuff we do, you didn't see."

"We do it to children all year," Tina said. "We evaluate them over four mornings with the MSA. That's how you do for the whole year, and we make incredible decisions based on that. "

"My kids made connections," Yolie said.

The level of defensiveness worried Jackie, considering the staff meeting was minutes away. "I don't want people who are working hard and doing their best to say, for what?" she said.

"This is more valuable than MSA," Tina said of the report. "It shows how you deliver instruction—not just for the MSA but to become independent thinkers. Ridgely Elementary's scores go up every year they do this piece."

At the staff meeting, teachers would complain to one another that Jackie was visiting their room when they were following the structured phonics part of Open Court or writing a BCR or giving a test, so how could she base a whole-school analysis on that? When she said, "Ninety-three percent of you have established routines, and that means behavior isn't a problem. . . . This is heaven," they wanted to know what school she was talking about. They felt that they used the explicit language—"making a connection"—ad nauseam already.

"*What's the point?*" Miss Johnson wrote in a note she passed to a co-worker. Whatever the point, eight thousand dollars had been poured into the multibillion-dollar school improvement industry, for information few in the room took seriously.

◆ ◆ ◆

As schools have changed the way they do business, private-sector firms have lined up to help them, at a large profit. Two billion seems to be the magic number: That's how much money is spent on materials for testing and test prep each year, from state exams to college boards, and it is also the annual revenue for educational software companies. It's also the most generous estimate of how much companies that provide tutoring under No Child Left Behind could make.[2] To keep track of it all, you might want to buy a five-hundred-dollar annual subscription to School Improvement Industry Week ("Web-Leveraged Information Services for the Marketplace Created by No Child Left Behind") and listen to its podcasts: "Expect Democrat Assault on Industry's Keystone— AYP." "Little Dog in the Big Dog Park? How Small Publishers Can Play Without Getting Bitten." "Two New Markets: Truancy Reduction and Student Newsletters."

Observers who aren't conspiracy theorists detect a symbiotic relationship among many of the private-sector beneficiaries of the school accountability movement. President Bush's brother Neil owns a company that sells educational software, including sales to school districts that pay for it with federal Title I money. Many believe that the relationship between the president and family friend Harold McGraw III— who ran Bush's transition team and whose company, McGraw-Hill, is one of the biggest curriculum and test providers in the world—has a lot to do with the administration's emphasis on scientifically based reading programs, such as McGraw-Hill's Open Court. Two chief architects of federal education policy, former Bush adviser Sandy Kress and former deputy education secretary Gene Hickok, now make a living lobbying for for-profit education corporations, including testing and test-prep companies. As several people involved in the crafting of No Child Left Behind told me, lobbyists for testing and school improvement businesses had a far greater role in the law's creation than did associations representing actual educators. And since the law passed, many of the people appointed to evaluate states' applications for reading grants have had their own business interests in the industry.[3]

Of course, firms that offer consultants and workbooks and software and magic-bullet curricula can make the most money from schools with the lowest scores. One of the best accounts of this came from *Baltimore Sun* reporter Alec MacGillis, who in 2004 documented how software companies employ hard-sell tactics (including lavishing perks on teachers who flacked their products), take credit for score increases where credit may not be due, hide study results that don't show what they want, and unapologetically target poor and minority children. "That's where the pain is. You go where the pain is, and you talk to the pain," one software saleswoman told MacGillis.[4]

When the pain was at Tyler Heights, plenty of people came to talk to it. The introduction of Saxon and Open Court were each accompanied by consultants hired by the county, who flew in as frequently as once a month for two years. Tina spent a thousand dollars to bring in a principal from Ocean City, who had a history of increasing scores and brought a whole set of MSA strategies to Tyler Heights, which were adopted immediately. And then there were the consultants from Virginia who the school system had Tina hire in 2004. Tina gave three representatives from The Urban Learning and Leadership Center a tour of Tyler Heights and presented the strategies she'd introduced. A consultant returned for two other brief visits. The organization promotes an approach it calls the SAME Pathway—"Social, Academic, and Moral Environment"—but Tina never got much of an idea what she should be doing differently. Basically, according to Tina and the organization's executive director, Harvey Perkins, the consensus of the consultants was, thousands of dollars later: We don't know why we're here. Keep doing what you're doing.

◆ ◆ ◆

In March, Tina headed to San Antonio for the annual elementary school principals' conference. She wandered through the massive exhibition hall, collecting as many samples as she (and I) could hold. "Are you a Title school?" the vendors would ask, their grins stretching and cartoon dollar-signs practically popping up in their eyeballs when Tina said yes. She attended a session by a principal from another Maryland county called "Effective Strategies for Meeting AYP," and said to herself, as she often does during these things, "We do all that": long reading blocks, standardized instruction, posters of strategies, behavioral plans, MSA practice packets. Over the course of three days she enthusiastically amassed ideas—perfect attendance incentives (grocery gift certificates for parents), conferences with kids about test scores, hand signals teachers could use with one another. On this last one, which she got from a principal who brought her Baltimore school from one of the lowest performers to the top in one year: I couldn't wait to see the look on Miss Johnson's face when she would be told to "clap fireworks" when a colleague presented a good idea.

The conference was rewarding for Tina, but one thing socked her in the stomach—and it wasn't the nacho bar or Texas barbecue. Tina decided to attend an early-morning presentation by the Virginia guys who had come to Tyler Heights to consult two years before. At "Differentiated Leadership: Leadership Standards That Facilitate Change," the program description promised, "participants will hear from presenters known nationally for their ability to help school leaders create and sustain the changes needed to reach full state accreditation and make Adequate Yearly Progress." Tina took notes as the PowerPoint progressed: "*We must be professional in our dealings with—staff.—parents.—community.—board.*" "*Be sure your stakeholders are behind you.*" "**Relationship bet./among adults most determining factor for success of students.*" Toward the end of the presentation, she saw on the screen, "*Where does following the S.A.M.E. Pathway lead?*" Photos of smiling, industrious children accompanied the next slide: "*Student Success!!*"

And then, on slide forty-seven of fifty-one: "*Success is Relative*," followed by . . . Tina's test scores! There were the Tyler Heights numbers, shooting up from 2004 to 2005.

Tina was furious. Like these guys had anything to do with third-grade math proficiency jumping twenty-four points? Fourth-grade reading jumping forty-nine? The next slide said, "*A review of annual test data indicates that of the 13 schools that have been served by ULLC, each has shown dramatic increases in student performance in all sub-groups of NCLB."* By then all Tina could think was:

1. Never believe a "study" again.
2. These guys are gonna get it.

The presenters had spotted Tina on the aisle and introduced her to the audience, and she was polite enough to quash her instinct to protest. But once the presentation was done, Tina approached the men at the front of the room. She felt they were evading her attempts at eye contact. All day she simmered, and then, walking to dinner, she spotted the men eating penne outside an Italian restaurant. Tina launched in about the supposed "moral element" of the SAME Pathway. Her voice was measured—Tina McKnight never, ever gets ugly—but her ire was evident enough that one of her targets tightly clenched his fork, suspended over the pasta.

"We didn't mean to imply we had to do with the scores—just that this could be replicated," the other consultant said. "My intent was to celebrate Tyler Heights as a school that has looked at school improvement through that lens." Back in Maryland, Tina called the executive director, seeking an apology, and took notes on the call. *"We've been talking you up everywhere we go,"* she scribbled fast. *"Some people out there are selling snake oil." "We gotta get out there and sell the real deal."*

♦ ♦ ♦

The staff of Tyler Heights weren't just consumers in the school improvement industry—for a while this school year, at no cost to their audiences, they were providers. At a conference for the county's Title I schools, the thirty-three chairs filled right away for "Soaring to Higher Heights: Achieving Success on the MSA," and a little "Wow" came across the room when the school's test scores popped up on the PowerPoint. They were asked to give the same presentation for principals, so one day in January, Tina, Mandy Panetta, and Sheila McDermott carted their equipment to the school system's big board room.

"You need tips?" one principal said to another as the trio set up.

"I don't need tips. I need a miracle."

"I hate all the data analysis micromanagement stuff."

"MSA is not on my radar."

Tina overheard this. "When you have nineteen new staff members, it better be on your radar," she said. The forty-five people who had arrived, mostly principals, talked about how many teachers they still needed to hire, custodians' schedules, traffic on I-97, and the poster Ms. Panetta had just tacked to the podium.

"Star Strategy," one said, mocking.

"I can't knock it. Their scores were good."

Lorna Leone took the podium. "Tina McKnight and the staff of Tyler Heights have been applauded and need to be continued to be applauded, with their staff, their population, for the great growth they have shown," she said. Tina introduced the demographics of the school on the PowerPoint, and then the reading scores. "Where's the applause?" Tina said. "We applaud ourselves all the time."

Mandy found it nerve-wracking to go around with this dog and pony show when the scores were probably going to drop, but the unease didn't show as she talked about the Star Strategy and MSA cards, Ask and Answer and hundred-dollar words, Mr. Trickster and BATS and students assessing one another's BCRs (something I never saw done). Sheila talked about daily journal writing and using ten picture cards each week from the Open Court book to practice vocabulary, so that kids would know what the objects were when they got to the DIBELS test.

When it was Tina's turn, she talked about "ownership of MSA vocabulary" and VSC checklists, and teacher planning templates, and showed off little five-dollar flip charts on Bloom's Taxonomy, which she said helped with "ratcheting up questioning." (I never saw those in use either.) She talked about learning position: "You have to be physically engaged in order to be mentally engaged."

"This is so serious," one principal murmured.

"We set our standards very, very high from day one," Tina said, and then narrated the lyrics to "Ain't No Stopping Us Now," which was playing on the boom box. As the song ended, Leone took over and said, "As a new area director, it brings tears to my eyes. What you saw this afternoon, you could pay a good dollar to go to a conference and hear."

Tina thought the same thing, and hinted to Mandy in the parking lot that that might not be a crazy idea. After all, several principals (principals of Blue Ribbon Schools!) came up to her afterward saying, "Awesome presentation," and asking for VSC checklists and lists of MSA words. That week she'd receive thank-you notes:

> Dear Tina and Tyler Heights,
> I was so impressed with your presentation this afternoon concerning your effective effort to ensure that all students succeed at Tyler! It was clear to me that you are not accepting excuses.
> Your dedication was evident. The children at Tyler Heights are in good hands. I commend you!

> Tina,
> I want to commed you and your staff for the fabulous presentation given to the Principals on Jan. 6th. Useful ideas were provided and explained well. I appreciate your willingness to share Tyler's promising practices.
> Congratulations on your scores. They are a direct reflection of your devotion.

As much as the praise jazzed Tina, it weirded her out a little too. Her colleagues were telling her that whatever the scores this year, she'd changed the school, that even 70 percent proficiency would be good, but still, she shared Mandy's worries about being the poster children for academic success. "I have some serious concerns," she told me in the car back to school. "I have some serious concerns."

In the fourth grade, the teachers weren't teaching the strategies—they didn't know them well—and the reading benchmark scores showed it. "In some ways it's the teachers holding the kids back," Tina said. Regarding math, she prayed that the talent development teacher, who had just arrived, would help. "We're really getting to the bottom level, targeting instruction to the individual students instead of to the class. We have to be there. It's forty-five days away. We have to be there. . . . Forty-five days is a lot of time. It seems like a little bit. If we get a lot of snow . . . I'm praying for no snow."

A few blocks from Tyler Heights, Tina rolled down the window to greet some middle schoolers horsing around in the street, as she often did. (Last month she saw one of her former students with a boy all over her; she got the girl in the car and drove her to school. "What's the number one rule at Tyler Heights?" Tina asked. "Respect self." "You're not respecting yourself when you let that boy be all up on you.")

Getting out of her Jaguar back at school—Tina explains that when you're a principal, car dealers give you great financing—she changed from her comfy black boots into comfier black mules. They still were not quite where she wanted to be stylewise—maybe her blacks didn't match?—but her foot problem wasn't getting any better and at least these particular shoes didn't make it any worse.

16

We Must Leave Them No Choice

In the Crystal Ballroom of a beachfront hotel, the keynote speaker in the Hawaiian shirt was trying to work 750 Maryland educators into a stir about standardized tests. Jim Popham, a former UCLA professor who once helped design exams and now made a living from revealing their faults, was explaining how most states test too broad a range of standards, don't provide clear enough descriptions of what's going to be assessed, and don't explain the results in a way that could help teachers and parents help children. Given how some questions are written, he said, it's hard to tell to what degree scores are affected by teaching or by other factors, such as inherent aptitude or family income. In the testing game, he said, "the only way to win is to engage in activities that are not good for children." At this the crowd clapped. They nodded when he said that expectations for adequate yearly progress were unrealistic. They shook their heads when he said that on some types of tests items covering the most important content—the material all teachers teach—are often thrown out when the test is revised, because a surplus of correct answers hinders the number crunchers' quest for a wide spread of scores.

The Maryland Assessment Group is a twenty-year-old nonprofit whose main event is this conference each November, where principals and teachers gather insight on testing. At various sessions they may learn a quiz-show game to help with multiple choice skills, strategies for the MSA's section on multiple-meaning words, the importance of high-level questioning, ways to give standardized tests in art, and "Data Analysis that Leaves No Child Behind." In the exhibit hall they stuff their tote bags with workbooks like *MSA Finish Line* from Continental Press and *Maryland Practice and Mastery: Reading* from Curriculum Associates ("your test scores will go up—or your money back") and *Achieve Maryland* ("authentic practice tests that mirror the MSA"), published by Harcourt, which produces the real test.

So it was strange to see an indictment of standardized testing from the featured speaker, especially considering a testing company was helping to subsidize the eggs.

The principals and teachers had no problem with it, because they largely agreed. Nearly every teacher I know rejects the assertion—delivered implicitly or at times explicitly—that before No Child Left Behind, they didn't know where each of their students stood academically. They hate being judged on student performance that they believe is due in large part to factors outside of their control.[1] (A popular e-mail making the rounds of teachers—Alia's mother sent it to her—was an analogy of a dentist whose effectiveness was going to be measured by how many cavities his patients had, no matter how much candy they ate, no matter the lack of fluoride in their well water, no matter how rarely they made appointments, no matter the glowing reviews from those who watched the dentist work.) While most teachers believe that standards and testing are needed in some form, only 18 percent in one national survey said that the exams they face are meaningful and used well by their districts. Eighty-five percent of the members of the nation's largest teachers' union believe there is too much reliance on standardized testing. Seventy-eight percent want changes to No Child Left Behind.[2]

They don't feel this way because they are lazy, dim, or unconcerned about children. They feel this way because they know what the tests tell us, and what they don't.

But the choir Popham was preaching to in the ballroom, supportive as they were, would never sing. All throughout the three-day conference they'd been leaving sessions and saying to one another, "But I don't get to make those decisions." In the national debate on educational accountability, the people who know the most about what goes on in classrooms have the least say. Teachers in general are not a revolutionary bunch, elementary school teachers especially, and at any rate national education reforms had rarely before had such an impact on the classroom. So educators hadn't yet found a way to pipe up. Would anyone listen if they had? The national unions are supposedly the teachers' mouthpieces, but their opposition to the law, which mirrored that of other education associations, has always been dismissed as a case of teachers wanting less work for more pay.[3]

Tina McKnight spent most of the speech in the hotel lobby, having borrowed a cell phone to manage a crisis involving a girl throwing book bags across Mrs. Facchine's room and slapping a classmate for looking at her. She returned to a cold plate of brunch and the tail end of a speech she probably would have found much to agree with. While Tina liked the new way of breaking down data to make sure no students were being missed, she sometimes hated what she and her staff had to do in the name of accountability. She certainly didn't like that her kids' test scores were now to be factored into her own performance rating—a policy that would have sunk her rating, had it been in place a couple of years back. She had no problem with high expectations, but the way she saw it, MSA didn't expect much.

Tina's attempts to question higher-ups or skirt rules were generally met with some version of "This is the way it's done" or "That's not county policy." Besides, she figured, the prevailing sentiment would be, look at the scores—something must be working. "You can get yourself in a lot of hot water" by being anything other than compliant, Tina said. "You carry out the programs and policy of the Anne Arundel County Public Schools—that's your job." Would attorneys be so discounted in a debate on the future of their industry? Would doctors? Why would the same people who call Tina McKnight a hero not want her honest assessment?

Time and again, the message comes across loud and clear that the opinions of educators do not matter in this discussion. "One of the things important to NCLB was to push the envelope—getting something out there that was not fully embraced by the practitioner community," someone who helped write the law told me. As Frederick Hess, an education analyst for a Washington think tank, wrote in a book called *Tough Love for Schools,* "We will not force painful improvement by convincing those who bear the costs of change that it really is a good idea. We must leave them no choice in the matter."

◆ ◆ ◆

Hess also wrote, "The choice is between an imperfect accountability system and none at all"—a common view among politicians and policymakers. But better-than-nothing is not good enough, when the education of millions of children is at stake.

Conversations on accountability and on No Child Left Behind have centered on practical matters of implementation. Why are the students who choose to transfer out of a school that did not pass the test usually not the children farthest behind? How can tutoring companies hired because the school failed yet again be meaningfully monitored? Anyway, should the tutoring requirement precede the transfer option? How many children should be in a subgroup for adequate yearly progress? Might gauging the growth of specific kids make more sense than calculating how one group of students performed in third grade compared to the previous year's third graders? Should we use adequate progress formulas that differentiate between schools that miss by one student and those that miss by many?

But more fundamental questions about where the accountability movement is taking our schools—questions about the limits of data and the real impact of schooling—have gone undiscussed.[4] A truly honest airing would address how a focus on the percent of students proficient rather than on actual scores can mask inadequacies, that there is no incentive to pay attention to children certain either to pass or to fail (only the kids "on the bubble" make the difference), that there is no incentive to teach anything you know won't be on the test. An honest airing would acknowledge how little the test tells us about students, and it would address the failure of accountability rules to do anything about some of the root causes of poor performance in schools: lack of preschool, lack of medical care, poor parent education, impoverished communities.

It's quite possible to believe in setting high standards and testing students, as I do, and still take issue with how the information is collected, how it is used, and what impact the process has had on teaching and learning. "The belief that the test ratings are fair and accurate is the linchpin of this whole system," education analyst Thomas Toch wrote as the school year started. "And that belief is weakening."[5]

Among the general public, awareness of No Child Left Behind has grown over the last four years—but only to the point where half of public school parents say they know at least a fair amount about it. Of those who are aware of the law, more think poorly of it than well, and just as many say it hurts schools as say it helps.[6] Parents oppose the reliance on a single test, the testing of English and math only, the inclusion of special ed students' scores in measures of progress, and even breaking out test scores by subgroup. The share of public school parents who say there is too much emphasis on testing has increased each of the last four years. That emphasis, they believe, induces "teaching to the test"—and not in a good way.[7]

Various groups have joined the call for concern, including the National PTA, which issued a statement opposing federal testing mandates, and the National Council of the Churches of Christ, which went so far as to say that No Child Left Behind was morally suspect. A coalition of a hundred education, civil rights, and social organizations, calling itself the Forum on Educational Accountability, issued a plea for Congress to change many elements of the law.

In the first four years of No Child Left Behind, questioning even a small provision put one at risk of being labeled as someone who could care less about children—or as a racist. When Connecticut's education commissioner fought to test her students only in every other grade, Margaret Spellings, who took over from Rod Paige as education secretary in early 2005, said on national television, "I think it's un-American—I would call it—for us to take the attitude that African American children in Connecticut living in inner cities . . . are not going to be prepared to compete in this world." At a conference for education writers, I asked an Education Department undersecretary about schools narrowing the curriculum in the name of No Child Left Behind, and she gave me no response beyond the accusation that I did not care about minority children. Jack Jennings, who runs a Washington think tank that analyzes the law and its consequences, said that when he asked his own questions he was told by a Bush adviser, "You aren't for poor people." One suspects that if you suggested 90 percent might be a more reasonable proficiency goal than 100, you'd be asked why you hate 10 percent of America's children.

From the time the law passed, there was general grumbling from state lawmakers in both parties, since education had historically been left to them and to localities. By the summer of 2005, bills in twenty statehouses were introduced that either allowed districts to opt out of the law (forgoing federal money), demanded payment for what they saw as an unfunded mandate, or insisted on changes in the rules. Nearly all those bills fizzled out, probably in part because Spellings allowed states flexibility on several provisions of No Child Left Behind. It wasn't enough flexibility for Connecticut, which filed suit in August 2005 over the federal government's failure to provide funds for the law's implementation.[8]

The people making the decisions about education have very little idea about what goes on in classrooms. "My boss visits schools," an aide to an influential congressman told me, and I thought about everything he *didn't* see. At a hearing on the Hill I once listened to Representative Bud McKeon say, "You hear all the negatives. The great thing about this job, we get to visit schools and see lots of great things. You can tell a good school right away, walking in." It's fortunate he has the power of omniscience, because in most instances, that's all the time people like him give. Those visits where he sees lots of great things—I cannot overemphasize how staged they are. If I were a principal, I'd want visitors to see the most difficult children on one of my school's most difficult days, so that people could understand just how complex things are. I'd also require politicians to stay all day, because you learn nothing from a walk-through. That is, of course, not the way it works. One school I know of in Maryland, when visited recently by a politician, went so far as to create a fake class, by assembling a handpicked group of top students and pulling in another teacher and calling her an "aide."

So I was not surprised when several people involved in the drafting of No Child Left Behind told me they had not foreseen some of the unintended consequences that cropped up, such as the narrowing of the curriculum or the way middle-class students would be more likely than poor ones to take advantage of the opportunity to transfer out of schools. Other potential shortcomings they had anticipated, such as the unlikeliness of every school reaching 100 percent proficiency by 2014. A congressional aide who helped write the law told me, "You want to be the principal who tells parents your kid won't be proficient in ten years? Will it happen? No. But we'll get closer than if we don't push it."

◆ ◆ ◆

On a Monday in early January, several helicopters touched down in a working-class neighborhood of Anne Arundel County so that President Bush could celebrate the fourth anniversary of No Child Left Behind. In the company of Margaret Spellings, Laura Bush, the governor's wife, congressmen, a host of journalists, and the staff and students of North Glen Elementary School, Bush proclaimed that the school was "a center of educational excellence," an example of the law's success.[9]

Over three years, North Glen's MSA scores had increased to the point where white students were not generally outscoring black ones, an improvement the former principal credited to Open Court, Saxon Math, and federal funds. "There's an achievement gap in America that's closing," President Bush said. "We don't need achievement gaps in this country. It's not good for us to have achievement gaps where certain kids can read in fourth grade better than others. . . . I'm here to thank the teachers, not only here, but around the state of Maryland and around the country, who are dedicating their lives to providing hope for our future."

At Tyler Heights, the teachers dedicating their lives to providing hope for our future joked: What if Bush had come here? Their scores had shot up just like North Glen's, though because there were almost no white kids at Tyler Heights, there was not an achievement gap to close, per se. Still, the lunch would have been good, Tina might have re-decorated, and they'd have managed to control their rage about the president's education policy—above all the idea that before this law they didn't know whether their children could read or write. They'd have hidden the naughty kids in a back room.

"Our kids wouldn't know who Bush was," Miss Johnson said.

"But they could tell you about author's purpose," Miss Milhoan said. McKnight's inbox that day was filled with e-mails from colleagues asking why Bush didn't come to Tyler Heights. "That's where he should have been," Tina said at a staff meeting that afternoon. "Oh well, next time. Oprah."

17

I Used to Be a Nice Person

Alia Johnson once wanted to be a marine biologist. At college in southern Pennsylvania, she took science classes and worked hard. But she didn't do exceptionally well, and at some point it just stopped seeming worthwhile. Alia had always enjoyed working as a nanny or babysitter. So she switched to an education major, graduated, and came to Annapolis and Tyler Heights. Alia realized pretty quickly that she couldn't save the children—everyone who begins at a Title I school thinks that you can at first—but you can *teach* them, she knew, if you provide structure and discipline and goals to meet. *"I like to try to give the kids with 'nothing' something to look forward to in life!"* she wrote on her MySpace page.

You couldn't always tell from her face—Alia doesn't smile a whole lot—but in general she was content, easily pleased by yet another rerun of *Shawshank Redemption* or a quiet walk or a good day at school. A dose of regret about her career choice stuck with her, though, especially when she flipped between the National Geographic Channel and Animal Planet to patch together a day of dolphin shows. Or when every one of her students failed a benchmark. Or when they were nasty to one another, and wouldn't listen to her, and her voice grew more and more defeated throughout the day, until she finally got home and plunked down on the couch—practically comatose, but alert enough to feel her optimism seep away. Cue another dolphin marathon.

"I wish I would have stayed in marine biology," she would say then.

Despite her sternness, her students this year really liked her; they blamed themselves when she snapped. "The only reason she's hard is if people be bad and get on her nerves," David said. But aside from a note from Summer that Alia had taped to the wall—*"Dear Mrs. Johnson, You are the nicest teacher in the hole wild world. And I will Not talk in class any more"*—they didn't show it a lot. And they noticed she was wearing down. "I like the old Miss Johnson," Roman said, thinking back to autumn. "She gave out Scholar Dollars and compliments. She was helpful."

Alia felt like a bitch. She hated the kids; she hated that she hated the kids. When she paged through old performance evaluations and read comments about how positive she used to be, when she found a teaching award she once won, she grew as nostalgic as Roman. "I used to be a nice person," she said.

Alia wanted to be nice again. Frankie was going to return soon from Iraq to Virginia, and Alia wanted to be near him. She wanted to teach in a school where children arrived each day with their homework completed, a school where boys didn't bicker just because one was handed an extra napkin with his cookie, where she wouldn't get so frustrated she'd have to call her mom five times a day. Maybe she couldn't be a marine biologist, but at least she could move to the beach.

When Alia, Mr. Al, and Jennifer Johnson arrived in 2001, they had promised one another they'd stay five years, and she wanted to honor the pact. Then, she always told herself, "I'm outta here." Alia began applying to school systems in southeastern Virginia. Asked about professional success, she wrote an essay about the test scores. They're measurable, she figured. People can check.

That Virginia's Standards of Learning exams were totally different than the MSA troubled Alia, but it pleased her too. Third graders in Virginia wrote what-I-did-on-my-summer-vacation essays that were assessed for writing skill, rather than BCRs only intended to demonstrate reading comprehension. Science and social studies were tested too, lots of facts teachers sometimes found random—which country sent Christopher Columbus to America, what Betsy Ross was famous for—but to Alia represented actual *knowledge*.

If she had her way, she'd teach children who would pass the state test as a matter of course. Or even better: children too young to be subjected to it.

◆ ◆ ◆

On a Wednesday in mid-February, when Alia told Tina that she was looking for a teaching position in Virginia for the next school year, the principal covered her ears. This was someone Tina always rated "outstanding" or at the very least "highly effective," the only person of color heading a Tyler Heights classroom, someone she could always count on to deliver instruction the Tyler Heights way—one-half of the team that had brought the third graders to *90 percent*. "I don't want to hear that," she said.

Administrators like Tina do hear it, again and again. Holding on to teachers, good teachers, is one of the biggest challenges for high-poverty, high-minority schools. Anywhere, actually: Despite a two-decade high in the percentage of teachers who say they are very satisfied with their careers, 27 percent plan to leave their jobs within five years.[1] Affluent schools are chock-full of the same teachers they had two decades ago, but with only four years behind her, Alia was among the longest-serving staff at Tyler Heights. Only two resource teachers, the custodians, some aides, Ms. McDermott in kindergarten, and Tina herself had been around longer. While it's possible (of course) for a new teacher to be excellent immediately and an old hand to be a dud, in general, experience, education, knowledge, and intelligence matter.[2]

At Tyler Heights turnover is high; teachers tell Tina they are leaving because of the commute or a move or a baby, but often they just want out—away from the kids, away from a boss who they feel regiments too tightly and adds layers of tasks without a good sense of what goes on in their classrooms.[3] The fringe benefit of high turnover is getting to pick your staff. But it's not easy. The recruitment office is up-front about the challenges at a school like Tyler when it asks candidates where they want to interview. Teachers can't be forced into assignments they don't want, and Tina often loses out in the race to grab promising new hires—unless they are passionate about teaching Tyler Heights' poor, minority children. As for minority hiring, which Tina was so eager for? In six years, she said, she had only been sent one Hispanic candidate to interview, the current ESOL teacher, and few African Americans.[4]

Tina did have some benefits to offer. The first was classes between about fourteen and twenty children, compared to twenty-five or so in other schools. Second, to make its Title I schools more attractive, Anne Arundel County gave teachers an extra $1,500 a year and principals $5,000—"combat pay," some people call it.[5] New teachers, like Miss Milhoan and Mrs. Facchine, got an additional $2,000 as a signing bonus, on the condition they stayed two years, and all Tyler teachers received another $1,500 for raising test scores. The financial incentive wasn't enough to be anyone's prime motivator—rather, as Ms. Panetta said in a newspaper article in September of 2004, it was "a nice little perk." Mrs. Rogers-Payne said, "It's not about the money. They couldn't pay us for all the work we do."[6]

Apparently not. A year later, the pre-K and fifth-grade teachers appearing with Mrs. Rogers-Payne in a photo accompanying the article were among the eight classroom teachers—half the school's total—who didn't return.

◆ ◆ ◆

Nikki Facchine was making copies one day when Tina came up and complimented her on the wonderful things she had heard from the visiting administrator who had conducted her first evaluation. Later that day, Nikki was called over the PA to the office, where she was told she was not qualified for her job.

One of the big changes No Child Left Behind brought to schools was the requirement that by the end of the school year, all teachers be "highly qualified" in the subjects they teach, by virtue of a college major, proficiency on a test, or other criteria determined by each state. The idea that French teachers shouldn't teach math and kindergarten teachers shouldn't teach high school makes sense, and in theory it's a good way to ensure that poor, minority children aren't stuck with unqualified teachers. The law has prodded districts to help their teachers acquire needed coursework and stop relying on just a warm body in a pinch. Generally the standard is not that impressive a bar to reach; what the law calls "highly qualified," I would simply call "qualified."

But occasionally a talented teacher misses the cut because of bureaucratic complications.[7] Mrs. Facchine completed education school at the University of Delaware, passed a standardized test of elementary school content, and got certified for kindergarten through eighth grade and special education in New Jersey. She taught there one year, got certified for kindergarten through eighth grade in Maryland, taught in a Baltimore suburb for the 2004–05 school year, then came to Tyler. Nowhere along the way did anyone let her know she had missed any steps, nor was she named on a list of unqualified teachers Tina had received earlier in the year.

Now, though, Tina passed on the news that Nikki would not be considered highly qualified until she passed a pedagogy exam, the K-6 Praxis II test in Principles of Learning and Teaching, or racked up enough points on a rubric Maryland had created to determine teacher qualifications under No Child Left Behind. The school had two days to prove that Nikki was qualified, or a letter would be sent to families saying she was not.

"Parents are going to say, 'Oh, that's why my kid's failing,'" Nikki said.

If it were some class she were lacking, some knowledge or experience she didn't have, she might have understood. But a test that probably mirrored half the tests she took in college? A test that in a year and a half in Maryland nobody bothered to tell her to take? She wasn't worried about passing—the Praxis would only ask her to write a few essays explaining how she'd teach certain topics. It was more about the insult, after a successful college career and two and a half years of teaching. Tina was heartbroken for her.

The two met in Tina's office to try to cobble enough points together on Maryland's experience rubric. States vary widely in what they require for what No Child Left Behind calls "HOUSSE"—High, Objective, Uniform State Standards of Evaluation. In Maryland, a teacher can gain points by taking or teaching classes, attending workshops, serving on committees and improvement teams, being a mentor, presenting at conferences, and so on. Here was one point for Nikki's graduate school credit, nine for undergraduate social studies, nine for science, six for art, twelve for reading—or did that count for language arts? Could her eighteen credits in Spanish be applied to language arts, since Spanish was a language? Was it true that her nine special ed credits and four technology credits didn't count for anything? Her year in New Jersey didn't count, because she'd taught middle school. It's too bad she didn't already have next semester's calculus class under her belt, because that would count—though what that had to do with teaching eight-year-olds to tell time, she had no idea.

They were up to seventy-four points out of the necessary one hundred when Tina got on the phone to Central Office. Nikki took a broken breath and tried not to cry. "Can I talk with anyone who's in certification? I'm working with a teacher to try to see if she can qualify for HOUSSE." Tina was put on hold. Nikki said, "I only taught for two years."

"You've been on our school improvement team, because everybody's on the SIT team," Tina told Nikki, and then motioned that someone had come on the line. "I just kind of needed . . . I'll be at the board today; maybe I could stop by. . . ." She hung up and turned to Nikki. "Boy, she's got a good secretary. She puts that wall there—won't commit to anything." Tina checked the list. "Okay. Align local content standards with state standards. Formally or informally? I think you do that every day. Developed content assessments—I say you do that too. Published an article in a textbook—no. Teacher of the year, no."

It was clear Nikki wouldn't make it. Even one Tyler Heights kindergarten teacher who had taught for nine years in Florida (four in Title I schools), taken three hundred hours of ESOL coursework, and completed all but one class for a master's equivalency missed HOUSSE by one point.

"This is the first document I've ever seen that says I need to take that test," Nikki said.

"Let me share with you the letter that is to go out."

"I don't want my parents to think I have no teaching experience."

"I wish there was more that I could do."

"Can you send another letter after I pass the test?"

"When is the test?"

"March fourth."

"And then it takes six to eight weeks for the results. Probably not. But there probably won't be any hoopla with the letter. I know how you feel and it bothers me. And it's not like you did anything wrong. It could have been avoided. It was paperwork—it's No Child Left Behind."

"Thank you," Nikki said softly, standing and pushing in her chair. "I appreciate your help." Later in the year, with states clearly in no position to meet the highly qualified teacher deadline, the Education Department would extend it until the end of the 2006–07 school year. But that didn't matter now. Nikki walked down the hall to the library, to go online and register to take the Praxis test. Tina began to type a letter to Nikki's kids' parents. Nobody specified that the letter had to go by U.S. mail. So she sent it home in the children's backpacks, where with any luck it would get as much attention as everything else crumpled up in there.

18

The Whole Scenario Can Change

The Oscar ballots at Price Waterhouse, the Coca-Cola formula, the Colonel's blend of eleven herbs and spices: Few secrets are guarded as closely as the Maryland School Assessment. Two weeks before the MSA test was to be given, the Tyler Heights staff gathered in the library, where Tracy Prater read aloud the rules the teachers would sign their names to:

> I understand that it is a breach of professional ethics to provide verbal or nonverbal clues or answers, teach items on the test, share prompts, coach, hint, or in any way influence a student's performance during the testing. I understand that making notes about, making answer keys for, writing about, or discussing with persons not involved in the test administration, the content of the actual test or any part thereof . . . is prohibited. I know that violations of test administration and security provisions may result in invalidation of test results, cost assessed to my district, and disciplinary actions against me by my district or certificate suspensions or revocations by the Maryland State Department of Education.

"You don't want to be a person whose integrity is being questioned," Tracy said as the forms were passed out. Some teachers in the back hadn't received theirs, and were talking.

"We're waiting," Tina said. "We're waiting. Signal."

Tracy—who at this time of year spends more time organizing testing as the school's assessment coordinator than in her nominal job as reading teacher—went on to explain that every Tyler Heights teacher would help proctor the test for the third, fourth, and fifth graders. Classes in the lower grades would be staffed by substitutes.

Students who arrived in the country within the past year were exempted from the reading test. A couple of other children, including Mateo, who had been around longer but knew so little English they would obviously fail, might be excused, on the grounds that the test would be too traumatic, and just given a zero. (As long as Tyler Heights met the 95 percent participation requirement, this wouldn't be questioned.) For students with accommodations, Tracy said, scribes "can only write exactly what the student says. We're trying to train the students to ask that it be read back to them." If a student with a scribe starts to write a BCR herself, you can't finish the writing for her later. If the child stares at the wall for five minutes, Mandy Panetta asked, can you say, "Is there anything more you can write?"

"I asked the county test director about that, and she said use your common sense. Say, 'Hello!' But you can't say, 'Are you finished?'"

What about accents, low talkers, fast talkers, one teacher asked. "Can you say 'I don't understand'?"

Tracy didn't bother to share the rule about barfed-on tests—transfer the answers to another form, put the exam in a Ziploc, and send it to the state—but she did touch on sticky notes. Teachers had just told the kids they wouldn't be able to mark up reading passages, as they were used to doing, so they practiced using Post-its instead. It turned out, Tracy said, that they *could* underline but couldn't use Post-its, because the adhesive might screw up the test results.

No detail was too small for consideration. "The difference between basic and proficient can be one point," Tina emphasized. "The difference between proficient and advanced can be one point."

Oh, and by the way, science benchmarks were coming next year. "They want results," Tina said.

◆ ◆ ◆

"They" were mentioned a lot at Tyler Heights. Usually, including in this case, "they" meant the officials of the Anne Arundel County Public

Schools. Sometimes "they" were the anonymous people—nobody really knew who—who would score the MSA one day. A week later, the teachers of Tyler Heights would learn about another "they" who was paying attention to the data: the U.S. Department of Education's Office of Civil Rights. Six months after Dr. Smith signed the agreement with the NAACP, which promised to improve educational measures for African Americans, three months after he'd left, and eight school days before MSA, Tina briefed her teachers about it, as the school system required.

"It states that—hold on to your seats, ladies—Anne Arundel County Public Schools will eliminate the disparity in test scores by June 2007," she told the Literacy Team.

"That's what we try to do every day," Mandy said.

"That's my take," Tina said. "There was a lawsuit threatened by the community, and the hope is that if there is a show of good faith, the people might pull back on the lawsuit. For me it doesn't really change a whole lot."

"Are the people filing the lawsuit putting in a community piece?"

"There is the expectation that schools can't do it alone," Tina said. "There is an effort to bring parents into schools." She said that administrators were discussing a possible parents' basketball league in Annapolis, which people would certainly show up for. Or maybe, Tina suggested, chess; she'd just seen Ted Danson teach inner-city kids the game in an overcoming-the-odds TV movie.

Teachers were insulted by the implied assumption that they were neglecting students and that they were lazy or discriminatory in who they disciplined or sought special ed for. "Beyond the statistical evidence," Mandy asked, "what is the basis of the lawsuit? Are they coming into schools and looking at what's being done? Or is it just the statistics?"

A statistic showing a chronically absent fifth grader failing MSA wouldn't say anything about her truancy, and the statistic about her truancy wouldn't say anything about the guidance counselor staging a manhunt. The statistic that would show a black fourth grader being identified as a special education student wouldn't show him arriving unable to read and traditional interventions not working. The statistic showing a third grader as a whole lot of suspensions wouldn't say anything about the tireless efforts of at least seven staff members to keep her on track.

"We've all said you can't just look at the label," Tina said. "If you've got a concentration of students and tried a bazillion things, you can't not identify them. The discipline data is troubling me. We're not going to make our goal of a ten percent reduction. But I'm not going to *not* give consequences because of the data. I just won't do it."

She added, "I'm not bothered by this agreement in any way. These are our goals too. We are where for reading?"

"Eighty-five point seven."

"And where for math?"

"Seventy-nine point six."

◆ ◆ ◆

Tina's to-do pile of papers and folders, which wasn't getting any smaller, sat in the middle of the conference table. There was one thing on the agenda for the Literacy Team meeting: testing.

"I think all the pieces are in place," Tina said.

She called out to her secretary, asking her to remind the subs to be at school on MSA day no later than 7:35, and turned back to the group. "Where are we with the kids? Where do you think fifth grade is right now?"

"They're fine," Mandy said. "It's just, the fifth grade is drama with everyone."

"You're talking big folks, little folks?" Tina asked.

"Both. I sense a little bit of burnout," Mandy said.

"Do you think we should give them a break with the mock next week?"

"Well, we told them they were going to do it."

"How about some extra downtime?" Tina suggested. "Extra recess?"

"I don't know."

"For right now, we have to compartmentalize the drama," Tina said. "It will just zap time and energy. We have to put it away for now. Kids can sense drama. But when you looked at their work, their BCRs, you were comfortable? We don't have to cross our fingers and our toes and our eyes?"

"Who's proctoring in fifth grade?" Mandy asked. She worried that Mrs. Williams's teammate was too laid back. "We need to make sure it's someone who's going to see to it that the level of work is demanded."

"It has to be someone who is going to demand that students work until time is called—they're not going to be slackers," Tina said.

They looked at the schedule and saw that someone from Central Office was assigned to the room, someone unknown. Mandy couldn't do it, because the kids in that class were mad at her—part of the drama. One resource teacher offered to switch from giving accommodations to a fourth grader named Jeffry, whom she'd helped all year. But since Jeffry was having his best year—he was not clinging to doorjambs while being dragged from the classroom—Tina figured they should leave that be.

"What about the men?" a teacher asked, but Mr. Al would be monitoring difficult kids in the library and Mr. Dillard would be on call for breakdowns.

"Is Julian in a small group?"

"He's one that could perform very well or could take an I-don't-care attitude," Tina said. "I will make a concerted effort to be in there. You know what I always say, the difference between basic and proficient is one point. We don't want the loss of focus to be that one point."

For fourth grade, a resource teacher made a list of what topics needed to be hit again, but it wasn't much. "You go in to Antes' room, she's drilling, giving out Scholar Dollars for correct answers— onomatopoeia—bam! Huffman's kids would not be able to answer the same questions, but they're trucking along," she said.

"They're still in the proficient band for the most part?" Mandy asked. "Yes."

"Third grade," Tina said.

"They've done everything," Mandy said. "There are four more focus lessons for next week."

"What's your pulse level in terms of stress? I thought the kids had a higher stress level last year, but then it came down because of the snow days."

"They're maybe not so stressed, because they don't check in."

"They're not all in that range," Tina said, diplomatically.

They talked about Mrs. Facchine's kids, the ones with emotional issues. Michelle, who was on the verge of nine suspensions, would start going home at lunchtime. "She'll be missing math," Tina said, "so she might have to do a compacted math lesson in the morning." Mike needed more confidence; Reggie needed the special ed accommodation—cross your fingers.

"So, students aren't too stressed," Tina said. "They're at a place where we know we've done all we can do to get them there. I don't know if there's anything else to say about it. Okay, I'm gonna shift gears, because Stanford 10 is staring us in the face. Last week we started the mock in second grade."

◆ ◆ ◆

The Maryland State Department of Education allows teachers who will be administering the MSA to look at the actual exam several days beforehand. (Tyler Heights teachers were prevented, however, by an agreement they signed with the state, from talking with me about what was on the MSA.) Many Maryland teachers don't even know this is allowed; none of the many education and testing experts I spoke with had ever heard of this in these high-stakes times; but some schools are urged by their districts to take full advantage of the opportunity. "If you're the examiner, you have to be prepared to deliver the test as accurately as you possibly can," Gary Heath, the assistant state superintendent in charge of testing, told me.

The instructions on the test are straightforward; why the teachers need preparation to give them, I don't understand. At any rate, I have found teachers less concerned with how a test would be delivered than with what their children would and wouldn't know. Which vocabulary words would trip them up? Would they be faced with questions about topics they'd never heard of? Would they be flummoxed by idioms that no child would ever use, or directions phrased differently than they had been in class? Could they answer BCR questions unlike those they had practiced? Could students who had mastered certain math tasks combine them successfully for multistep problems? How would they handle reading passages longer than the ones in practice tests? Could they maintain focus during tests that required them to stay on task longer than they had ever done?

The time between teachers seeing the test and giving it is too short, Heath told me, to make a difference in the results. "Even if I gave it to people two weeks ahead of time, and you teach your kids all these questions, how successful do you think that would be? It wouldn't." For a week, the vocabulary words sat in teachers' heads like unmentionable elephants; when one of them showed up on a Saxon Math problem, teachers weren't sure if they could explain it or not.

"We may as well not teach this week, because we can't teach them what's on the test," Alia said. Much of the test was the same as last year's. What was different was Alia's confidence that her students could pass.

◆ ◆ ◆

The Social Committee gave all the teachers in MSA grades fruity bath gel as a pick-me-up gift, but too many third graders had failed their practice tests for the tensions to be easily assuaged by a hot soak. When Miss Johnson asked her students a week before the test what made two poems similar, all the students offered was that they both had authors and titles. Roman handed in a BCR that ended, *"So I know my answer is why I conclude."* Dena wrote, *"Alexander and the boy are alike because The boy in the poem has 5 stanzas, Repetition, and Rhythm."* Too many children were starting their summaries, *"I know this is a summary because . . ."* Elena capped off a math lesson on arrays by asking, at the very end, "What's an array?" When asked what text features a menu contained, Summer said, "Dialogue!"

"Are you guys thinking, or just saying the first thing that comes out of your mouth?" Miss Johnson asked. "Is anyone talking in this menu?"

"We are," Summer said.

"I'm very frightened," Miss Johnson muttered.

Last year in Baltimore Mrs. Facchine's students had been the lowest of the low, yet only two—one mentally retarded, one with Asperger's syndrome—failed the MSA. So she knew the bar for passing was not high. Still, she told her husband not to expect the $1,500 bonus. "We're just training them to answer one type of question," she said, while the MSA would expect them to go beyond the literal. "We're not teaching them to think. We're teaching them to regurgitate."

Alia's nerves about her kids, meanwhile, were overtaken by something bigger. Frankie was coming home the Saturday before the test, and she was going to meet him in Norfolk. Alia had read all about the adjustment problems soldiers and sailors had on returning from Iraq; their relationship wasn't as well-defined as she'd have liked and she tried to prepare herself for anything. Somehow, the MSA just didn't seem so important anymore. So she decided to let go, the way people attach their grief to helium balloons and send it skyward. She had a great weekend with Frankie and on Monday participated in the staff tug-of-war (tiny Tina as the anchor) and kickball game that had been scheduled instead of a staff meeting. "De-stress before the test," Tina called it, though Alia's idea of de-stressing would have been more like grading papers while sitting on the couch and watching the news.

While the third-grade teachers used the few days before MSA to cram in skills, Mrs. Williams's class went ahead with Open Court and took time, as usual, to stray. The day before the test, while the third graders did a BCR on author's purpose and practiced online at testfactory.net, Mrs. Williams explained the inaccuracy of musket balls in the American Revolution and the provenance of "don't fire till you see the whites of their eyes." She explained the different spellings of honor and honour, theater and theatre, and, strangely, schedule versus skedule. Mrs. Williams figured that the high MSA score was Tina's goal, but it didn't mean much to her personally. Last year she watched her students answer lots of problems wrong on the test, and then three-quarters of them passed. She didn't feel there was a whole lot of correlation between a good education and the MSA—an opinion she once voiced in a letter to the editor of the local paper.

"I'm confident that my students, if they continue as they've been doing, will be successful," she said. "These kids can read and write and think. Will the MSA show that? Maybe, maybe not." Mrs. Williams had done some practice, but little enough that when the other fifth-grade teacher said, "We just did four BCRs in a row, bang bang bang," she wondered if her class might do worse, making her look bad.

◆ ◆ ◆

The truth was that the students of Tyler Heights didn't have to do all that well for the school to make adequate yearly progress under the law. Months before, Tina had found out the proficiency requirements given the state's formulation of confidence intervals, statistical ranges of acceptable pass rates based on the number of students in a group. When groups are small, the intervals are larger, and vice versa. Tyler Heights' cushions were big. While Maryland's target for reading was 63 percent of students proficient, for example, according to the information Tina received just half needed to pass for Tyler Heights to make AYP, including only one-third of Hispanic students and three of ten special ed kids. What's more, Tina knew that the benchmarks the third graders had done so poorly on were, historically, more toughly graded than the MSA.

Tina didn't tell her staff about the breathing room. "I don't want any teacher, even in the back of her mind, thinking, 'I don't have to work hard and we can still make it,'" she told me. Besides, the school's own stated goals were higher, 85 percent for reading and 80 percent for math—no confidence intervals there.

Pass rates in the seventies Tina could handle, write off to a statistical fluctuation. But even if Tyler Heights still made AYP, falling would hurt. "That is going to be really difficult for this school," Tina told me. "People will think it was luck. They'll think, 'They can't hang on to it.' They'll think, 'Those kids can't learn.' We will let ourselves down. We'll let a lot of people down. There's a lot of pressure there. A lot of people are looking at Tyler Heights. Before, we didn't have any reputation in the community. We were the worst school. We have made believers of this school, and we need to hang on to that." She needed to hang on to her teachers too: "Attracting people to this school is always incredibly challenging, even with the scores. I just worry about people having to keep going, keep their energy up. Even my energy. This is a real crucial year for us."

Based on student-by-student analyses from teachers, Tina predicted 73 percent proficiency in reading and 76 percent in math. She expected nearly a quarter of the students would be advanced in math. Half the ESOL kids, she figured, would be fine.

"The thing is, we can do all the projection we want," she said. "But if it's an off day for some kids, or the items are written in a different way where the kids understand the concepts but don't know what they want them to do, this scenario can change. The whole scenario can change."

♦ ♦ ♦

Two days before MSA's Wednesday start date, Tina drooped a bit from nausea and teary-eyed allergies—not her full-blown after-the-daffodils weepies, but still. A stomach bug had spread through the school too, hitting more than fifty students, teachers, and Tina. When she got dressed Monday, black hadn't seemed right, so she changed twice, finally settling on turquoise.

The last couple of weeks everything had piled on. Clogged toilets in the primary hall. News that, yet again, Tina would not get an assistant principal for next year. Difficulty finding long-term subs for the fourth-grade teacher about to give birth and the art teacher headed to surgery. The change in command at the Naval Station, which provided lots of assistance to the school, assistance Tina hoped wouldn't be lost in the shuffle. The back-and-forth to get Reggie's dad to approve his special ed accommodations, which he did just in time. On Monday, Tina was confronted by an irate parent who refused to keep her first grader out of school, as the nurse had insisted, despite a fever and scaly scalp. (The nurse, the mother told Tina, was a quack who got her diploma from Kmart.) On Tuesday, Tina was still faxing back and forth with the state to secure a last-minute scribe for a fifth grader with an infected hangnail.

Troubles lay outside school as well. Tina's son, who was in medical school in North Carolina, had grown ill and distant at the same time, and she felt like she couldn't pull away from the MSA and her mother long enough to visit him. A week before, the local power company had announced a 72 percent increase in local energy rates, which Tina feared would put home care for her mom just out of reach. As it was, the family squeaked by because Tina handled Sunday duty, sparing the cost of an aide.

That her mother wasn't getting any better despite all the energy Tina put into her care was a difficult realization for such a goal-oriented person. Even more difficult was when Tina arrived on Sunday and her mother asked, "Who are you?"

Tina was such a master compartmentalizer that it didn't occur to her until Tuesday, twenty-four hours before the MSA, that there could be a wee bit of stress behind her tummy trouble.

"I'm realizing it might not be a virus," she told me.

19

Never Give Up Trying

Cyrus's tricksters were driving Miss Johnson crazy the morning before MSA. On the multiple-choice problems the class was doing for practice, Cyrus marked the wrong answers with dark lines instead of tiny ticks. "If you do that on your test, you'll get them all wrong," Miss Johnson said.

At home Cyrus's work was scrutinized closely. If it was not neat or correct, he said, he had to do it over. At school he felt like he could do no right. Yesterday before recess, Cyrus gave two correct answers but was so quiet Miss Johnson didn't hear. She chastised him for ignoring her. Coming back from recess he was last in line by far, his face tucked so deep into his leather jacket he could barely see.

Today, Cyrus was spaced out—"traveling," Mrs. Marshall called it. As his classmates continued in the MSA practice workbook, he stood over the trash can, cleaning his nose. Slowly he folded a paper towel open and shut, open and shut. He blew gently to release the hanging snot. Cyrus's head hurt. His stomach hurt. His scalp itched too—all symptoms he attributed to the MSA.

"I'm glad I'm sick," he would tell me quietly at lunch. "Then I won't have to take the test."

I told him that he'd have to take it when he came back.

"Then I'll run to the ocean," Cyrus said. "I'll go in the ground. But then I'll die."

It was hard to tell if Cyrus was truly terrified or just a drama king—the kids, Miss Johnson pointed out, took advantage of the big deal being made of MSA to crank their melodrama up high. Cyrus tipped the meter toward terrified when he added, in a tiny voice, that he could already picture logging on to the computer to see an embarrassing set of scores. "They want me to go to college," he said, "they" meaning his parents, his teachers, everybody. "I wish I were still in pre-K."

◆ ◆ ◆

As the rules demanded, Miss Johnson had covered up everything in the classroom that might help on the test—the math meeting board, the BATS formula, YoJo's tips, the hundred-number chart. On the back board she had written *"Good Luck! Do Your Best!"* and a smiley face. Up front she wrote, *"Study MSA Terms! MSA is tomorrow! Get a good sleep!!"*

The third graders at Tyler Heights had been bathed in encouragement for weeks. They worried but looked forward to showing off how smart they were. Mr. Al, the resident artist, made a banner of somebody reading the MSA test book while dreaming of a desert island. All through the classrooms signs made by children in the younger grades offered cheer: *"I know you will do great!" "you numer 1." "MSA rock!!!on!!!"* Polaroids of the third graders who had done their homework each day were posted on the "Smarties" bulletin board in the hall. (The first week there were twelve kids, then twenty, then back to twelve.) Students' Top MSA Tips were posted on the lockers:

1. *Never give up trying.*
2. *Use BATS for BCR.*
3. *You should use light tricksters so you can get credit.*
4. *Get readly of school.*
5. *Eat and helpty breakfast.*
6. *Get reparded for school.*
7. *Take turns will a partner to test me.*
8. *Always have a nice sleep.*

9. *Use process of elimination in case you get stuck on a question that is an 50/50.*

As Miss Johnson's class worked in the practice book, she walked around the room to check, finding mistakes everywhere. To Autumn, she said, "Explain to me how these two words have the same sound. Don't shake your shoulders at me. How can 'dead' have the same sound as 'ck'? I think you maybe need to go back and figure that out."

To Lilia she said, "What's a word that has the same sound?"

"Synonym."

"What's a word that has the same sound?"

"Rhyming?"

To Avante she said, "U-blank-e. What does that mean to have u-blank-e?"

"Long u."

"So try again."

"Prune."

"Do 'prune' and 'juggle' have the same sound?"

"No."

To everyone she said, "Is 'olive' a compound word? 'Live' is a word but can you 'o' something? Can you see 'o'? Can you play 'o'? 'Fantastic.' 'Fan' is a word but 'tastic'? 'Plastic,' yes, but 'tastic'? Malcolm, write your name. David, I ask that that go away." He had pulled out his science book. "Using your whisper-phone on this part would be very helpful, because when you say it with your lips, you hear it with your brain."

"I'm ready," Avante proclaimed.

"I'm not," Autumn added.

"Everyone in this classroom has gotten everything you need to take this test," Miss Johnson said. "If you're not ready, it's because you chose not to listen." Across the hall, Miss Milhoan told her class not to worry, and she meant it. "What's the big C word I have in you?"

"Confidence," Montell said.

"You've done great on the mock tests, I've given you the information you need, and you have all your strategies," she said. "I know that you're going to make me proud. You don't see me freaking out, so you don't have to."

Miss Milhoan went up to get something from her desk, and there was a bout of chatting, which grew loud quickly. "When I give an inch, you guys take a mile," she said.

"What's that?" someone asked. Javy said that meant they went too far, a flash of smarts that netted him a Scholar Dollar.

◆ ◆ ◆

Miss Johnson was helping her class distinguish "patch" as a verb from "patch" as a noun when Autumn blew her nose, loud. She went to the bathroom—her stomach hurt—and returned after a while, laying her head on the desk.

"This is why you might be nervous for the MSA test," Miss Johnson said.

It might have also been that Autumn's cousin was shot and killed the week before, something she hadn't told anyone at school. It might have been that she had not properly cleaned the bathroom over the weekend; her punishment was to clean the whole house for a week. All she could think about was her cousin and the infuriating fact that her brothers would be spared their chores. For others too MSA had competition for attention. David was preoccupied with having gotten in trouble for something someone else did. Roman was preoccupied with having gotten in trouble for something he did do. "Bad places," was all he'd say about it.

Some kids had new reasons to breathe easy. Juan was understanding more English each day. Vision testing had determined that Summer needed glasses and Eddy was practically blind, and Sam's Club came through in time. Jamila and Elena both were getting far better grades than they had at the start of the year, and Malcolm was on a roll, no breakdowns.

But in general, students were going stir-crazy from test prep. Kickball had been reinstated, but the third graders still lumped around shortstop, screamed at one another, and ran to the next base whenever they felt like it. ("I've given up," Mrs. Facchine said Monday as she watched.) Referrals after winter break were nine times higher than last year, and suspensions were three times higher—a small number of third graders were the primary offenders, and nearly one-third missed the third-quarter behavior incentive party. Even students who could normally be counted on were guilty of minor offenses.

Of the students predicted to score advanced in reading, all but one were sliding. Estela, glum from problems with her siblings and her best friend's suspension, refused to continue with math facts if she got one wrong and was befuddled about when to use hundred-dollar words. ("It's so confusing in my head," she told me.) Namika would not sit in class, stomped around, and neglected her work. Tisha said she was upset she hadn't seen her dad for a while but seemed plagued by something darker as well, and her grades showed it. Sydney had begun handing in scribbles instead of paragraphs.

Boredom prevailed. One day, before writing a BCR about a play, Lilia asked, "Miss Johnson, can we play the play?"

"Tomorrow, can we be the characters?" David asked.

"If we have time, because we have to take the mock MSA."

With Sydney's squiggles, Miss Milhoan suspected her mom's remarriage, but certainly part of it was ennui. As a little girl, Sydney said her mom told her, she used to read *"loooong stories"* and as a toddler wanted to be able to read so desperately that she destroyed books out of frustration. But now she didn't like to read, didn't like school at all. "I wish we did more science, more fun things in math," she told me. "I want to write stories about who I am. Why can't I write on the overhead sometimes? We just sit there. Why do we have to write five BCRs?" For the past week Sydney would bring in square roots she learned at home, but not her homework. Twice she'd forged her mom's name on notes.

"We pray to God that Sydney will snap out of it," her parents wrote to Miss Milhoan.

"Well," the teacher said, "I've prayed to God and it hasn't worked."

"I've prayed to god, to saints, for a miracle," Miss Johnson said, "and they still can't go back to the text when they're writing a BCR."

◆ ◆ ◆

Two hours into the day before the MSA, Miss Johnson's class had written BCRs about what they could conclude about where Joe was, and what skills were needed to set records, and how they knew *The Diary of a Worm* was a journal, when she put another assignment on the over-head. The passage was about Blackie, who hid to have puppies. The BCR question asked, *"What can you conclude about who Blackie is?"*

David's eyes were closed. Avante raced through the assignment and then wrote a note, illustrated by a smiling sun: *"Dear Ms. Johnson, You are the best Guidance Miss Johnson. You make me smile very happy. And thanks for making me to BCR."* Tisha hadn't gotten any farther than *"I can conclude that Blackie is a dog."* Lilia's response was simply sloppy; she couldn't for the life of her stay inside the box, and then she would panic. It didn't help that she was answering in yellow and orange crayon.

"You know that's not acceptable," Miss Johnson said, crumpling Lilia's paper. "Don't play with me. Don't do that tomorrow. What can we conclude that Blackie is? Savannah, please sit up." The girl had fallen asleep. ("I just want to lay down in my comfy bed," she would tell me at lunchtime, weary from MSA practice and the preferential treat-ment she imagined a suspended sibling was getting at home.) "Can I write a 'So I know'?" Autumn asked. The third-grade teachers had de-cided that the 'S' in their kids' BATS wasn't cutting it, and they'd told them to skip it. But the students could never remember: S or not? "Don't do an 'S' unless you can think of a magnificent, awesome 'S,' " Miss Johnson said. "It's just wasting your time. You can proof and pol-ish it while you're waiting."

Proofing and polishing was a drag. Roman raised his hand for the fourth time, asking to call his mother, who'd forgotten his lunch money. Denied, he wandered to the sink for the third time, as if mag-netically drawn there. Malcolm asked to go to the nurse, which Miss Johnson permitted; Autumn asked to go to the nurse, which she did not allow. Avante folded his note carefully and wrote, *"From: Avante To: Guidance."*

Miss Johnson checked papers at the front of the room and said, "You're on track. Very nice. Stand up and take a stretch."

Avante walked up to Miss Johnson and asked if he could deliver the note. She marched him back to his seat, where he refused to do more work. Malcolm returned from the nurse, with news he was going home with a fever. Miss Johnson collected his glasses and said, "I need you to be here tomorrow to take it unless you're really, really, really, really, really, really sick. Okay? Feel better."

At lunch, his classmates professed their envy. Jamila wished she could go home too. She felt "exaggerated" about the MSA, she said, icky all over. Like her classmates, she mistakenly thought promotion to fourth grade, as well as a good report card, depended on a good MSA score.[1] (Good thing she had no idea her teachers didn't expect her to pass the reading test.) Jamila's mother, wanting her to feel comfortable with the test, made sure she practiced the MSA definitions. She got them correct, but her confidence was still shaky. Whenever she thought she'd do well on something, she was wrong. And the more she practiced, the more scared she got.[2] "If I don't do well—I don't know, to tell you the truth. If I don't do well . . ." She trailed off.

Elena, who was also expected to fail reading but had written Miss Johnson a note expressing her confidence *("I will do my best on the MSA test and I will get 100% if I don't pass the reading test I will pass the math test. Also, I am talking about the real test")*, said she was prepared. So did Roman: "I'm good." "I'm just a little nervous. BCRs," Tisha said, shaking her head. Avante widened his eyes, took a bite of ketchup pizza, and said that despite his earlier pronouncement that he was ready, "My heart feels like it's beating from here to there." He pointed to the back wall of the lunchroom.

◆ ◆ ◆

In the computer lab after lunch, Dantay rushed and guessed through a math practice test, scoring 55 percent. "That doesn't give me a lot of hope," Miss Johnson told me. To Dantay she said, "Do you think that's good? Do you think that's a passing score?"

"No."

Jamila got a fifty-seven and sighed, then decided to be excited because she had gotten the ten probability questions right. Cyrus took a long, long time. David aced it.

Back in class Lilia said, "Miss Johnson, if we check with our calculator tomorrow and it's not correct, can we cross it out and . . ."

"Isn't that what you're supposed to do?" Autumn was playing with her fraction card. "Autumn, this would be part of listening to pass the MSA test. How about a novel idea to the four of you—put your shoes on."

"Can we do this on our own?"

"No, that's why it says 'guided class practice.'" A problem asked how the pattern 163, 173, 183 was achieved. "Minus three? Minus thirteen?" said Roman, who was expected to score advanced in math.

"It's not minus anything," Miss Johnson said.

"Plus three?" said Autumn, who was expected to score basic.

"Plus nine?" said Elena, who was expected to score proficient.

At the end of the day, Miss Johnson said, "I'm giving you a very important sticker. Make sure your parents see it." On the sticker a shaggy dog dozed in a nightscape of stars. "IMPORTANT TESTING TOMORROW!" it said. "PLEASE GET A GOOD NIGHT'S SLEEP!"

"I never get a good night's sleep," Lilia said, as the students lined up to leave.

20

We Celebrate the Bottom

When Miss Johnson's third graders entered Tyler Heights on Wednesday they were greeted by hugs from the guidance counselor. "Are you ready?" Jennifer Johnson asked. "I know you're ready!" They looked a little numb and nervous—tired too, from staying up to vote for *American Idol*. At their desks, they were eating strawberry Pop-Tarts and chocolate milk when Mrs. Tabor came on the television, saying that YoJo sends his best wishes. Then Ms. McKnight appeared, wearing a purple suit and an orange shirt, an orange silk flower pinned to her lapel. "This is Tina McKnight, the principal of Tyler Heights Elementary School. You have done all the work to be prepared for today. You are ready, you are smart, you're going to do very, very well."

The students did morning work—figuring out which digits were in the tens place—as Mrs. Tabor and Ms. Prater wheeled a cart through the hall. Room by room, they handed out dollar-store plastic baskets filled with water bottles, mints, MSA vocabulary cards (the kids were permitted to look at the words, not the definitions), and calculators. Unlike yesterday, Cyrus felt fine. Jamila still felt "exaggerated," though she was far better off than the fourth grader who had become hysterical in Dunkin' Donuts before school. A girl named Marisol had arrived quite ill, despite a doctor's note, and Ms. McKnight sent her home. The principal peeked in on the teachers' lounge, where a buffet breakfast was set up for the staff—as it would be for each of the four MSA days, thanks to Title I funds and the home cooking of the Literacy Team. She checked the intermediate hall to make sure everything was in order. "There was a full moon last night," she said. "I never believed in the full moon stuff until I became a principal."

Miss Johnson sent her students two by two to the bathroom. For day one, the children faced eighty-seven minutes of testing, punctuated by two short breaks. When everyone had returned, she pressed play on the boom box, and the room filled with calming music she had brought from home. The CD was designed to induce sleep, but maybe it could help soothe nerves instead. Miss Johnson led her students through the meditation script. They caressed their bellies and earlobes and collarbones. They touched their elbows to their knees. They clasped their hands together up high and lowered them, tongues pressed to the roofs of their mouths. Teachers fetched all the children entitled to accommodations. Then at nine a.m. sharp, the students of Tyler Heights Elementary School began selecting the answers that would tell the world how much they had learned that year.

◆ ◆ ◆

In the 2005–06 school year, America's students would take forty-five million standardized tests, and states would pay more than a half billion dollars, to meet the testing requirements of No Child Left Behind.[1] The market was dominated by a few big companies, including Harcourt Assessment (creator, with the Maryland State Department of Education, of the reading MSA) and CTB/McGraw-Hill (the math MSA). The Maryland School Assessment, given since 2003, was designed to meet the requirements of No Child Left Behind and improve upon the state's old system. Over the previous decade, Maryland students in grades three, five, and eight had proved knowledge and skills by carrying out multistep tasks and writing about them. Some teachers like the former test for its emphasis on problem-solving and its breadth—in addition to reading and math it covered writing, social studies, and science. But the scope seemed too broad to adequately prepare for, many thought the test failed to assess actual knowledge and skills, and the hands-on experiments were complicated to administer. In the end the test provided little useful information about each child, because students took the test in groups and because the results took so long to return.

The MSA and its companion for older students, the High School Assessment, require no goggles, no soil samples, no groups—just pencils and paper, multiple-choice and short written responses. State officials say the MSA is a fine, fair measure of student achievement on the Maryland standards and hired an independent nonprofit, called Achieve Inc., to confirm that. The American Federation of Teachers rates Maryland about average, saying that between half and three-quarters of its tests are "aligned to strong content standards." In 2005, a Washington think tank rated the state English and math standards a "C."[2]

The reading MSA, which for third graders takes three hours over two days, is in essence two tests. Some items, called "criterion-referenced," are specifically written to test students on Maryland's standards. "Norm-referenced" items are taken from Harcourt's Stanford 10 series and used to see how students compare to children elsewhere in the country. The MSA also contains items that are being field-tested for future tests and don't count toward a child's score. (The Tyler teachers prayed that the easiest BCRs weren't the field-test ones.)[3]

In a world where people assume students' test scores tell you what you need to know about what students have learned, it's important to understand what's on these exams. "If it's in the content standards, we're going to measure it, if we at all can," Gary Heath, the state's testing director, told me. Few in the general public see for themselves if he is right, beyond the sample items released on the state website (eight questions for third grade, taken from a 2003 exam). Parents have a right to see their child's answer booklet, though that option is not really advertised and few know about it.

The state superintendent and the testing director, in consultation with the attorney general, decided not to let me sit in Miss Johnson's classroom during the MSA. I knew my request was a long shot, as the state does not allow journalists to witness testing, but given an unblemished eight years covering Maryland schools, I thought it was worth a try. I offered to sign a promise that I'd sit far from the test and not look at it.

"There's nothing that I take more seriously than making sure my tests are secure," Heath told me when he called to say no. (This was after he said, "It's not a secret, it's just a test. It's not like it's a big mystery what's going on in there.") His greatest concern was that somebody might publish test questions. Because some items are repeated from year to year, this would supposedly compromise the security of the test and force the state to go to the expense of creating new items. Given that teachers see the test and that students are under no obligation to keep its contents secret, I found this concern hard to justify.[4]

As for Heath's comment that what can be measured *is:* I may miss some subleties—I am not a psychometrician, after all. But I have covered Maryland schools since before the MSA began and know enough about what is on the test to assess this assertion. The reading exam requires children to demonstrate some word skills, comprehend and explain a variety of texts, and understand vocabulary and text features. It omits an awful lot of the grammar and usage skills listed in the state content standards. It doesn't test reading aloud, speaking, or listening—except, unintentionally, for the students who have the test read to them and scribed. Nor does it test the use of references like dictionaries, thesauruses, and the Internet. While the BCRs require students to write, those questions don't test writing, per se, but reading comprehension.

Heath told me some standards are simply too complicated to test.[5] Agreed. And I don't enumerate this (abridged) list to suggest that the reading MSA is a bad test. That it requires BCRs sets it ahead of reading tests that use only multiple-choice questions, which are quicker to answer, and cheaper and quicker to grade.[6] Then again, many states whose reading tests are only multiple-choice have separate writing exams, at least in some grades.

All in all, testing experts say that a lot of state tests aren't as valid or challenging as they should be; they are reluctant to name any specifically. Certainly some children might never have been able to write a cohesive paragraph before they were forced to at least try on the MSA, and many educators feel like the test is okay, as far as it goes. But it is crucial for people to understand exactly that: how far it goes.

◆ ◆ ◆

Day One, the compound words were a cinch, the third graders said. But they had problems with the way expressions were phrased and with simple vocabulary words. "Is 'mound' a wave?" Emily asked me over lunch, even though she was the top student in the grade, even though "mound" had been a vocabulary word in Open Court weeks before. "Is 'ill' sleepy?" another asked.

"I feel sad because the whole Maryland sees my test," one boy said. "The president too, and everyone hates him."

Miss Milhoan felt her students did pretty well; the other two teachers weren't so sure. At one point in the test Roman asked Miss Johnson, "Can I get a dictionary?" and she thought, Is he for real? She watched as Dantay raced through with misplaced confidence and as Savannah became derailed by a classmate who snapped, when she turned the page, "You're not allowed to go ahead!" (Her sensitivity would strike again, when she failed to complete the last problem in the first section of the math test. She froze up, refused to continue, and was taken to another room to finish.) Autumn, though, forgot to play dumb and took her time, filling in right answer after right answer. Avante and Cyrus finished on time and would later insist they got everything correct.

The forty-five minutes allotted for the last section, with its long stories and poems, was not enough for Jamila. Miss Johnson had no tolerance for drama and suspected Jamila had lied earlier about needing a bathroom break. (Her instinct was right. "I just had to get out of there," the girl told me later, breathing in deeply and shaking her head.) So when the timer buzzed and Jamila cried on hearing "Pencils down," Miss Johnson told her, "Don't even start."

◆ ◆ ◆

Jamila's partially finished test booklet and all the others would eventually make their way to a Harcourt scoring center in Atlanta and be scanned into computers. Multiple-choice questions would get scored automatically, while the BCRs would be read on the screen and graded by humans, against rubrics they were provided. The BCR that took Jamila ten minutes to write, a good scorer could grade in seconds.

Typically throughout the industry, test scorers—including those Harcourt hires for MSA—must have a bachelors degree. Scorers are usually hired seasonally and paid by the hour—retired teachers, people in between jobs, new college grads. Test scorers generally get a few days of training, after which they must score sample exams, to make sure their grading is in line with the norm. Once real scoring begins, their work is checked along the way, to make sure they do not drift. Each response is graded by at least two scorers; too much difference between them—or a particularly creative answer—sends the answer to a third set of eyes. Testing officials say these precautions ensure validity. Talk to scorers and the picture is a little fuzzier than one would hope for, in a system where, as Tina McKnight kept pointing out, the difference between passing and failing is just one point.[7] "We think these tests are so objective, but you still have a table full of scorers saying, 'I *think* I know what this kid means,'" one former scorer told me. "We erred on the side of not being punitive."

One woman who worked several years for a major company, including as a director, told me, "You sit in this room—it's like a warehouse. Click—accept. Click—accept. It's horrendous." The tables were filled by "lots of weird, weird people—that's the only job they could get." She recalled a contingent of middle-aged men who were obsessed with the war in Iraq and easily aggravated into a lesser score by any doodle or phrase that looked like it could be Islamic, emblematic of a heavy metal band, or Spanish. In the case of tests that were a graduation requirement, she said, the scorers appreciated the gravity. "For elementary schoolers, they were just like, 'Eh.'"

In all, she said, "For most students who spoke English well and didn't have a disability and were able to write legibly, the process was fair."

◆ ◆ ◆

The staff of Tyler Heights had worked very hard to create a controlled, distraction-free environment for students. During the test, however, an observer, one of many sent across Maryland by the state education department, came into classrooms and read over shoulders. She spent a lot of time by Raychelle, a student so flustered by hovering that Miss Milhoan never attempted it. Here was this lady turning pages in their books, copying down their answers, stressing them out. Raychelle tried to cover up her answers with her arm. Well, Miss Milhoan thought, at least her first answer was good. The teachers were told the observer wanted to see whether kids were confused and if they had enough time and how questions were worded, but why couldn't she do that after the tests were completed?

"BCRs come tomorrow, so that make me proud," Savannah had said after the first day of the reading test. By "proud" she meant "scared." The next day, after the test, she said, "Those BCRs be making me nauseous." No problem comparing poems or explaining whether a crafts project would be good for third graders, she said—they'd practiced those a zillion times over the year. But, she told me, she had not understood a passage about a Native American garden. Her classmate, Autumn, expressed confidence; then again, on a question that asked her to retitle a poem, she told me she started with, *"I think this is a good name because it has rhyme and stanzas."* Trevon said he almost cried when he saw a question about Native Americans using their resources, and lots of unfamiliar words. Perhaps a closer emphasis on social studies would have helped. Resources are covered in the state third-grade standards, Native Americans in the county curriculum. One question set Eddy, who was taking the test with Mrs. Davidson, rolling his pencils off the table. Then his MSA vocabulary card. Then his papers. Mrs. Davidson called Mr. Dillard, who took Eddy for a walk.

His teacher had lied, the boy said. She said there wouldn't be anything on the test they hadn't done in class.

Back in the ESOL room, Elena was stuck on a word. "Is there a camera in the room?" she asked Mrs. Davidson.

"No."

"So why don't you tell me what this word means?"

The morning before, Elena had carefully marked up the reading passage with notes and wrote a lengthy answer, but by today she was worn out. "Do you think one detail is enough?" she asked Mrs. Davidson, who was not allowed to respond.

When the math test came the following week, the third-grade teachers thought their kids did fine. Mrs. Williams, on the other hand, watched her fifth graders spend their leftover minutes second-guessing themselves and changing right answers to wrong ones, time and again. "It was murder," she told me, but the rule at Tyler Heights was for kids to work until time was called, and she didn't want to be caught not enforcing it.

◆ ◆ ◆

While the six hours Maryland's third graders sat for testing seemed like forever to the children, assessment experts emphasize it is merely a snippet of time, a snapshot taken on a yearlong trip, and should be treated as such.[8] America's policymakers, eager to use test results as the basis for reform, either haven't gotten this message or choose not to heed it. They dismiss, too, the concerns of many academics that standardized tests tell you not just about what a child learned in school but about other factors such as family income, inherited aptitudes, a child's level of effort, or even, particularly for the emotionally disturbed, mood.[9]

Test scores are not always analogues of the "achievement" and "performance" Americans want from students, despite the way those terms are used today. Certainly the tests do not measure imagination, nor do they fully capture the abilities of an advanced intellect. While there are analysts who so strongly believe that America's test scores predict workforce earnings that they have tied monetary value to each point, others assert that research shows no direct connection between scores and what the country ultimately wants its schoolchildren to become: well-paid, college-educated, responsible, motivated, and productive workers and citizens.[10]

Then there is score pollution: the idea that scores to some degree measure not just children's abilities but the degree to which their schools zoomed in on the test beforehand. All that time spent on MSA workbooks, months of BCRs answering the types of questions that teachers predicted would be on the test (because they have seen the exam three years now, and the format doesn't change much), even the appearance of YoJo, some experts would say, makes it impossible to truly compare Tyler Heights' scores with a neighboring school that does not adhere to a laser-sharp focus. They question if a test taken after such hard-core preparation is even a valid sample of what students are truly capable of.[11]

Issues with how data are collected and evaluated complicate the picture too. While children may receive an individual "scale score" at home, the numbers reported under No Child Left Behind are the percent of students scoring proficient in a given school, group, or so on. That percentage can go up while the mean score actually goes down, obscuring problems.[12] (Or the other way around.) So far, improvement in proficiency under No Child Left Behind is calculated by comparing the scores of this year's third graders to last year's third graders: a wholly different group of children. Because the proficiency levels must increase over time in order for a school to make adequate progress, a school where a class of low-skilled students follows in the footsteps of a group of whizzes faces an extra hurdle. A child's score improvement is not acknowledged in official calculations—just whether she is basic, proficient, or advanced. If Miss Johnson brought a student from a kindergarten reading level to a second-grade reading level in one year, the child would theoretically still fail. Between the start of third grade and the time they sat for the MSA, Elena and Jamila had improved vastly; if they scored basic, as expected, their growth would not be reflected in the bar charts of Tyler Heights' performance.

Given states' flexibility to set their own rules, within parameters set by the U.S. Department of Education, further muddying ensues.[13] Not only do states differ in what they expect students at each grade level to know and choose their own tests, they set their own bar for proficiency, or "cut scores."[14] States vary widely in how big a population such as African American or special education must be before the group counts toward the adequate yearly progress calculation. (If there are as few as five Hispanic children in a Maryland school, for example, they count as a subgroup; some states, however, exempt groups as large as fifty.)[15] States can get permission from the Department of Education for several other allowances that, like the confidence intervals, make adequate yearly progress easier to achieve.[16] "Safe harbor" grants adequate progress to subgroups that have decreased the number of children scoring basic by a specified amount but are still below the AYP bar. "Proficiency indexing" gives schools partial credit toward AYP for students scoring below proficient but not at the state's lowest level. "Error bands" allow states to give students who just miss the cut the statistical benefit of the doubt.

These allowances surely explain part of the discrepancy between states' performances—a high of 71 percent of schools would fail to make AYP in Florida this year, while in Wisconsin only 4 percent did.[17] They may also shed light on why results on the country's only national standardized test have not been as rosy as those on state assessments, where pass rates have been increasing in the vast majority of cases.[18] For example, 81 percent of Maryland fourth graders passed the reading MSA in 2005, but only 32 percent of those tested on the National Assessment of Educational Progress scored proficient. (Another 33 percent achieved a level NAEP sets between proficient and wholly inadequate.) A government-appointed board gives NAEP to a sample of thousands of American fourth, eighth, and twelfth graders at various sites around the country and reports results nationally and by state and large city. To hear Education Secretary Margaret Spellings tell it, students are doing great, and we have the administration to thank. "We have made more progress, particularly with our early grades, with our nine-year-olds in reading and math, the core subjects that are measured by No Child Left Behind, in the last five years than in the previous twenty-eight years of our education report card combined, and I don't believe that's an accident," she said of the most recent NAEP test.[19] When President Bush visited Anne Arundel County in January 2005, he lauded NAEP scores as the best ever. But Spellings's "last five years" included three before No Child Left Behind took effect; by many measures, NAEP scores did not increase any more than they had before. (In some grades and subjects, they were stagnant.) And Bush only pointed out the categories in which the scores *were* the best ever.[20]

That NAEP would differ from state results shouldn't be surprising, because teachers don't prepare students for NAEP. They don't know what's on it the way they do their state tests, and it may test things that aren't even covered in a certain grade in a certain state. Some say the NAEP bar is too high. Another possibility is that tests like the MSA are scored too easy.

Or that they *are* too easy. This is what Miss Johnson's third graders insisted at lunch the last day of the test, as celebratory music played from Mr. Al's boom box. Savannah said she was excited. Autumn, though she still had a headache, proclaimed herself "impressed."

"That's the word I'm looking for," Tisha said.

Later that day, Ms. McKnight would say, "MSA, that's just the bottom of what kids should know. It's not like we were calling them brilliant. We're still shooting for the basement. We celebrate the bottom right now. I pray we don't have to keep celebrating the bottom."

21

It Feels Like a Different School

Dear Parents and Guardians,

The MSA tests are over! We were so proud of the way our third, fourth and fifth graders worked throughout the entire week of testing. It is a real challenge for students to endure almost two and a half hours of testing each morning for four days in one week. Our Tyler Heights intermediate students did that and did it well. They did not give up. They stayed focused. They used their test taking strategies. They gave the MSA test their best effort. We could not have asked for more of them. . . .

On April 5th, the second graders will begin to take their standardized tests. . . .

Now we can get back to a more normal routine of learning. We have more than 60 days left in the school year. Our students have weeks and months of learning left in the school year. The MSA tests are over, but we are just beginning the rest of the school year.

You didn't have to read the school newsletter—or the teacher bulletin, in which Ms. McKnight wrote, "The learning is often a little more fun at this time of the year and that is acceptable"—to see that Tyler Heights changed after the MSA. At the end of March, yellow black-eyed Susans mounted on construction paper lined the walls of Miss Johnson's room, accompanied by acrostics students wrote about spring the moment that testing finished. Jamila's said:

> *Sunshine on flowers*
> *Perfume smell in the air*
> *Roses bloom*
> *Insects come*
> *Nice flowers*
> *Good day for Games.*

On the back table sat plastic Petri dishes with little pebbles and sprouting peas. "Look at the peas!" the students said with a gasp after returning to school one Monday morning. "The peas look like grapes!" "They drank the water!" The children would also briefly examine mealworms through hand lenses and, with the help of their teachers and Ms. Borinsky, select their own projects to do in pairs for the school science fair. The classrooms' counters were crowded with the evidence that within weeks would tell them, among other things, whether an egg would explode in vinegar or water, whether gel or paste toothpaste would better clean ceramic tile, and whether a marigold fed milk would grow as well as one fed water.

"It feels like a different school," David said.

After Miss Milhoan's students learned about the Chesapeake Bay in *National Geographic Kids* and *Time for Kids,* she showed them the watershed on a map, then they made posters, with fish that had X's for eyes. *"Please don't throw trash in Chesapeake Bay. 1. The sea animals will die. 2. We won't have seafood."* For two weeks they came into class talking about algae and pollution. The third graders wrote letters of encouragement to the second graders about to take the Stanford 10: *"You can rock the Standfor 10. Show you teacher what you got!!!!"* *"Stand For 10! Take everything that is helping you take the test series."* They wrote thank-you notes to the Career Day visitors: *"Dear Josh and Mr. Grooms: What happens if there was a fire in my house and I was still in it!"* *"Thank you for coming. You can to the goodest school in Anne Arundel County."* And persuasive letters, part of the county writing curriculum:

Dear Ms. Milhoan,
I need your help! I need a Break. Can I have homework 2 days a week. I will get more sleep, I will do Better on tests, and I will do all my homework. That's all the reasons way you sud give me a Break.
Your student,
Montell

Dear Miss Milhoan,
I think we should watch more movies. One reason is that we work hard everyday. Another reason is that we have to wait 6 hours until we go home. The next reason is that we have to wait 4 hours till recess time and till we can play. Sometimes fifth grade can watch movies when they finished there homework. Can we pleas watch more movies? So those are reason why you should let us watch more movies.
Your student,
Emily

The fourth graders spent two days—except for the afternoon the project was interrupted for a math benchmark—solving a fictional murder at an elaborate crime scene Miss Antes had set up. They searched for clues, matched fingerprints, read up on the suspects. They tested clothing stains to determine if they were marker or food color, burned thread and analyzed the ashes to see if it was cotton or wool, and pH-tested Coke to look for poison. For Mother's Day gifts Miss Johnson's students wrote nice thank-you letters, which were mounted on construction paper and laminated. They wrote and illustrated haikus.

Mountains are high up
You could hurt your self on one
Mountains are rocky

Math wasn't much different in content after the MSA, but the mood was far more relaxed. Miss Johnson's students got really excited for function tables, acting as "math detectives," their teacher explained, who had to figure out what number comes out of the other end of the equation machine.

"This is fun!" Roman said.

"That's why they call it *function* tables," Lilia said.

During a unit about child entrepreneurs in Open Court, Miss John-son drew her own invention on the overhead: the Rubbernecker, a bub-ble that shields a roadside accident from gawkers. (She kept her other creation, toes-free socks, to herself. That one had come out in stores be-fore she got to invent it for real.) The students then thought up their own inventions. Savannah wrote in her flowery print, *"My invention is a shirt with a short sleave and a long sleave and a skirt with stockings,"* and drew a fashion-designer workstation complete with sewing machine, lamp, cell phone, and sketchbook. Avante wrote, *"My job is to give away stuff animal because some people like to sleep with a stuff animal."* Tisha drew a grinning, boxy creature dusting a tall shelf of books: *"I will in-vent a robot maid that does not break."* Summer invented a candy bar called Magnificent, with each section a different flavor; Lilia came up with a business suit that doesn't get wet, even in the ocean; Malcolm created an outdoor cafeteria; Roman designed Nikes that let you run faster than NASCAR; Cyrus's magnifying glass animated objects.

They went whole days, sometimes, without writing one BCR.

One student was missing from the fun. A week after MSA, Autumn became one of the 18 percent of Tyler Heights children to leave the school, having been pulled out to live with a relative hours away. It was a small relief that she was no longer around to crawl on the floor dur-ing math and tell people they were ugly. But it was a shame she was missing this part of the year, given that she had seen science and social studies as the light at the end of the MSA tunnel and gasped with ex-citement when Miss Johnson announced the class would write an acrostic. It was a shame that her academic standing would be jeopard-ized, as it often is for kids who move (a big part of the Tyler Heights population).[1] It was even more of a shame to find out that when Miss Johnson's class was writing poems and sprouting beans, Autumn wasn't enrolled in any school at all.

◆ ◆ ◆

After MSA, Tyler Heights celebrated Dr. Seuss's belated birthday with a host of special visitors reading to each class. At the talent show, stu-dents modeled the navy tops and tan skirts and pants that would be re-quired next year. Dena, who wouldn't even look at the camera for a class picture and whispered her answers in class, sang "Pieces of Me," swaying and confident. Mrs. Facchine smiled big. The girl could be a space cadet in class, but here she knew every word and sang with the flourishes of an *American Idol* contestant. When a fourth grader named Lanetta sang sweetly, Ms. McKnight commanded the audience to stand up for an ovation. "There shouldn't be a dry eye in the house," she said.

Many teachers cringed throughout the show. The song choice for the group dances—in "Hollaback Girl," Gwen Stefani vows to beat up her rival, and in "Run It," Chris Brown promises to do it all night long ("Babe pretty thick wit the kick that's sick that need to be hit," and so on). Gardell singing, "I can go all night till six in the morning." The thuglike posing and symbol-flashing. Miss Johnson was nostalgic for last year, when there was a great drumming number, a touching rendition of "Lady in Red" by a second grader, and impressive dancing. "Letting them be hard—it's not cute," she said. In the final act, four fifth-grade boys in white T-shirts and jean shorts sang and swayed, the mike kicking in and out, to "World's Greatest" by R Kelly. The boys sang half-heartedly and off-key. But the lyrics were positive and the melody emotional, and Ms. McKnight hopped up on the stage, proclaiming it the best talent show ever.

The abundance of activities in April and May spilled outside of school as well, as field trips piled on. The bus rides themselves were a source of excitement; a simple drive over the Severn River sent the children into paroxysms of glee. At the community college, an amateurish musical of "The Emperor's New Clothes" brought the adults pain—especially when the main characters sang, "The one thing we cannot endure is the poor taste to be poor"—but seemed to amuse the students. On a family field trip to D.C., the children raced from rockets to insects to bones. At the natural history museum, Avante stood still for longer than I'd ever seen, chewing on his jacket while staring in awe at topaz and crystals.

To reward Emily for putting up with such difficult classmates and being the only one to never, ever give her a hard time, Miss Milhoan took her to T.G.I. Friday's for macaroni and cheese and a slushie. To reward Malcolm for what had turned into a great year, Miss Johnson and

Ms. Benefield swore him to silence so his classmates wouldn't get jealous and took him to the aquarium in Baltimore. He enjoyed the dolphin show and the shark tank and the stuffed koala Miss Johnson let him pick out from the gift shop, but what really captivated him were the things children all around him took for granted: the tall geometric buildings, the revolving door, the leftover pizza he got to take home from Hard Rock Café. He thanked Miss Johnson, over and over and over all day, and made her eighty dollars well worth it.

A week later, on a hot bright day in May, the whole school made its annual excursion to the Naval Academy to watch a demonstration of the Blue Angels. The children could feel the planes fly by all the way through to their bones. They had done this before and were a little bored, except for Dantay, who had had to beg his mother for the two dollars it cost to attend. As the lights dimmed for the last activity of the long day, a showing of *Chicken Little* in the Navy auditorium, the boy who almost never talked leaned on my shoulder and whispered, "I'm so happy I'm here."

◆ ◆ ◆

Objective (a) of Indicator 1 of Topic A of the Maryland Voluntary State Curriculum for third-grade reading was to "read, use, and identify the characteristics of nonfiction materials to gain information and content knowledge." But Miss Johnson didn't read her students a picture book about Anne Frank for official reasons. She just wanted them to like a book. They did, very much. So after that she gave them each a Helen Keller biography she'd found in the book closet, a book Miss Johnson knew would suit their reading levels, and taught them how to handle a book without cracking its spine. "This book is good," Summer said. "This book is interested."

Miss Johnson gathered her students on the carpet and, in a discussion that reminded her of how she used to teach reading, asked how Helen's parents found out she was blind, how they found out she was deaf, how the girl communicated what she wanted. With a degree of interest and recollection they hadn't shown all year, the students answered: Helen rubbed her cheeks when she wanted her mom. She mimed eyeglasses for her dad. She pushed away when she wanted nobody.

Earlier in the day, racing through the last units of Open Court, Miss Johnson had read her students a story packed with complicated vocabulary (*condescending, contempt, Persian, forsaken*) and syntax: "The Country Mouse opened her heart and hearth in honor of her old friend," Miss Johnson read. "There was not a morsel that she could not bring forth out of her larder—peas and barley, cheese parings and nuts— hoping by quantity to make up for what she feared was wanting in quality, eating nothing herself, lest her guest should not have enough." She explained some words and not others. Five minutes later, when she asked discussion questions, the students drew blanks. Now with the Helen Keller book they couldn't stop commenting. For the first time, they sat on the carpet without fussing over who touched who and who looked at who. "You guys remember a lot since we last read this two weeks ago," Miss Johnson said.

After thirty minutes, she sent them back to their desks. When they have free time during the school day, she told them, they should read chapter 3. Then she had to explain what free time was.

◆   ◆   ◆

MSA results would not be back until June, probably after school ended. When it came to the official measures available to the teachers, Open Court tests and the benchmarks, the third graders still looked weak. On the math benchmark in mid-May, they all passed the multiple choice, but the teachers hadn't seen the test ahead of time to prepare students and one BCR was just a mess. Asked to convert twenty-eight inches into feet and inches, answers included five feet a hundred thirty inches, twenty-six feet six inches, and twenty-three feet twenty-eight inches. Only one of Miss Johnson's students got it right. The BCRs were no better. "I know that <u>equivalent</u> mean that feet and inches are made out. I know that <u>measurement</u> is to <u>measure</u> things like a snake or your feet," one said. "I know <u>Measurement</u> mean a <u>inch</u> or a <u>feet</u>. My answer is correct <u>because</u> 28 feet is amost a foot. <u>$400,</u>" said another.

For the third marking period, only two students in Mrs. Facchine's class and none in Miss Johnson's got an A in reading. One of Miss Milhoan's students got an A; the rest got C's or worse. At the awards ceremony, one student in each class made A/B honor roll—compared to thirteen students in fifth grade. When Ms. McKnight gave away golden dollars to the children who'd done all their homework, none of Miss Johnson's students were among them, and the teacher held back recess for every violation. Eventually, Summer, the only student whose mother signed her agenda every day, would get back on track with homework. She was the only one. Rather than have her play on the playground by herself, the whole class worked through recess and Miss Johnson let Summer pick anything she wanted out of the teachers' lounge snack machine. (She chose Smartfood.) Nobody had changed the Polaroids on the Smarties bulletin board since before MSA.

For his lousy report card, Avante lost his video games. For hers, Jamila was grounded—sort of. At a Little League game for a relative, her mother told her to go play on the playground. "But I'm punished," Jamila said, and her mom sent her anyway, and that was the end of that. If only Miss Johnson could be assured Tisha's mother would let her off that easy. In class when nobody else could figure out sixty-seven minus twenty-eight, Tisha saved the day with thirty-nine; when Miss Johnson misread a question and counted an hour and a half forward from 6:15 instead of an hour and a half back, Tisha pointed it out. Smart or not, though, she hadn't done her homework for a month. Miss Johnson could let it go, but then a bad report card would take her mom by surprise. She could tell Tisha's mom, but she feared the fallout at home. In the end, Miss Johnson figured, lifting Tisha out of her cruddy world would be up to her and her alone. "You told me you wanted to be a doctor," Miss Johnson said. "To be a doctor you have to get out of here, and you won't get out unless you do your best. This work isn't your best."

Sydney, the bright, bored girl who had started handing in incoherent messes instead of BCRs before the state test, wasn't any better after. Miss Milhoan and her parents met for more than an hour and agreed that the teacher would check off a three-point rubric each day assessing whether Sydney had done her work. Because the girl's parents didn't want her singled out, Miss Milhoan had to use the rubric for the whole class.

"These kids don't want to please their parents," Miss Milhoan told me. "They don't want to please me. They don't want to please themselves." She said to her class, "One friend hasn't done his homework in forty-two days."

"You think I'm a deadbeat?" Montell asked.

"Some of you have tendencies sometimes, but none of you are like that all the time."

Juan, who could multiply two-digit numbers in his head and had learned a dictionary's worth of English since arriving at Tyler Heights a year ago (including the proper uses of "psych" and "kidding"), raised his hand. "Miss Milhoan, I play outside one and a half or two hours, then I come inside and watch TV, and then I do my homework at six o'clock."

"I'm glad you have a system, because your homework is always done."

◆ ◆ ◆

On the first Tuesday in May, the library was crowded with circuits and volcanoes and a birdhouse and an awful lot of plants, dead and alive. Over the past month the third graders had learned that LeBron James Bubblicious held its flavor longest, eggs in vinegar lose their shell and cook a little, a bowling ball rolls faster than a ping-pong ball, grass may grow fine without light for a while but its color will fade, marigolds fed milk will get so moldy and stinky that the smell lingers in your class-room forever, and the plant you ignore might just grow more than the one you talk to.

The process, which took place entirely at school, was not easy—the students had to work in pairs but could not get along, and they were so unfamiliar with the scientific method that each step was a brand-new challenge. But they were proud of their work and stood tall in front of their trifold posters as the judges inspected. On Jamila and Tisha's poster the girls had written, *"Our question is Do earthworms prefer light or dark?"* They had found this in a kids' science book. *"Our hypothesis is that we think earthworms prefer the light."* But the worms hadn't. When the girls shone a flashlight on them, they crawled away. *"Our data shows that when we put the lamp on the worms they crawl to the dark,"* they wrote. (Like nearly all the projects, theirs was short on *why.*)

One of the judges came over to Jamila and Tisha, carrying a clip-board to take notes. "Did your project turn out like you expected it to?" he asked.

Tisha was being goofy, swinging the flashlight they had used on the worms. Jamila stood stick-straight, a serious look on her face. She had practiced answering these questions. "No," she said. "The reason they like the dark is we were supposed to have night crawlers. Stop using that flashlight. You're running it out."

"I'm not running it out."

"What would you have done differently if you had to do it over again?" the judge asked.

"I would have had a different hypothesis," Jamila answered.

The answer drew a laugh, so she used it with every judge that came after.

◆ ◆ ◆

Shedding the pre-MSA orderliness did not do good things for the discipline situation at Tyler Heights. One third grader, unable to control her outbursts, was sent home for the rest of the year. Among those who were left, there were fights, there was sass, and even regular bribes of extra recess couldn't stem the tide. Avante was having such trouble keeping himself in check that one teacher told him she'd kiss Miss Johnson's feet if he didn't pay attention to kids who bothered him for a week. Though Mrs. Facchine is not black, two of her students called her a nigger. (One later changed the insult to "stupid white woman.") Even Lilia, who had been one of the sweeter girls in the grade, started to act nasty and talk back. Miss Milhoan tried to reason with her students. "Does your mom go to work and get in fights because someone took her pencil?" she asked. "Do you think all the teachers are best friends? No, but they don't push each other and argue all day."

If the third-grade teachers had that kind of trouble controlling their emotions, it would have been a messy place, as they had a lot to work with in May. Miss Milhoan first thought her biggest problems were that she and her boyfriend, now engaged, were having trouble finding a new apartment; some colleagues thought the Social Committee, which she chaired, forgot a wedding gift for one teacher; and Ms. McKnight seemed to suggest that she hadn't done enough to pull up her students' grades. How could she even judge this, Mandi wanted to know, when the principal had spent so little time in her classroom? Days later her mother fell ill, cancer in her lungs and brain. Mandi drained her sick days and her wedding account to go to Ohio and be with her in the hospital. It looked like a matter not of if but when. She was simultaneously glad to be with family, terrified of what was happening to her mother, and eager to return and get report cards done, as she missed her kids.

"Where were you?" they asked when she returned.

"I went home to Ohio because my mom is very sick."

"Oh," they said. She thought, That's all I get?

Mrs. Facchine's students reacted the same way when she told them her husband was having his tonsils removed. His health had been a mystery for a while, this was very stressful for her, and though she realized it was stupid to count on the empathy of a group of nine-year-olds—particularly this group of nine-year-olds—it still hurt. And nightmares about yelling at her students to get in line had driven her to insomnia.

Then there was Miss Johnson. Frankie was a day away from closing on a house for the two of them to share when he received news he might be kicked out of the Navy because his neck circumference was screwing up his body fat ratio (yes, really). So the house deal fell through. Weeks later, delivering some of her things to an apartment she had found for them in Virginia, a driver not paying attention hit her at an intersection. The cop who arrived at the scene asked why she was crying. She did not say, "Because I have no job and no money and only sort of a home and only sort of a boyfriend who may or may not have to go back to war and a rash on my hand I have self-diagnosed on the Internet as dermatological lupus and a classroom full of belligerent kids waiting for me in Annapolis." She did not say, "Because I never want to be around kids again ever, even my friends' kids, who I know are nice." She did not say, "Because I need a luck transplant."

She did not say anything. Back at Tyler Heights, her steady veneer chipped a little more, as she found herself crying to (of all people) the principal. "One more thing," she said later that day, "and I'll have to poke my eyes out."

22

Teaching Might Be Fun Next Year?

Gardell shouldn't be in class with Roman—the combination is just trouble. Sydney shouldn't be in class with Cyrus. Malcolm shouldn't be with Felicia, Avante shouldn't be with David, Jerold shouldn't be with Javy, Michelle shouldn't be with Savannah, and Raychelle shouldn't be with either of them. Come to think of it, there are six kids who clash with Michelle. And Ferric—already his mom insisted he be kept away from half the kids in his class, prompting Nikki Facchine to wonder if she should hang his desk from the ceiling.

The third-grade teachers sat around a table in the conference room, sorting slips of color-coded paper (blue for low academic skills, pink for average, and orange for high) and trying to come up with recommended class lists for the next year that had a good balance. There were a lot of third graders they just couldn't imagine hacking it in fourth grade. Reggie might make it, they thought, given his new special ed identification, but then again, he was absent five days out of ten recently. One springtime arrival, a girl in ESOL, was catching up; another, a boy who couldn't read, would probably be held back.

Mandi Milhoan was concerned about Jerold—he had been recommended for retention in first grade and second grade, but his parents never approved it. The first and second quarters, when there was a lot of review, he always did okay, but he floundered when new material was introduced later. Alia said, "Gather documentation. But Tina will pass him on."

When Tina joined the meeting, Mandi made the case to hold back Felicia. She had failed every math test. As far as Mandi could tell, she hadn't learned any of the third-grade curriculum. But Tina pointed out the nineteen of thirty on Felicia's last benchmark—a score Mandi had largely attributed to good guesses. "Maybe she's improving," the principal said. "What will we do differently to do better if she stays in third grade? What will we be doing differently to encourage Felicia to do more work? If we retain her to do the same thing, that doesn't help her. How will she take seeing all her classmates going to fourth grade and being with second graders?"

"I have seen no improvement," Mandi said.

"Has she known so long that she would be retained that she hasn't tried?" Tina said. "If we don't aggressively try to put supports in place for her emotional instability, it'll just be more of the same." As for retention, "the data don't support it." Maybe next year, Tina said, Felicia should eat breakfast one-on-one with an adult in school at the start of every school day.

Yolie Marshall came in. Dantay, she said, hadn't made improvement in reading intervention. His Open Court scores fluctuated depending on how much one-on-one attention he got that week. He didn't return the permission slip for summer school, just like he never did for after-school tutoring. It took a month and a half to schedule his parent-teacher conference; Dantay's mom changed it five times. She never gave a contact number or signed his progress sheets.

"He needs a student support plan before we end the year," Tina said.

"He cannot read," Alia said. "If something is not done for him, he will get passed along and not be able to read when he gets to middle school."

◆ ◆ ◆

Uniforms, Tina McKnight thought, might help behavior next year. She had heard they raise test scores; she knew they made things easier on parents; at the very least Hispanic girls would no longer get teased for showing up in odd castoffs or, worse, long party dresses.[1] While a newspaper article took a jab at the policy Tyler Heights and a middle school were going to adopt next year—"drab khaki pants and mood-dampening polo shirts," the reporter wrote—parents really wanted the dress code and the students didn't seem to mind.[2]

A preponderance of navy and tan clothing wasn't the only change Tina was expecting at Tyler Heights for the 2006–07 school year. (Some would come to pass and some wouldn't.) She was going to get an assistant principal after all, for half the week. Alia was not the only one leaving—one-third of the classroom teachers would have to be replaced. With a science MSA for fifth and eighth graders looming in two years, she would have to find thirty minutes a day for the subject—plus make sure the fifth graders knew how to type, since the pilot-test MSA they'd face next year would be on the computer.

The third graders were going to be sent home for the summer with a huge reading and math workbook and would, Tina said, receive an incentive for completing it. "I personally feel like our kids have been trained to work for a reward. . . . I don't think they work for the joy of learning," Mandy Panetta said. "I think there was a place in our school for tangibles," Tina said, and they had their intended effect. Now kids were surprised when they didn't get a prize. As it was, the treat system would be complicated next year by a new school system rule that insisted food served as rewards meet minimum requirements for protein, vitamin A, ascorbic acid, niacin, riboflavin, thiamin, calcium, and iron. However, Tina said again, "We can't stop them cold turkey."

A new contract would add two more hours of teacher planning each week. In a memo, Tina wrote, *"Regularly scheduled collaborative times will be mandated and will require 100% participation,"* and later she would specify during which of those sessions teachers were to plan for reading, during which they were supposed to write tests, and so on. (For Mrs. Williams in fifth grade, that was the last straw; she decided to find another job. "Tina would be a great infantry general moving the troops in a consistent fashion," she said. "But this isn't the military.")

With the Literacy Team, Tina brought up the idea of using some of the Total Quality Management techniques she'd seen at a conference. Students could mark their progress on certain goals from the state curriculum on wall charts and in data notebooks—kindergartners, for example, could color charts of how many words they'd learned. The teacher would adapt instruction accordingly. Mandy pointed out that pacing guides leave teachers little room to switch course, data notwithstanding.

"I think we're going to see some changes in regards to that," Tina said. First there was the county's new obsession with professional learning communities, in which data-driven decision-making is key, and then there was the new superintendent, Kevin Maxwell, who was anticipated to have a lighter hand than Dr. Smith. "I'm going out on a limb," Tina said. "I probably can already guess that constraints you had in the past are probably not going to be there. Differentiation and PLCs are going to drive things in this county." Along those lines, Tina had all sorts of ideas. She wanted to have a class of students who were in special ed all the time, not pulled out, and have students taught more from the levels their brains were at rather than their chronological ages. Rules were expected to change for special ed; no longer would a student have to fail before he was eligible, and funds could be used on students who didn't have diagnosed disabilities too.

Perhaps, Mandy suggested, where students were unable to understand the grade-level readings, the assessments could be written with easier passages that still taught the reading comprehension concepts at hand. Here the zeal for differentiation showed its limits. "I hear everything you're saying," Tina said, "and I absolutely agree. We all know as educators we should be targeting students' strengths and needs. The research shows it. But then we practice something else. . . . We can't throw it all out, because Anne Arundel County signs our paycheck."

As for SpellRead, the expensive program the county had mandated at the end of last year: Logistical constraints meant that kids missed time in just about every other subject, and even then, half the lessons went unfinished. Some students in SpellRead improved their DIBELS scores, just as many didn't—though whether that meant they weren't learning wasn't clear, the teachers felt, because of the limitations of the test. The program was not a clear success, not in the least, but Tina had a feeling she was stuck with it, if only because she wanted to keep the SpellRead teacher on staff.

The third-grade teachers had come up with a plan for next year's students, most of whom, according to DIBELS, would not arrive on grade level. (According to their second-grade teachers, they needed help with problem-solving, vocabulary, probability, synonyms, context clues, and vowel sounds.) Mandi and Nikki thought they would divide children into reading sections by ability, give them books at their levels, and discuss them in small groups—a format called "guided reading" and similar to what Literacy Collaborative had offered. They'd compact the weekly Open Court story into two or three days instead of dragging it out over five. They would set up activities for the students to rotate through, activities that would incorporate science and social studies into reading. They hoped to make their way through the county writing curriculum, real writing, they said in a conversation that had the same enthusiastic tone as their students discussing summer plans for the swimming pool.

"I'm not doing BATS next year," Mandi said. "I don't care what they say. I think BATS is what killed these kids."

"So teaching might be fun next year?" Nikki said.

"They might like to read? They might be able to read? We won't be guessing about their reading level?"

They presented their proposal to Tina, who liked it—just enough loosening of the Open Court ties to help the kids without stepping too far away—and had more ideas for next year. She hoped for weekly minute-long checks of how well students read aloud. Teachers would rewrite the Open Court tests so they more closely matched the MSA and benchmarks. The new gifted teacher would lead interventions that emphasized critical thinking.

If this year's MSA scores were good enough, Tina figured that the students would have a solid enough grasp of the basics that she could ease up on the laser-sharp focus. Field trips and Career Day wouldn't all have to be shunted off to the end of the year. "We're not going to do as many BCRs," Tina swore, though nobody was sure if they should believe her.

♦ ♦ ♦

In early campaigning for the 2006 elections, candidates capitalized on the complaints they were hearing from parents about the accountability movement. In states such as Texas, Florida, Connecticut, and Minnesota, gubernatorial and congressional candidates criticized the emphasis on testing.[3] In Maryland lieutenant governor Michael Steele's campaign for Senate, the Republican made a sport of trying to distance himself as far from President Bush and his party as possible. That exercise included a television ad charging that No Child Left Behind made teachers teach to a test—a strange position for someone who a year earlier had issued a report recommending that schools be rated based on "academic performance" (usually code for test scores) and teachers be paid based on their "demonstrated effectiveness" (again, test scores).[4]

While Tyler Heights planned for the 2006–07 school year, conversations about school began on the national level, as No Child Left Behind was due for renewal soon. There was little doubt that—at the earliest in 2007 but possibly not before the 2008 elections—the law would be reauthorized in some form, a form that still emphasized standards-based testing. But on the details, politicians and policymakers were beginning to appear divided. Congressional Democrats said the law was too punitive, and that the administration never funded it properly. In the early spring of 2007, a coalition of Republican lawmakers, inundated with complaints from educators at home, said they had changed their mind about No Child Left Behind—and introduced a bill to allow states to opt out of what one called the law's "shackles."

Some people pressed for more testing. President Bush wanted reading and math tested every year in high school, instead of just once. A commission on higher education recommended testing college students, so universities could be held accountable too.[5] For others, the issue wasn't whether students should be tested in more subjects in more grades but rather whether one set of tests per school year, instead of a variety of measures, should be the basis of a whole accountability system.

The consequences for the schools' not making test-score progress were under discussion—whether schools should have to provide tutoring *before* they have to allow transfers, how to monitor the quality of tutoring firms. Legislators were also expected to pay attention to the inconsistency across states, whether in how they calculate graduation rates or set their standards or determine how big a school's subgroups must be for them to count toward adequate progress.[6] Some policymakers saw the answer to inconsistency in standards that would be set at the national level rather than state by state, a long-controversial notion that had been gaining backers throughout the year.[7]

The topic that got more attention than any other as reauthorization grew near was what was called a "growth model"—judging progress by evaluating the scores of each child over time.[8] This model, which a few states already use for their own information, makes far more sense than comparing pass rates of one set of students against those of the previous year. It does, though, have complications: States would need data systems far more complex than the ones they are already having difficulty setting up. It would be hard to track children who moved. There are concerns that such a system that could be used to attribute test-score gains to individual teachers might encourage them to narrow the curriculum even more and might not properly capture teachers' effects on students at any rate.[9] "Value-added" systems, as they are called, also tear at the fiber holding up the accountability movement: that *all* students be held to the same standard.[10]

Growth models would not solve some of the philosophical problems with the current system. The Education Department has authorized two states, North Carolina and Tennessee, to pilot-test the model and still insists on uniformity: Instead of expecting children in the same grade to be on the same level, it expects them to grow at the same rate. Or more, because the 100 percent proficiency goal for 2014, while widely considered unattainable, is also politically untouchable. To close the gap for children who are behind, Margaret Spellings said, a year of progress for every year of instruction is not enough.

The administration left the door open for suggestions, and then again it didn't. "I think as this law has matured, various new, better ways are emerging, and I'm very open-minded to those," Secretary Spellings would say over the summer. Two days later, she said, "I like to talk about No Child Left Behind as Ivory soap. It's 99.9 percent pure or something. There's not much needed in the way of change."[11]

◆ ◆ ◆

The third-grade teachers sat in the conference room and tried really hard to think what had gone well over the last nine months.

As part of the school improvement process, Miss Johnson, Miss Milhoan, and Mrs. Facchine had to assess how the year measured up to the goals that had been set. The MSA results wouldn't be back until after school ended, so they couldn't evaluate whether they'd hit the target of 85 percent proficiency in reading (no way, they figured, given the awful benchmark scores) or 80 percent in math (perhaps) or a variance between subgroups of no more than 10 percent (who knows).

They could, however, enumerate the good and the bad. Coming up with what Alia would list in her report as "Challenges" had been easy:

> *Having 85% of the students reaching the proficiency level for reading has been a challenge. The students have a difficult time decoding and comprehending the written text.*
>
> *Inconsistent intervention service due to other needs of staff members.*
>
> *More constructive criticism would have been helpful to make sure the new teachers were correctly implementing the curriculum.*
>
> *Behavior issues and academic concerns were a challenge to address due to the lack of training (for teachers new to T.H.E.).*
>
> *Teaching reading was an overall challenge due to the low ability level of the majority of the third-grade students. A condensed curriculum and more supplemental or leveled materials would help to identify the specific areas of concerns.*
>
> *Implementing the science and soc. studies has been a challenge due to the time constraints, MSA prep, and the overall behavior concerns.*
>
> *The students also have great difficulty writing independently.*

What had gone well?

"Students learned MSA strategies and MSA words," Alia said.

"They definitely know the hundred-dollar words," Mandi said.

"Student work was contained in MSA folders," Alia said, and wrote that down under "Successes." "*BCR strategies were effectively taught on a daily basis,*" she wrote too.

"They excelled in math, I think," Mandi said.

"How about, 'Teachers worked collaboratively?'" Nikki said. "Teachers continued to work throughout the year and didn't quit in January."

"Teachers worked as a cohesive unit," Alia said.

"Teachers were able to plan effectively."

"Math goals were met," Alia said.

"Munir can read now, and he couldn't read a lick when he came in," Mandi said.

"Some of them made connections between stories they read," Nikki said.

"They didn't know they lived by the bay, and they do now," Mandi said. "They know the state they live in."

"I would say they definitely have more background knowledge," Alia said. "They could tell you what to do to handle a situation. Not that they could *do* it." This would go down as *"Overall classroom management and school safety was maintained."*

"A lot of them have better interpersonal skills. Well, not all of them," Mandi said.

"A small minute sliver of them," Alia said.

"A majority won't make it in the world unless they drastically change soon," Mandi said. Then the substitute who was teaching her class appeared in the doorway and beckoned her into the hall. Felicia was getting suspended, again, for kicking a first grader on the way to the nurse.

Alia explained to her teammates the procedures for the end of the school year. Empty your shelves and cover them, clean off your desk, even clean the drawers because Tina might look there too. Keep your erasers, because you might not get new ones. Push the furniture to the front of the room and put your name on every piece. Put in a requisition form for scissors and crayons, though it might be denied. Leave up the MSA words and the concept/question board until the very end. Order *National Geographic Kids.* Write a field trip proposal.

Nikki and Mandi thought about the Mint, for the money unit. Mandi filled out a form to take kids to the theater: *"Students will learn about a play firsthand and incorporate it into the VSC."* Music came through the walls, kids practicing for the final awards ceremony.

"I want to be a music teacher," Alia said.

"I want to be a lawyer," Mandi said.

"I want to be an FBI agent," Nikki said, crouching under the table with her finger-gun pointing over the edge.

23

Don't They Look Good?

At fifth-grade graduation on the second-to-last day of school, Mateo's mother spent five dollars to buy a sheet of paper with a photo of him grinning against a tree and a list of his favorite things—math, reggaeton music, cake, fishing, a book about the rain forest, *Scary Movie 4.* For another five dollars, she bought a frame to go with it. Bertha took her seat with the other hundred family members and snapped a photo of Mateo as he entered with his classmates, wearing a new double-breasted suit and silver tie, his hair gelled extra swoopy.

Mateo had had a good spring. Tina had decided to exempt him from the MSA in reading, taking the basic score and risking the fallout, and he felt okay about how he did on the math test. An A on a science quiz, a journal entry about frontier life that was as long as anyone else's—though he missed that it was supposed to be fictional and just wrote about himself—and third place in the science fair for an experiment on density. His partner, Thomas, had run the show, but still. Best of all, a Personal Success certificate from Mrs. Williams at the awards assembly, for "scholarly growth." He didn't know what that meant, but the page was ringed with colorful pencils, and he liked it.

After the Pledge of Allegiance and a reading from Dr. Seuss's graduation standard, *Oh, the Places You'll Go!,* the students took the stage one by one to announce their goals. In the computer lab, they had filled in a Mad Libs of sorts: *"When I grow up I want to be a _____. I want to be a _____ because _____. I will achieve this goal by _____ and _____."* Mateo, who hates talking in front of people, had practiced, a brick on his desk serving as a podium, a rubber girl figurine a makeshift microphone.

In front of the real audience, Zavier announced that he wanted to be a millionaire. Thomas, never to be one-upped, said trillionaire. There was an aspiring movie star, two singers, two artists, a rapper, and a dancer. There were three veterinarians, two scientists, a mechanic, a surgeon, two nurses, a teacher, an author, a chef, and a policeman. There were five models and eight athletes, including Mateo, who spoke carefully. "My name is Mateo Martinez. When I grow up I want to be a professional soccer player. I want to be a professional soccer player because I like this sport. I will achieve this goal by completing school and practicing soccer." Then he repeated the whole thing, in Spanish.

After a speech by the middle school principal—mostly procedural, barely inspirational—and two songs, Tina took the mike.

"Good morning, Tyler Heights!"

"Good morning, Ms. McKnight."

"Good morning, Tyler Heights!!"

"Good morning, Ms. McKnight!"

"You know I'm about energy and responding. When I came to Tyler Heights, the boys and girls in front of you were in kindergarten. It felt like I gave birth to them. They didn't realize it, but they were helping me to be a good principal. I don't know if I could have picked a greater group of young ladies and young men to help me become a better principal. They have worked hard, and don't they look good?"

The fifteen students who had attended Tyler Heights since kindergarten were called to the risers and awarded with golden dollars. Thomas and Gregory, for getting all A's all year, got gift cards to Barnes & Noble. The students with the most Accelerated Reader points were honored.

"What are McKnight's ten easy rules?" the principal asked the crowd. "Do them with me: Read, read, read, read, read, read, read, read, read, read. If you follow those ten simple rules, you *will* achieve what you mentioned earlier." At the end of her talk, Ms. McKnight said, "I leave you with these words—and replace it with where you're going: We will soar to higher heights, every day at . . ."

"Tyler Heights."

"Try again. Where are you going? We will soar to higher heights, every day at . . ."

"Tyler Heights."

"Annapolis Middle. Soar to higher heights at Annapolis Middle. Let's try again."

♦ ♦ ♦

Before school ended for the summer, Ms. McKnight gathered the third graders in the library to tell them about the math and reading practice workbook they were to complete over the summer. Your teachers will check up on you three times by phone, she said, and so might she. The school was offering a free uniform shirt for students whose parents tracked their workbook progress and a pizza party for those who completed the thick book.

At the final awards assembly, four third graders made the A/B honor roll. Malcolm got a Personal Success award for getting his grades up, and Jamila got one for coming *this close* to honor roll. She also received certificates for perfect attendance and excellence in PE, which she splayed on the table. Later Jamila's mom would take them to work to show her boss and let her daughter pick what she wanted to do all summer (swim every day). Her dad promised her fifty dollars. For now, the joy was simple: the feeling of doing well. "I listened in class," Jamila whispered to me at the ceremony. "I had a few attention—tantrums. But I got it back together."

Miss Milhoan gave out awards like "Makes Me Laugh in the Morning" and "Tries Your Best." "At the beginning of the year I made up awards," Mrs. Facchine said, watching. "I'm not going to anymore. The kids don't deserve it. I must be the meanest person in the world." She was not so mean that she didn't smile when the third graders performed. "Big, big dreams, lots of big dreams, things I wanna do someday. Big, big dreams, lots of big dreams, big dreams are okay," they sang. "They're actually cute," Mrs. Facchine said.

"Oh, you're so good. I love it," Ms. McKnight said when they finished. She guided them off the risers in unison—third step to the second, second to the first, first to the floor—and praised them for their organization in getting back to their seats. "You are perfect. Excellent, excellent job." Later she went to Miss Johnson's room, where the kids were watching SpongeBob on TV. They had already sat through *The Wizard of Oz*, with chips and cookies. Alia figured there was a curricular connection: One of the Open Court units had covered Imagination. Her mind was half elsewhere, anyway. During the movie she had gotten on her cell phone to schedule an interview with a principal in Virginia, a school with 100 percent parent participation and almost no poverty and, because it went only through second grade, no big state test. "If I could get this job, it would be freakin' cake," she had told her mother.

The kids' thoughts were elsewhere too: on a celebratory dinner at Cactus Willies (Jamila), ice cream sundaes (Cyrus), a television marathon on Mom's tall, fluffy bed (Summer), the dolphin snow globe that had been a secret, special gift from Miss Johnson (Malcolm). Ms. McKnight knew the MSA scores were at Central Office that very moment, probably being used to write principal evaluations, and she wondered when they would arrive at Tyler Heights.

Miss Johnson turned off the TV for Ms. McKnight, who held up a piece of paper. "Has anyone seen this?"

"Hundred book reading log."

"Why do you think I'm here?"

"To tell us to read books."

"What do you do?"

"Read a hundred books and come back to school."

"And what do you get?"

"You get to eat breakfast with you."

"What else will happen?"

"You'll get smarter."

"Louder."

"You'll get smarter!"

After Ms. McKnight left, the students watched SpongeBob try to free a purple jellyfish, until Miss Johnson flipped the television to *The*

Jungle Book. "Row three, go to your mailbox and get your report card," she said. "Do not take those out of the envelope until you get home." Avante took his out, and Miss Johnson squeezed it back into the small envelope. "Hopefully next year in fourth grade, you'll make better choices," she told him. "Don't let it 'fall out' again."

One of the resource teachers came on the announcements. "Have a wonderful and safe summer. You will be missed. We look forward to seeing you next year. And remember Ms. McKnight's rules for success. This is the first call for bus one-eighty-nine." The first students to leave were Avante, Tisha, and Jamila. Miss Johnson gave each a half-hug on their way out the door. "Have a nice summer. Good luck in fourth grade. Have a nice summer. Good luck in fourth grade." Over the loud-speaker came a plea for a lost lost-library-book form. Miss Johnson asked the kids to stack the chairs at the front of the room.

"This is the first call for bus forty-two." Savannah and Lilia stopped stacking and left. As her students filed by, Alia thought: five years here. She waited for the sadness to sink in; it hadn't yet. In two days it would, before Tina checked her emptied room and gave the okay to leave. She would throw up all morning; she would collapse onto the counter as Mandi and Nikki tried to comfort her. But now, composed, she ripped the emergency procedures and respect rules off the cinderblock, then the gummy blue adhesive, and continued her semiformal good-byes.

"Students on bus three-eleven may walk on the silver line to the multipurpose room," the announcement came. Malcolm and Dantay headed out. Miss Johnson rolled up the flag. The students who walked home waited in line. David asked, "What's the green bag for?" Miss Johnson wondered why he was asking now, when the bag had sat there under a table near the doorway all year. "It's stuff for emergencies," she said.

"Coloring stuff?"

"No, stuff for the teachers."

Cyrus's mom popped in to pick him up. "Hello!" she said.

"Are we getting ice cream?"

"I don't know."

Students who walked home or were picked up were called on the

PA. Manny, Summer, and David got their hugs and left. Miss Johnson pulled a personalized wooden wreath, decorated with the universal symbols of teachers (apples, pencils), off her door. Mrs. Facchine came in and said, "That was so anticlimactic."

The music teacher remedied that. She wheeled a stereo on a cart into the hallway, pressed play, and set the *Hallelujah Chorus* booming throughout Tyler Heights. A little boy and his mother, stragglers, plugged their ears as they headed out of the building.

◆ ◆ ◆

"Okay, take it easy, Tina," the principal said to herself the following Monday morning. "Settle down."

She was at her desk trying to access the MSA scores she was told were available on e-mail: no delivery man this year. The scores were supposed to have come back Friday; that they didn't meant more sleepless nights.[1] (Test-driving a Volvo convertible over the weekend wasn't enough to distract her.) If the benchmark scores were any indicator, she wouldn't like what she was about to see. Then again, she had looked at the third graders' BCRs on the test. They were brief but probably good enough for the modest target of proficiency. "If noneducators score the test and just look for key words, we should be okay," she said.

A week before, Tina had given each of her staff members a certificate in the library, as rain poured outside. "It was an incredible, wonderful year," she said then. The logistics of a whole-school field trip and the behavior of the children, the kindergarten children pulling up their DIBELS scores: "The number of times I was overwhelmed with what we were able to do is countless. . . . Everyone does their job a hundred percent. I know we all complain. But if you put all of those pieces together—those excellent pieces—you wind up with a school that is a wonderful school. And people take notice."

Now, Tina's left hand rested on her desk while she reached forward with her mouse with the right—looking for the data that would make people take notice again. She searched through her archive file, then the public folder, then unread mail. "I saw something that said Outlook. Click on that. Outbox. This is ridiculous. Why can't they just send it?" She picked up the telephone to call the school system help desk. She talked to herself and to the phone. "Click on folder. Click on plus sign. Hi, this is Tina McKnight, and I can't get to my scores. I've gone to public folders and they're not there. Two minutes ago? Okay."

And there it was.

2006 MSA and Alt-MSA scores
Subj: Release of MSA scores
Memo from Acting Deputy Superintendent,
dated June 13, 2006.

"Faster, please! The public folder icon isn't appearing at the very bottom. No, it's Ernestine McKnight. Sorry, I'm not even hearing . . . Grab Tracy! They're coming! They're there!" By now several people had gathered in Tina's office. "I might have to drive over to the board and pick them up. I'm on the phone with the help desk."

The person on the other end of the phone began to operate Tina's computer remotely, so the little arrow moved around magically. "I want to go to 'All Students,'" Tina said. The arrow went to "All Students." Tina put the phone down and said, "Okay, people. Now I'm afraid to open them." Her hand braced her chin as the file opened. "Tell me I'm looking at them right!" No, she wasn't. Flustered, she hadn't noticed the schools were in alphabetical order. The moment it took to scroll down to "T" felt like ages.

"C'mon," Tina said. An antivirus pop-up appeared. An Adobe update pop-up appeared. And then: "These are our scores! These are our scores! Am I looking at it right? Yes! Yes! What is that, an average? I don't believe it!"

Eighty-two percent of the fifth graders were proficient in reading and 74 percent in math. (No huge surprise, Tina thought. The top kids were all over the place, at least one writing a BCR about how stupid the question was in the first place.) For fourth grade, 90 percent in reading and 87 percent in math. And the third graders, the children everybody fretted most about, the ones who had seemed to make the least progress all year, the ones who bombed benchmark after benchmark: 90 percent in reading, 90 percent in math.

"It wasn't a fluke," Tina said. She stomped her feet like a drumroll as the teachers around her hugged and cried.

◆ ◆ ◆

During the jubilation, Alia was at her new apartment in Virginia, trying to fit her belongings onto practically one shelf. She had hoped to keep them in the second bedroom, but Frankie had taken a roommate. There was a good chance she'd get this job she interviewed for, as a second-grade teacher, a half hour from her new home. The MSA was far from her mind.

Alia was glad to have seen her students grab up books at the year-end giveaway—chapter books about UFOs and Abe Lincoln and swamp monsters and prairie girls. "Look!" Jamila said. "A hundred fifty-two pages!" Back in the classroom Miss Johnson let them read, and except for Avante (who was sleeping) and David (who was asking to go to the bathroom, then the nurse, then the bathroom), they were rapt. She was glad that the third graders had gotten through all of the carefully mapped-out math lessons, and while they were still counting on their fingers, when they put their minds to it they could solve basic problems. She was glad they got through most of Open Court, though speeding through toward the end, and that they knew the meanings of a whole lot of terms like *text feature* and *author's purpose* and *dialogue*.

But there was so much in the county curriculum that they didn't get to. They covered a small fraction of the writing lessons. Persuasive letter, haiku, yes; research report, fable, and set of directions, no. They covered a small fraction of the social studies lessons. Economics, some; maps and Native Americans, a little; politics and government, even littler. Physics, life science, earth science, barely; matter, yes; magnification, no. Even on the MSA stuff, drilled over and over, Alia hadn't been sure. There were a few good answers on the last benchmark, taken a month and a half after MSA, the first day in June: *"I know that boys and girls club is a set of directions because it gives you steps in order. Some example how I know it is directios because it has 123456. Also it's telling you what to do."* But more showed no improvement over September: *"The author made the story more easier to understand is by the contest and making more fun and easier."* These kids knew so much less than her students the year before.

Asked what they learned really well over the year, Alia said, "Probability." That's it. (Mandi Milhoan was more generous, suggesting all of math.)

So when I called Alia to tell her that in each subject, 90 percent of third graders had passed the MSA—a number that would wind up being the state's highest, in math, for schools with the same share of poverty and second highest, by a nose, in reading—she laughed.

"That's funny," she said.[2]

◆ ◆ ◆

When Tina and the teachers crowded into her office and looked at the scores on the computer, there was nothing about individual students' scores. It would be a couple of weeks before they learned the identity of the five third graders who scored advanced in math and the one in reading, the three children who didn't pass the math test, and the four—only four!—who didn't pass in reading. One would be Dantay, who was barely reading on third-grade level. Another was Jamila, despite her progress. Perhaps she should not have begged off to the bathroom during MSA after all, because for the two of them, Tina's frequent warning that "the difference between basic and proficient can be one point" came true after all. There was no information about what the schoolwide proficiency was; it would be a month before they found out the numbers to post in each room: 87.4 percent for reading, 80 percent for math. They'd have to wait, too, to find out that the school was one of the 71 percent in America that had made adequate yearly progress under No Child Left Behind. There wouldn't be as many phone calls of congratulation this time around, and a *Washington Post* article featuring the "crown jewel of Anne Arundel elementary schools" wouldn't show up for four months.[3]

It would never become clear why exactly the fifth-grade pass rate in math had fallen four percentage points, when Mrs. Williams had been certain the students knew much more than last year's group. It was a mystery, too, how the third graders did so well, given their performance in every other arena. Was the MSA just scored too easy? Did the children hide their abilities all year? Alia was not the only teacher who laughed on hearing the scores. Nikki and Mandi did too.

Tina, though, saw enough data on the screen to know that Tyler Heights was not a one-hit wonder. She saw enough to know that she could leave the building this summer for a trip to Costa Rica with her niece, and, more immediately, that ice cream was in order. First she sent a staffwide e-mail:

> Hello
> Time to play our favorite song—Ain't no stopping us
> Now! once again.
> Tina

"Now we can lie back on that focus," she then said, and headed out with her team for soft-serve.

Prologue: Ain't No Stopping Us Now

1. Nearly two of five children within the Annapolis Middle School boundaries attended private school. Daniel de Vise, "A Fight to Fill Empty Desks at Md. School," *Washington Post,* January 30, 2006.

2. Twenty-two percent said schools are to blame. Lowell C. Rose and Alec M. Gallup, *38th Annual Phi Delta Kappa/Gallup Poll of the Public's Attitudes Toward the Public Schools* (Bloomington, Ind.: Phi Delta Kappa International, 2006).

3. National Commission on Excellence in Education, *A Nation at Risk: The Imperative for Educational Reform* (U.S. Government Printing Office, 1983). The call to action was one of about ten issued at the time, with names like *Making the Grade, Action for Excellence,* and *Meeting the Need for Quality.*

2: America's Schools Will Be on a New Path of Reform

1. The history of education reform in this chapter is informed, in part, by personal interviews and by Christopher T. Cross, *Political Education: National Policy Comes of Age* (New York: Teachers College Press, 2004); Diane Ravitch, *Left Back: A Century of Failed School Reforms* (New York: Simon & Schuster, 2000); Noel Epstein, ed., *Who's in Charge Here? The Tangled Web of School Governance and Policy* (Denver: Education Commission of the States and Brookings Institution, 2004); Patricia Albjerg Graham, *Schooling America: How the Public Schools Meet the Nation's Changing Needs* (New York: Oxford University Press, 1995); and David T. Gordon, ed., *A Nation Reformed? American Education 20 Years after A Nation at Risk* (Cambridge, Mass.: Harvard Education Press, 2003).

2. On the extent of the gap, see Abigail Thernstrom and Stephan Thernstrom, *No Excuses: Closing the Racial Gap in Learning* (New York: Simon & Schuster, 2003), and Paul E. Petersen, ed., *Our Schools and Our Future: Are We Still at Risk?* (Stanford, Calif.: Hoover Institution Press, 2003). To see how test-score gaps grow over the summer and school year, see Martha S.

McCall et al., *Achievement Gaps: An Examination of Differences in Student Achievement and Growth* (Portland, Ore.: Northwest Evaluation Association, November 2006).

3. In Lowell C. Rose and Alec M. Gallup's *38th Annual Phi Delta Kappa/Gallup Poll*, 19 percent of Americans surveyed in 2006 said the achievement gap was related mostly to the quality of schooling received, and 77 percent blamed other factors. Forty-nine percent said it was schools' responsibility to close the gap—a decrease from previous years—and 46 percent said it was not.

4. David C. Berliner and Bruce J. Biddle contended the worries were alarmist and unfounded in *The Manufactured Crisis: Myths, Fraud, and the Attack on America's Public Schools* (Reading, Mass.: Addison-Wesley Publishing, 1995). The most recent call to action is from the National Center on Education and the Economy, *Tough Choices or Tough Times: The Report of the New Commission on the Skills of the American Workforce* (Hoboken, N.J.: Jossey-Bass, 2006). A straightforward status report can be found in Jim Hull, *More Than a Horse Race: A Guide to International Tests of Student Achievement* (Alexandria, Va.: Center for Public Education, January 2007).

5. Eloquent arguments against the connection can be found in Patricia Albjerg Graham, *Schooling America*; Henry M. Levin, "High-Stakes Testing and Economic Productivity," in Gary Orfield and Mindy L. Kornhaber, *Raising Standards or Raising Barriers? Inequality and High-Stakes Testing in Public Education* (New York: Century Foundation Press, 2001); and in two works by Larry Cuban: *The Blackboard and the Bottom Line: Why Schools Can't Be Businesses* (Cambridge, Mass.: Harvard University Press, 2004) and "A Solution That Lost Its Problem: Centralized Policymaking and Classroom Gains," in Noel Epstein, ed., *Who's in Charge Here?*

6. Other goals: that all children "start school ready to learn," 90 percent of high schoolers graduate, teachers be able to improve their knowledge and skills, every school be free of drugs and violence, schools better involve parents, and every adult be able to read.

7. It can be found at www.ed.gov/nclb/overview/intro/presidentplan/proposal.pdf.

8. Boston College professor Walt Haney had a hard time interesting the media in his August 19, 2000, article on dropouts, "The Myth of the Texas Miracle in Education," when it was published. Reporters told him it was too political before the election, he said. *Education Policy Analysis Archives*, 8(41). For a critical look at Texas test scores, see Diana Jean Schemo and Ford Fessenden, "A Miracle Revisited," *New York Times*, December 3, 2003.

9. Nicholas Lemann explained the politics in "Letter from Washington: Testing Limits," *New Yorker*, July 2, 2001.

10. The law is at www.ed.gov/legislation/ESEA02. If you don't have a few hundred hours, try a summary: Frederick M. Hess and Michael J. Petrilli, *No Child Left Behind Primer* (New York: Peter Lang Publishing, 2006).

11. Over half of elementary schoolers born to immigrants are poor or "economically disadvantaged." The share of whites and blacks in poverty fell slightly over the last two decades, but for children of immigrants it increased. Randy Capps et al., *The New Demography of America's Schools: Immigration and the No Child Left Behind Act* (Washington, D.C.: Urban Institute, September 2005).

12. Daniel de Vise, "A Shared Journey Takes Separate Paths," *Washington Post*, August 13, 2006.

13. Abigail Thernstrom and Stephan Thernstrom, *No Excuses*, p. 4.

4: A Bank Teller Could Pick Up the Lesson

1. Laura Loh, "Plotting a Strong Course in Education," *Baltimore Sun*, June 22, 2003.

2. On how "reformers have confused setting standards with standardization," see Larry Cuban, "A Solution That Lost Its Problem."

3. Compared to others, high-poverty and high-minority schools have double the share of teachers with less than four years' experience. Daniel P. Mayer et al., *Monitoring School Quality:*

An Indicators Report (Washington, D.C.: National Center for Education Statistics, December 2000). Inexperienced teachers also teach disproportionately in high-ESOL schools. Clemencia Cosentino de Cohen et al., *Who's Left Behind? Immigrant Children in High and Low LEP Schools* (Washington, D.C.: Urban Institute Program for Evaluation and Equity Research, September 2005).

4. For how the law nullifies this requirement with a loophole, see Heather G. Peske and Kati Haycock, *Teaching Inequality: How Poor and Minority Students Are Shortchanged on Teacher Quality* (Washington, D.C.: Education Trust, June 2006). According to another study, only three states—Ohio, Tennessee, and Nevada—thoroughly analyzed the situation as required. Peske et al., *Missing the Mark: An Education Trust Analysis of Teacher-Equity Plans* (Washington, D.C.: Education Trust, August 2006).

5. See Patricia Albjerg Graham, *Schooling America*.

6. Education analyst Frederick M. Hess wrote about the "utter disinterest of colleagues in what others were doing" when he taught high school in *Tough Love for Schools: Essays on Competition, Accountability, and Excellence* (Washington, D.C.: AEI Press, 2006).

5: Was It a Big Scratch or a Little Scratch?

1. Dana Markow and Suzanne Martin, *The MetLife Survey of the American Teacher: Transitions and the Role of Supportive Relationships, 2004–2005* (New York: MetLife, 2005).

2. See Lareau's *Home Advantage: Social Class and Parental Intervention in Elementary Education* (Lanham, Md.: Rowman & Littlefield Publishers, 2000, second edition) and *Unequal Childhoods: Class, Race, and Family Life* (Berkeley, Calif.: University of California Press, 2003).

3. On the importance of community reforms to school improvement, see Richard Rothstein, *Class and Schools: Using Social, Economic, and Educational Reform to Close the Black-White Achievement Gap* (Washington, D.C.: Economic Policy Institute, 2004) and *Reforms That Could Help Narrow the Achievement Gap* (San Francisco: WestEd, 2006).

6: Chapter Books Are Not Bad, People

1. Stephanie Desmon, "On-Site Trainer Is Seen as Key," *Baltimore Sun*, October 29, 2000, and Laura Green, "New Approach Has Students Learning Better," *The Capital* (Annapolis), May 13, 2001.

2. Other required elements are reading fluency, vocabulary, and reading comprehension. The study on which this is primarily based is the National Reading Panel's *Teaching Children to Read: An Evidence-Based Assessment of the Scientific Research Literature on Reading and Its Implications for Reading Instruction* (Washington, D.C.: National Institute of Child Health and Human Development, 2000). For a counterargument, see Gregory Camilli et al., "Teaching Children to Read: The Fragile Link Between Science and Federal Education Policy," *Education Policy Analysis Archives*, 11(15), May 8, 2003. See also Michael Pressley, "The Rocky Year of Reading First," *Education Week*, December 14, 2005.

3. *CSRQ Center Report on Elementary School Comprehensive School Reform Models* (Washington, D.C.: Comprehensive School Reform Quality Center, November 2005). On the "methodological nihilism" that may occur if programs are jettisoned for lack of foolproof evidence of their benefits, see Michael Feuer, "Moderation: A Radical Approach to Education Policy," *Education Week*, June 14, 2006.

4. Educational psychologist Gerald Coles charges that studies proving success from commercial programs are often financed or conducted by the publishers themselves. *Misreading Reading: The Bad Science That Hurts Children* (Portsmouth, N.H.: Heinemann, 2000). Chapter 3 addresses Open Court.

5. The impassive title of the report, *The Reading First Program's Grant Application Process,* belies the juiciness within—particularly the collusionary, smarmy e-mails to and from the Reading First director, Chris Doherty. About state officials who preferred a certain program, he wrote, "Beat the [expletive deleted] out of them in a way that will stand up to any level of legal and apologist scrutiny. . . . They are trying to crash our party." *Final Inspection Report ED-OIG/I13-F0017* (Washington, D.C.: U.S. Department of Education Office of Inspector General, September 2006). See also Pressley, "The Rocky Year of Reading First."

6. Online transcript of the Charlotte "What's Working in Reading" conference, presented by the CMS Partners for School Reform, January 19, 2001. For his role in changing the way reading is taught, Lyons was named the fourth most influential person in education, behind Bill Gates, President Bush, and Kati Haycock, who runs an education think tank that pushes for higher achievement. Christopher B. Swanson and Janelle Barlage, *Influence: A Study of the Factors Shaping Education Policy* (Bethesda, Md.: Editorial Projects in Education Research Center, December 2006).

7. A month later, Open Court publisher McGraw-Hill awarded Smith its prestigious Harold W. McGraw Jr. Prize, along with a twenty-five-thousand-dollar check.

8. E. D. Hirsch Jr., *The Knowledge Deficit: Closing the Shocking Education Gap for American Children* (New York: Houghton Mifflin, 2006) and "What Do Reading Comprehension Tests Measure? Knowledge," *American Educator,* Spring 2006.

9. "It's a crime that we give kids reading not for meaning," Tina McKnight said of "decodable" books. In a bestselling 1955 polemic, Rudolf Flesch agreed. "Every single story, every single sentence that goes into these books has to be carefully prepared and carefully checked to make sure that each word is one of the 637 that the poor child is supposed to have memorized up to that point—or if it's the 638th word, that it appears in just the right context for optimum guesswork and is then repeated seventeen times at carefully worked-out intervals." This, he wrote, "is *not* the language used in telling a story, making a narrative interesting, or conveying information intelligibly." *Why Johnny Can't Read: And What You Can Do About It* (Cutchogue, N.Y.: Buccaneer Books, 1955), p. 8 and pp. 84–85.

10. Jeff Archer, "An Agent of Change," *Education Week,* July 9, 2003, and Darragh Johnson, "A Classroom Crusade," *Washington Post Magazine,* November 10, 2002.

11. In a county teachers' union survey the previous May, 54 percent of members said Eric Smith was committed to raising student achievement, and 7 percent said he "considers and implements employee input on teaching methods." In a 2006 national survey, 46 percent of superintendents said it is crucial to involve teachers in policymaking. Jean Johnson et al., *Reality Check 2006: The Insiders: How Principals and Superintendents See Public Education Today* (Washington, D.C.: Public Agenda, 2006).

12. Frederick M. Hess gives a thorough analysis of reformist superintendents in *Spinning Wheels: The Politics of Urban School Reform* (Washington, D.C.: Brookings Institution, 1999).

13. People wouldn't have the benefit of a critical analysis of the Charlotte scores, whose trends turned out to match those of North Carolina overall, for another year. See Ann Doss Helms, "Test Score Gap Stumps, Rouses CMS Officials," *Charlotte Observer,* February 20, 2003.

14. See J. H. Snider, "Superintendent as Scapegoat," *Education Week,* January 11, 2006. The average tenure for urban superintendents is just over two years.

15. That night was all about the joy of bedtime reading and family bonding, so it was strange to see the headline on the local paper's coverage of the event: "Reading Programs Help School Improve Test Scores," Pete Holley, *The Capital* (Annapolis), November 17, 2005.

16. Steven L. Layne, "Aliteracy Poem," *Life's Literacy Lessons: Poems for Teachers* (Newark, Del.: International Reading Association, 2002).

17. A decline in literary reading through adulthood is a national problem. *Reading at Risk: A Survey of Literary Reading in America.* Research Division Report #46 (Washington, D.C.: National Endowment for the Arts, June 2004).

7: This Is Just Like the Real Test

1. Lynn Olson, "Benchmark Assessments Offer Regular Checkups on Student Achievement," *Education Week*, November 30, 2005.

8: Market Discipline Is the Key

1. Linda Perlstein, "Talking the Edutalk," *Washington Post*, January 18, 2004.

2. Jeff Archer, "Leaders Go to School on Business Practices," *Education Week*, August 31, 2005.

3. Jenny LaCoste-Caputo, "Student Testing Is Causing a Shift in Tech Spending," *San Antonio Express-News*, June 21, 2005.

4. While the U.S. Department of Education website states, "Annual testing provides teachers with a great deal of information," this varies widely. For a state-by-state look at how, see "Technology Counts 2006: The Information Edge," a May 4, 2006, special issue of *Education Week*.

5. *Reinventing Education: Entrepreneurship in America's Public Schools* (New York: Dutton, 1994). While secretary of education, Rod Paige seconded this notion in an October 6, 2003, letter to the editor of the *New Yorker*: "Good schools do operate like a business. They care about outcomes, routinely assess quality, and measure the needs of the children they serve."

6. "The Blueberry Story," *Education Week*, March 6, 2002.

7. The best analysis of the shortcomings of the business analogy for schools is Larry Cuban's *The Blackboard and the Bottom Line*.

8. R. Murray Thomas writes that it's "silly to imagine that the only variable affecting students' success on tests is their teacher's ability and diligence. Success depends also on a test-taker's motives, interests, energy level, inherited neural structure, schooling background, family support, emotional control, peer influences, immediate testing context, and more." *High Stakes Testing: Coping with Collateral Damage* (Mahwah, N.J.: Lawrence Erlbaum Associates, 2005), p. 100. For more on the pitfalls of tying teacher pay to scores, including in systems that measure a student's individual growth, see Henry I. Braun, *Using Student Progress to Evaluate Teachers: A Primer on Value-Added Models* (Princeton, N.J.: Educational Testing Service Policy Information Center, September 2005).

9. Peter Whoriskey, "Fla. to Link Teacher Pay to Students' Test Scores," *Washington Post*, March 22, 2006. Only 20 percent of superintendents and 17 percent of principals surveyed in 2006 said tying pay to student scores would be very effective in improving teaching. Jean Johnson et al., *Reality Check 2006: The Insiders*.

9: You Gotta Be Tough

1. *Teaching Interrupted: Do Discipline Policies in Today's Public Schools Foster the Common Good?* (New York: Common Good and Public Agenda, May 2004).

2. According to one study, watching how a kindergartner interacted on the playground could predict more about his first-grade academic achievement than a test could. Anthony D. Pellegrini, *Recess: Its Role in Education and Development* (Mahwah, N.J.: Lawrence Erlbaum Associates, 2005), p. 144.

3. Sixty-eight percent of teachers in low-minority schools say the atmosphere at their school is very orderly, safe, and respectful; thirty-five percent of teachers in high-minority schools say that. Steve Farkas et al., *Stand by Me: What Teachers Really Think about Unions, Merit Pay and Other Professional Matters* (Washington, D.C.: Public Agenda, 2003). According to *Teaching Interrupted*, 82 percent of teachers and 74 percent of parents blame parents for not teaching discipline.

4. Seventy-eight percent of teachers say kids are quick to remind them of their rights and threaten that their parents can sue them. *Teaching Interrupted.*

5. For more on the rigid focus on discipline in high-poverty, high-minority schools, see Jonathan Kozol, *Shame of the Nation: The Restoration of Apartheid Schooling in America* (New York: Crown Publishers, 2005).

6. Pam Belluck, "And for Perfect Attendance, Johnny Gets a Car," *New York Times*, February 5, 2006. Schoolwide incentives like these, and lesser ones, tend to be more common in low-income schools.

10: What Gets Taught Is What Gets Tested

1. A rural Kentucky administrator said about his district's change in lice policy, "The more your students are out of school, the less likely you are to meet the academic goals of No Child Left Behind." Robert Tomsho, "Kink in Federal Law Is Prompting Schools to Stop Picking Nits," *Wall Street Journal*, July 1, 2006.

As for the spelling bee, a Rhode Island administrator said that any event that allows one kid to win and others to lose is contrary to leaving no child behind. Ronald Blais, "School District Cancels Spelling Bee," *Woonsocket Call*, January 27, 2005. The bee was later reinstated after lots of publicity. The following year, Secretary of Education Margaret Spellings seemed to suggest that the answer was more assessment: "We need to take a look at our data across the whole spectrum and we ought to say—for people who say, 'Wah, wah, we can't have spelling bees because we have to focus on math and reading'—let's measure the spelling." Lois Romano, "Tweaking of 'No Child' Seen," *Washington Post*, August 31, 2006.

2. One study found that 33 percent of school districts had cut time spent on social studies, 29 percent cut time on science, and 22 percent cut time on art and music to make more room for reading and math. *From the Capital to the Classroom: Year Four of the No Child Left Behind Act* (Washington, D.C.: Center on Education Policy, March 2006). See also *NCLB: Narrowing the Curriculum?* (Washington, D.C.: Center on Education Policy, July 2005).

3. Many years after Canada left, recess returned to Atlanta, in the guise of "unstructured break time" or "wellness initiative." Patti Ghezzi, "Atlanta Schools Bring Back Recess," *Atlanta Journal-Constitution*, September 21, 2006.

4. Pellegrini's *Recess* is the most convincing I've seen. See also David Elkind, *The Power of Play* (Cambridge, Mass.: Da Capo Lifelong Books, 2006).

5. On the reduction of in-depth reading and writing, see Linda McNeil and Angela Valenzuela, "The Harmful Impact of the TAAS System of Testing in Texas: Beneath the Accountability Rhetoric," in Gary Orfield and Mindy L. Kornhaber, *Raising Standards or Raising Barriers?* Patricia Albjerg Graham wrote in *Schooling America* of reduced curricular scope: "Gradually the tests, which are much more limited than the standards generally, have become the focus. If the item is not on the test, it is unlikely to be taught." See also Robert L. Linn, "Assessments and Accountability," *Educational Researcher*, 29(2) March 2000.

6. Center on Education Policy, *From the Capital to the Classroom: Year Four.*

7. Jim Mueller, quoted in Kathleen Kennedy Manzo, "Older Students Play Catch-Up on Uncovered, Vital Lessons," *Education Week*, June 14, 2006.

8. For the relationship between background knowledge and reading skills, see E. D. Hirsch Jr., *The Knowledge Deficit.*

9. House Committee on Education and the Workforce hearing, "No Child Left Behind: How Innovative Educators Are Integrating Subject Matter to Improve Student Achievement," May 18, 2006.

10. Lowell C. Rose and Alec M. Gallup, *37th Annual Phi Delta Kappa/Gallup Poll of the Public's Attitudes Toward the Public Schools* (Bloomington, Ind.: Phi Delta Kappa International, 2005).

11. See *Arts in Education Standards, Curriculum and Assessments* (website of the Education

Commission of States, 2006) and Kristine Hughes, "The Art of Testing," *Teacher Magazine*, January 1, 2005.

12. *How Have High School Exit Exams Changed Our Schools: Some Perspectives from Virginia and Maryland* (Washington D.C.: Center on Education Policy, June 2005).

13. One forceful critique of how standardization harms writing can be found in Linda Mabry, "Writing to the Rubric: Lingering Effects of Traditional Standardized Testing on Direct Writing Assessment," *Phi Delta Kappan*, 1999, p. 80.

14. "Studies have shown that when teachers are pressured to increase students' performance, they become less autonomy-supportive and more controlling." M. Gail Jones et al., *The Unintended Consequences of High-Stakes Testing* (Lanham, Md.: Rowman & Littlefield Publishers, 2003), p. 85.

15. Children who don't have many analytical conversations in the home need them in the classroom—with their teachers and with one another. Relying on short answers precludes this. See Jane M. Healy, *Endangered Minds: Why Children Don't Think—and What We Can Do About It* (New York: Touchstone, 1990).

16. Appearing with Eric Smith at the Charlotte "What's Working in Reading" conference four years earlier, the surgery was gallbladder removal but the analogy was the same. Much later, in conversation with me, Smith would use the example of heart surgery.

17. Mary M. Kennedy, *Inside Teaching: How Classroom Life Undermines Reform* (Cambridge, Mass.: Harvard University Press, 2005), p. 54.

11: I Didn't Even Know That Was an Option

1. In a 2000 study, children in single-parent families had lower test scores and more behavior problems. Transience was even more significant. "Children who did not change schools in the year before they were surveyed had scores on a scale of behavior problems six times lower than children who changed schools two or more times. After accounting for other factors . . . the findings suggest that changing schools more than once in one year was the single biggest predictor of school problems in children ages 12 and under." "How Do Children Spend Their Time? Children's Activities, School Achievement, and Well-Being," *Research on Today's Issues*, 11 (National Institute of Child Health and Human Development, August 2000). See also *Elementary School Children: Many Change Schools Frequently, Harming Their Education* (Washington, D.C.: General Accounting Office, 1994).

2. See R. Murray Thomas's *High Stakes Testing* or Linda McNeil and Angela Valenzuela in *Raising Standards or Raising Barriers?* McNeil, a curriculum theorist at Rice University, wrote on p. 129, "[B]ehind the rhetoric of rising test scores is a growing set of classroom practices in which test preparation activities are usurping a substantive curriculum. These practices are more wide spread in those schools where administrators' pay is tied to test scores and where test scores have been historically low. . . . It is a curriculum aimed primarily at creating higher test scores, not a curriculum that will educate these children for productive futures. . . . It is creating an even wider gap between the curriculum offered to the predominantly white, middle-, and upper-middle-class children in traditionally high-scoring schools and those in traditionally minority and poor schools."

In a 2006 survey, 72 percent of superintendents and 47 percent of principals in mainly minority schools said children aren't taught enough math and science, compared to 37 percent and 26 percent in mostly white schools. Jean Johnson et al., *Reality Check 2006: Is Support for Standards and Testing Fading?* (Washington, D.C.: Public Agenda, 2006), p. 4.

3. In one study, " 'frequent, responsive mother-child language interaction' was the most critical factor in raising mental ability." Jane M. Healy, *Endangered Minds*, p. 91.

4. Children ages eight to sixteen from low-income homes are more likely to have televisions in their bedrooms than middle-class and affluent children, while they are far less likely to own computers and have Internet access. (All but one of Miss Johnson's students had a television in

their room.) Low-income children spend fifty-four minutes more each day watching television, thirty minutes more watching videotapes, and twenty-seven minutes more playing video games than high-income children. Emory H. Woodard IV with Natalia Gridina, *Media in the Home 2000: The Fifth Annual Survey of Parents and Children* (Philadelphia: Annenberg Public Policy Center, 2000). Children who spend thirteen hours or more per week watching television did worse on verbal and math tests than those who watched less, according to NICHD's "How Do Children Spend Their Time?" Even while controlling for other factors, more television watched at age one or three increases attention problems at age seven. Dimitri A. Christakis et al., "Early Television Exposure and Subsequent Attentional Problems in Children," *Pediatrics*, 113(4) April 2004.

5. On the connection between these disadvantages and mental deficits, see Jane M. Healy, *Endangered Minds*, pp. 238–39. Dolores Acevedo-Garcia et al. compellingly analyze the disparities of the living conditions of young minorities and whites in *Children Left Behind: How Metropolitan Areas Are Failing America's Children* (Boston: Harvard School of Public Health, January 2007).

6. For a thoughtful look at the cultural issues impacting the academic achievement of black students in particular, see chapter 7 of Abigail Thernstrom and Stephan Thernstrom, *No Excuses*.

7. See E. D. Hirsch Jr., *The Knowledge Deficit*, particularly chapter 2. "Many specialists estimate that a child or an adult needs to understand around 90 percent of the words in a passage in order to learn to understand the other 10 percent of the words. Moreover, it's not just the words that the student has to grasp the meaning of; it's also the kind of reality that the words are referring to." P. 25.

8. Hirsch wrote, "[T]he only way to improve scores in reading comprehension and to narrow the reading gap between groups is systematically to provide children with the wide-ranging, specific background knowledge they need to comprehend what they read. . . . If we do not spend large amounts of time reading aloud and discussing challenging material with children—material that is well beyond their ability to decode with understanding—we miss a critical opportunity to increase their knowledge of language and of the world." P. 21.

9. Keith E. Stanovich, "Matthew Effects in Reading: Some Consequences of Individual Differences in the Acquisition of Literacy," *Reading Research Quarterly*, 21(4), Fall 1986, p. 381.

10. Theoretically a school with high overall scores still has cause to worry about making adequate yearly progress, because each subgroup that comprises a certain number of children must make AYP too. In Maryland that number is five. But the state also provides a "confidence interval," or cushion, which means that in schools where the subgroup is more than five children but still small, as at Crofton, very few must pass to make AYP. The superintendent's goals for county schools made no such allowances. For more on confidence intervals, see chapter 20 of this book.

12: Where's the Sand Table?

1. Eight percent of U.S. kindergartners live in households where all members above age fourteen do not speak English as a first language. Randy Capps et al., *The New Demography of America's Schools*, p. 16.

2. On the gap, see Valerie E. Lee and David T. Burkam, *Inequality at the Starting Gate: Social Background Differences in Achievement as Children Begin School* (Washington, D.C.: Economic Policy Institute, 2002).

3. Glenn Cook, "Spurred by NCLB, Elementary Schools Get Serious," *American School Board Journal*, 191(5), May 2004. Superintendent Andre J. Hornsby of neighboring Prince George's County, issuing a similar decree, said, "We need to get rid of all the baby school stuff they used to do," in Nancy Trejos, "Time May Be Up for Naps in Pre-K Class," *Washington Post*, March 15, 2004.

4. See the works of educational theorist John Dewey, Tufts University child development expert David Elkind, and Temple University psychologist Kathy Hirsh-Pasek. In a book written with Roberta Michnick Golinkoff, Hirsh-Pasek presented a study in which academic preschool gave children no scholastic advantage: "Children who had been in the academic environment were more anxious and less creative than the children in the other group." *Einstein Never Used Flash Cards: How Our Children Really Learn—and Why They Need to Play More and Memorize Less* (New York: Rodale Press, 2003), p. 12.

5. Since Junior Kumon launched a program for four- to six-year-olds in 2003, enrollment increased by nearly 50 percent. Kaplan also offers a pre-K reading program, unsubtly titled SCORE! ("A good pre-K program can lead to a good pre-med program," the website promises.) See Sherry Saavedra, "Tutored at 2—Too Much, Too Soon?" *San Diego Union-Tribune*, February 28, 2006.

6. The Committee for Economic Development emphasized financial benefits in its June 2006 policy statement, *The Economic Promise of Investing in High-Quality Preschool: Using Early Education to Improve Economic Growth and the Fiscal Sustainability of States and the Nation.*

7. Federal officials aggressively promoted DIBELS—and, some have alleged, required it as a condition of grant approval. Its creators later served as Reading First consultants. Kathleen Kennedy Manzo, "National Clout of DIBELS Test Draws Scrutiny," *Education Week*, September 28, 2005.

13: I'm Giving Him Everything He Can Get

1. Where tests are given in English, some schools have gotten rid of bilingual education. Where tests are given in native languages, some teachers have cut back on English instruction. Mary Ann Zehr, " 'No Child' Effect on English-Learners Mulled," *Education Week*, March 1, 2006.

2. On the decrease in gifted services, see Michael Winerip, "No Child Left Behind? Ask the Gifted," *New York Times*, April 5, 2006. On how the allocation of attention hurts the scores of high-achieving students, see Randall Reback, *Teaching to the Rating: School Accountability and the Distribution of Student Achievement* (New York: Barnard College Department of Economics working paper, May 2006). For neglect of the middle, see Patrick Welsh, "Class Focus," *Washington Post*, November 13, 2005.

3. Lowell C. Rose and Alec M. Gallup, *38th Annual Phi Delta Kappa/Gallup Poll.*

4. Mary M. Kennedy, *Inside Teaching*, p. 18.

5. "[A]n overwhelming amount of evidence from research on child development, social psychology, and student learning indicates that such a one-size-fits-all expectation is ridiculously naïve and bound to fail." R. Murray Thomas, *High Stakes Testing*, p. 68.

6. Ten states translated tests in 2006, mostly into Spanish and not necessarily for reading *and* math: Colorado, Delaware, Kansas, Massachusetts, New Mexico, New York, Ohio, Oregon, Pennsylvania, and Texas. Illinois and Virginia simplified the English used on the math test and Kansas and Oregon did so for math and reading. Mary Ann Zehr, "Scholars Seek Best Ways to Assess English-Learners," *Education Week*, January 11, 2006.

7. The 3 percent was an increase from years past, granted by the Education Department after many complaints. Those adapted tests often wind up being a bizarre, inappropriate burden for the severely disabled. Children who can't speak, go to the bathroom, or sometimes even lift their heads—children for whom reading may forever be impossible—are given reading and math tasks to perform. For an excellent portrayal, see Daniel de Vise, "Trying Times for Special Ed," *Washington Post*, April 26, 2005.

14: I See Motivation All Over This

1. Testing expert Thomas Haladyna writes that it is ethical to train students in test-taking skills and motivate them but unethical to develop a curriculum based on the test content, teach objectives based on test items, and use the kind of directed score-boosting workbooks like those at Tyler Heights. Some might argue such a curriculum is based not on the test but the state standards; however, items from the standards teachers thought wouldn't be on the test weren't emphasized. Thomas M. Haladyna et al., "Raising Standardized Achievement Test Scores and the Origins of Test Score Pollution," *Educational Researcher,* 20(5), June–July 1991. The authors of *Freakonomics* don't go so far in their censure but do say that teaching to the test and using previous years' questions "certainly violates the spirit of the test." Steven D. Levitt and Stephen J. Dubner, *Freakonomics: A Rogue Economist Explores the Hidden Side of Everything* (New York: William Morrow, 2005), p. 27. These targeted activities are far more likely to take place in high-minority schools. George Madaus et al., *The Influence of Testing on Teaching Math and Science in Grades 4–12* (Chestnut Hill, Mass.: Center for the Study of Testing, Evaluation, and Education Policy, Boston College, 1992).

2. Each standard deviation from the mean will increase house prices 7 percent, according to David M. Brasington and Donald R. Haurin, "Educational Outcomes and House Values: A Test of the Value Added Approach," *Journal of Regional Science,* 46(2), May 2006.

3. "MSA scores alone provide only a partial picture of your child's academic performance. But together with your child's classwork, homework, and other test scores, MSA results will give you a good snapshot of your child's performance." *A Parent's Guide to Achievement Matters Most* (Baltimore: Maryland State Department of Education, revised January 2004).

4. For a good look at parental attitude toward scores and transfers in one district, see Stephen Paske, "School Daze," *Milwaukee Magazine,* October 2005.

15: Some People Are Selling Snake Oil

1. The webpage, which advertised the company's Instructional Assessment Tool, at the time failed to mention that those numbers represented only Ridgely's third graders. Fifth-grade proficiency dropped, and the following year the third-grade reading pass rate fell halfway back.

2. Testing materials figure from research firm Eduventures LLC, Boston, Mass. On tutoring, see Karla Scoon Reid, "Federal Law Spurs Private Companies to Market Tutoring," *Education Week,* December 8, 2004.

3. On Neil Bush, see Walter F. Roche Jr., "Bush's Family Profits from 'No Child' Act," *Los Angeles Times,* October 22, 2006. On McGraw, see Stephen Metcalf, "Reading Between the Lines," *Nation,* January 28, 2002. On Kress, who lobbied for McGraw-Hill before Bush became president, see Emily Pyle, "Te$t Market," *Texas Observer,* May 13, 2005. On the reading panelists, see Bess Altwerger, ed., *Reading for Profit: How the Bottom Line Leaves Kids Behind* (Portsmouth, N.H.: Heinemann, 2005).

4. Alec MacGillis, "Poor Schools, Rich Targets," *Baltimore Sun,* September 19–21, 2004.

16: We Must Leave Them No Choice

1. For a look at how education insiders say No Child Left Behind fails to account for factors out of schools' control that impact test scores, see Thomas Toch, "Measure for Measure," *Washington Monthly,* October–November 2005.

2. In one Public Agenda study, 53 percent of teachers said standardized tests are a "seriously flawed" measure of achievement, 80 percent said having standards improves academic performance, and 87 percent said grade promotion should require a test. Steve Farkas et al.,

Stand by Me. In a 2006 National Education Association member survey, 17 percent wanted No Child Left Behind to be repealed. Testimony of NEA president Reg Weaver to the House Committee on Education and the Workforce hearing "No Child Left Behind: Can Growth Models Ensure Improved Education for All?" July 27, 2006.

3. On p. 20 of *The Knowledge Deficit,* E. D. Hirsch Jr. wrote, "American educational expertise . . . has a monolithic character in which dissent is stifled." The NEA, joined by eight school districts, sued the federal government in April 2005 over No Child Left Behind, charging that NCLB was an unfunded mandate. The suit was dismissed in November 2005, and the plaintiffs appealed in March 2006.

4. For elaboration on criticisms see Thomas Toch, "Measure for Measure"; George Madaus and Marguerite Clarke, "The Adverse Impact of High-Stakes Testing on Minority Students: Evidence from One Hundred Years of Test Data," in Gary Orfield and Mindy L. Kornhaber, *Raising Standards or Raising Barriers?;* and Gail L. Sunderman et al., *NCLB Meets School Realities: Lessons from the Field* (Thousand Oaks, Calif.: Corwin Press, 2005).

5. Toch, "Measure for Measure."

6. Of the 49 percent of public school parents who in 2006 said they knew a great or fair amount about NCLB, 42 percent viewed it favorably and 47 percent unfavorably. Lowell C. Rose and Alec M. Gallup, *38th Annual Phi Delta Kappa/Gallup Poll.* See also *Open to the Public: The Public Speaks Out on No Child Left Behind* (Washington, D.C.: Public Education Network, 2006).

7. Forty-five percent of public school parents said there was too much emphasis on testing—a number that increases every year—and 17 percent said there was not enough. Seventy-four percent said this emphasis encourages teachers to teach to the test, compared to 60 percent in 2005—and most of them said that's a bad thing. *Ibid.*

8. The suit, *Connecticut v. Spellings,* was unresolved as of March 2007. Information on state opposition to the law is available from the Center on Education Policy and the National Conference of State Legislatures, as well as in Lorraine M. McDonnell, "No Child Left Behind and the Federal Role in Education: Evolution or Revolution?" *Peabody Journal of Education,* 80(2), April 2005, pp. 19–38.

9. Liz Bowie and Julie Hirshfield Davis, "Bush Brings Praise to Md. School," *Baltimore Sun,* January 10, 2006, and Daniel de Vise and Michael A. Fletcher, "Arundel School Basks in President's Praises," *Washington Post,* January 10, 2006.

17: I Used to Be a Nice Person

1. Dana Markow et al., *The MetLife Survey of the American Teacher, 2006: Expectations and Experiences* (New York: MetLife, 2006).

2. The degree to which these factors matter is not easily pinpointed. Many current studies are disturbingly meta: Teachers whose students score higher can elicit higher scores from students. For a research summary, see Jennifer King Rice, *Teacher Quality: Understanding the Effectiveness of Teacher Attributes* (Washington, D.C.: Economic Policy Institute, 2003).

3. Teachers most likely to leave the profession are those with degrees from highly selective colleges and good scores on college boards, in schools with high concentrations of disadvantaged children, under thirty, and with less than five years of teaching. Certainly the last three elements were common among Tyler Heights classroom teachers. *Attracting, Developing and Retaining Effective Teachers: Background Report for the United States* (Washington, D.C.: National Council on Teacher Quality and U.S. Department of Education Office of International Affairs, May 2004).

4. Blacks make up 23 percent of the county student body but only 8 percent of the teaching staff. Daniel de Vise, "Most Blacks in Low-Rung School Jobs," *Washington Post,* May 15, 2006. Hispanics are poorly represented too.

5. Five percent of U.S. school districts offer financial incentives to teach in disadvantaged schools. Center on Education Policy, *From the Capital to the Classroom: Year Four,* p. 166.

6. Liz F. Kay, "Teacher Bonuses Tied to Dedication," *Baltimore Sun*, September 13, 2004.

7. Assistants were affected too. The woman employed for four years at Tyler to make sure one boy didn't molest any classmates (who would also help teachers make copies and staple) had to get a job working the lunchline because she didn't have an associate's degree or equivalent or hadn't passed an academic test.

19: Never Give Up Trying

1. In 2001, sixth graders rated grade retention as the single most stressful life event, higher than the loss of a parent, an operation, wetting in class, or going blind. Gabrielle E. Anderson et al., "Children's Ratings of Stressful Experiences at Home and School," *Journal of Applied School Psychology*, 25(1), July 6, 2005.

2. Perhaps she could have benefited from the Freeze-Framer, a product whose maker, HeartMath, promises reduced anxiety and improved scores for schoolchildren. According to promotional materials, "This easy-to-use educational technology objectively monitors the heart's rhythms and . . . helps students learn to balance their mental and emotional systems—critical for successful learning and test taking."

20: We Celebrate the Bottom

1. Thomas Toch, *Margins of Error: The Education Testing Industry in the No Child Left Behind Era* (Washington, D.C.: Education Sector, January 2006). The $517 million is far less than is spent on test prep itself and does not include extra-NCLB tests, such as DIBELS, benchmarks, or the Stanford Achievement Test for Tyler's younger students. Harcourt administered more than nine million annual tests for twenty-two states in 2005–06 alone; the following year, the math MSA would be added to its roster as well.

2. *Smart Testing: Let's Get It Right*, Policy Brief 19 (Washington, D.C.: American Federation of Teachers, July 2006), and Chester E. Finn et al., *The State of State English Standards 2005* and *The State of State Math Standards 2005* (Washington, D.C.: Thomas B. Fordham Foundation, January 2005).

3. Charles P. Pierce offered a look at how a Harcourt test item was constructed in "Testing Times," *Boston Globe Magazine*, March 2, 2003.

4. One of his comments to me, "If you interview the kids about what's on the test, I'll come after you with everything I've got," kind of belied the "It's not a secret" one.

5. Eva L. Baker and Robert L. Linn discuss "construct underrepresentation" and the inclusion on exams of the easiest standards to test in "Validity Issues for Accountability Systems," Susan Fuhrman and Richard Elmore, eds., *Redesigning Accountability Systems for Education* (New York: Teachers College Press, 2004).

6. It costs pennies to score multiple-choice answers compared to fifty cents to five dollars for each written response, according to Thomas Toch. See also Lynn Olson, "State Test Programs Mushroom as NCLB Mandate Kicks In," *Education Week*, November 30, 2005. Olson reported that Mississippi went to all multiple-choice for 2005–06, except for its writing test, and Kansas got rid of everything that couldn't be machine-scored. Fifteen states would use only multiple-choice the following year in reading and math: Arizona, California, Georgia, Idaho, Iowa, Kansas, Mississippi, North Carolina, Oklahoma, Oregon, South Dakota, Tennessee, Texas, Virginia, and Utah. Betty Sternberg, then the Connecticut commissioner of education, charged that the U.S. Department of Education encouraged her to convert to all multiple-choice and get rid of the state's writing assessment in order to handle the testing volume. "Testing: Making It Work for Children and Schools," hearing of the Aspen Institute's Commission on No Child Left Behind, May 9, 2006.

7. For a first-person account that echoes what I heard from many scorers I interviewed, see Amy Weivoda, "We Hung the Most Dimwitted Essays on the Wall," *Salon*, June 5, 2002.

8. "[A]ll major professional associations involved in educational testing, as well as the National Research Council, emphasize that decisions about student promotion, retention, program or curricular placements, and graduation must be based on more than a single test score." Gary Orfield and Mindy L. Kornhaber, *Raising Standards or Raising Barriers?*, p. xi. W. James Popham wrote, "The commonly held idea that educational tests are super accurate really needs to be squashed. . . . A test score should be seen only as a rough *approximation* of a student's actual achievement level." *America's "Failing" Schools: How Parents and Teachers Can Cope with No Child Left Behind* (New York: RoutledgeFalmer, 2004), p. 16.

9. On the link to income, see *ibid*. On background knowledge see E. D. Hirsch Jr., *The Knowledge Deficit*. Stephen W. Raudenbush contends that differences in proficiency in early grades reflect children's cognitive abilities when they entered school, in *Schooling, Statistics, and Poverty: Can We Measure School Improvement?* (Princeton, N.J.: Educational Testing Service Policy Evaluation and Research Center, April 2004).

10. Robert Gordon et al. contended that an increase in earnings from a 14 percentile point increase in scores would be worth about $72,000 to $169,000 per high school graduate, for a nationwide gain of up to a half-trillion dollars per year. *Identifying Effective Teachers Using Performance on the Job* (Washington, D.C.: The Brookings Institution, April 2006). For characteristics not reflected in test scores see Graham, *Schooling America;* Thomas Toch, *In the Name of Excellence: The Struggle to Reform the Nation's Schools, Why It's Failing, and What Should Be Done* (Oxford, U.K.: Oxford University Press, 1991); and R. Murray Thomas, *High Stakes Testing.*

11. Robert L. Linn, in "Assessments and Accountability," wrote on page 4 that educators' past experience with a given test means that "policymakers can reasonably expect increases in scores in the first few years of a program with or without real improvement in the broader achievement constructs that tests and assessments are intended to measure." On comparing scores given varying levels of test prep, see Thomas M. Haladyna et al., "Raising Standardized Achievement," and Brett D. Jones and Robert J. Egley, "Voices from the Frontlines: Teachers' Perceptions of High-Stakes Testing," *Education Policy Analysis Archives*, 12(39), August 9, 2004. Joan L. Herman wrote that "if teaching and learning focus, in the extreme, only on what is tested and on the formats in which it is tested, the test ceases to be a sample of performance. The test becomes the domain, and the generalizability of the results—and what meaning can be drawn from students' test performance . . . becomes suspect." "The Effects of Testing on Instruction" in Susan Fuhrman and Richard Elmore, eds., *Redesigning Accountability Systems for Education* (New York: Teachers College Press, 2004), p. 151.

12. See Charles Murray, "Acid Tests," *Wall Street Journal*, July 25, 2006.

13. Maryland has been pointed out as a state that provides honest public reporting, but in general states have a perverse incentive to gloss over problems. Kevin Carey, *Hot Air: How States Inflate Their Educational Progress Under NCLB* (Washington, D.C.: Education Sector, May 2006). See also *No Child Left Behind Act: Improvements Needed in Education's Procedures for Tracking States' Implementation of Key Provisions* (Washington, D.C.: Government Accountability Office, September 2004); Lynn Olson, "Shifts in State Systems for Gauging AYP Seen as Impeding Analysis," *Education Week*, November 30, 2005; and Gail L. Sunderman, *The Unraveling of No Child Left Behind* (Cambridge, Mass.: The Civil Rights Project at Harvard University, February 2006).

14. Maryland uses the "bookmark" method to determine cut scores. A panel of teachers ranks test questions in order of difficulty and marks a dividing line between what basic and proficient students would know, and between proficient and advanced. Their recommendations are reviewed by committees that include psychometricians, legislators, businesspeople, professors, principals, and more.

15. Those children are still counted toward a school's total AYP calculation. But making the minimum subgroup size that large can take away the risk of a special-needs population

jeopardizing the school's AYP status. The Associated Press revealed that nearly two million children's scores are discounted in this way, in an April 17, 2006, article by Frank Bass et al.

16. For other allowances not listed here, see Frederick M. Hess and Michael J. Petrilli, *No Child Left Behind*, pp. 126–31.

17. Editorial Projects in Education Research Center, *2006 AYP Score Card for States and D.C.*

18. Jaekyung Lee, *Tracking Achievement Gaps and Assessing the Impact of NCLB on the Gaps* (Cambridge, Mass.: Civil Rights Project at Harvard University, 2006).

19. *The Diane Rehm Show* interview by Laura Knoy. National Public Radio, August 28, 2006.

20. For how NAEP data were compared and interpreted, see Martha S. McCall et al., *Achievement Gaps;* Daniel de Vise, "State Gains Not Echoed in Federal Testing," *Washington Post,* October 24, 2005; Lynn Olson, "NAEP Gains Are Elusive in Key Areas," *Education Week,* October 26, 2005; and *Education Watch State Summary Reports* at edtrust.org.

21: It Feels Like a Different School

1. Moving schools especially hurts when students are not in one place long enough to be fully tested for special services. This happened with Jada, the frequently absent girl in Mrs. Williams's class who had been in and out of Tyler Heights before. The same time Autumn left, Jada's mom pulled her out midday.

22: Teaching Might Be Fun Next Year?

1. No correlation with test scores has actually been proven.

2. Ryan Bagwell, "Two Public Schools in County Pushing for Uniforms," *The Capital* (Annapolis), April 23, 2006.

3. On statewide polls showing concerns about testing and about NCLB as a campaign issue, see Terrence Stutz, "Most Say School Testing Overemphasized," *Dallas Morning News,* February 22, 2006; Peter Whoriskey, "Political Backlash Builds over High-Stakes Testing," *Washington Post,* October 23, 2006; Alyson Klein, "No Child Left Behind on the Campaign Trail," *Education Week,* October 25, 2006; and Elena Schor, "No Child Left Behind Stirs Conn. Campaigns," *The Hill,* September 21, 2006. On the impact of the power shift in Congress, see Alyson Klein, "Political Shift Could Temper Resolve," *Education Week,* September 27, 2006.

4. *The Governor's Commission on Quality Education* (Annapolis, Md.: Maryland Office of the Governor, September 2005). Steele chaired the commission.

5. Karen W. Arenson, "Panel Explores Standard Tests for Colleges," *New York Times,* February 9, 2006.

6. Ellen Forte and William J. Erpenbach enumerated states' continuing requests for flexibility in *Statewide Educational Accountability Under the No Child Left Behind Act—A Report on 2006 Amendments to State Plans* (Washington, D.C.: Council of Chief State School Officers, December 2006).

7. Lynn Olson, "Nationwide Standards Eyed Anew," *Education Week,* December 7, 2005, and Chester E. Finn et al., *To Dream the Impossible Dream: Four Approaches to National Standards and Tests for America's Schools* (Washington, D.C.: Thomas B. Fordham Foundation, August 2006).

8. *No Child Left Behind: States Face Challenges Measuring Academic Growth That Education's Initiatives May Help Address* (Washington, D.C.: Government Accountability Office, July 2006).

9. For more, see Daniel F. McCaffrey et al., *Evaluating Value-Added Models for Teacher Accountability* (Santa Monica, Calif.: Rand Corporation, 2004).

10. Thomas Toch wrote in "Measure for Measure," "The idea that there should be one standard for all students, regardless of race or income, and that all schools should be held re-

sponsible for meeting those standards, is the gravity that holds the liberal and conservative sides of the school reform movement together. . . . Dropping the standards approach entirely makes no sense politically or policy-wise."

11. The first quote was from *The Diane Rehm Show,* August 28, 2006. The second came in a conversation with reporters at the Education Department on August 30.

23: Don't They Look Good?

1. The scores had been delivered to the state on time; other states weren't so fortunate. On logistical mistakes by testing companies, see Michael Winerip, "Standardized Tests Face a Crisis over Standards," *New York Times,* March 22, 2006; Robert A. Frahm, "State Risks Millions over the Test," *Hartford Courant,* May 4, 2006; and Valerie Strauss, "Hundreds Worldwide Hit by Loss of AP Tests," *Washington Post,* August 18, 2006. A survey published in Thomas Toch's *Margins of Error* found that 35 percent of states had faced a significant error by a contractor in scoring tests since 2000, and 20 percent didn't get results on time.

2. Linda McNeil and Angela Valenzuela in *Raising Standards or Raising Barriers?* wrote of high school teachers, "[A]lthough practice tests and classroom drills have raised the rate of passing for the reading section of the TAAS at their school, many of their students are unable to use those same skills for actual reading. . . . After children spent several years in classes where 'reading' assignments were increasingly TAAS practice materials, their middle school teachers in more than one district reported that they were unable to read a novel even two years below grade level." P. 133.

3. Daniel de Vise, "Uniforms Only Scratch the Surface: Dress Code Caps an Annapolis Elementary School's Dramatic Turnaround," *Washington Post,* October 19, 2006.

ACKNOWLEDGMENTS

Tina McKnight deserves a medal not just for what she does every day (and night) for children but also for the bravery it took to open her school to the world. Thank you, Tina, thanks beyond measure. I am indebted to the teachers of Tyler Heights, who welcomed me with utter honesty and were a hell of a lot of fun. Thanks to the students for hugs and insights, and to the parents who spoke with me. At AACPS, Eric Smith facilitated the project; Jane Beckett-Donohue vouched for me.

Gail Hochman, my excellent agent, believed in this book and made sure it landed with a group who believed too: George Hodgman, the most enthusiastic, energetic editor imaginable, and the team at Henry Holt. Henry Kaufman watched my back. My fellow reporters on the K-12 listserv of the Education Writers Association know their stuff, and share. Thanks as well to the many educators, policymakers, analysts, academics, and test scorers around the country who allowed me to pick their brains.

Kaye Hausmann and Hanna Rosin kept me sane. David Plotz, Hank Stuever, and Rick Perlstein offered wisdom on the manuscript. John Miller did all of the above and much, much, much, much more.

ABOUT THE AUTHOR

LINDA PERLSTEIN spent five years covering education for *The Washington Post* and is the author of the acclaimed *Not Much Just Chillin': The Hidden Lives of Middle Schoolers.* She speaks nationwide to educators and parents. She grew up in Milwaukee and now lives with her husband in Baltimore and western Virginia.